With great appreciation

J. Stanley Lemons

First

The FIRST BAPTIST CHURCH in AMERICA

J. Stanley Lemons

First

The FIRST BAPTIST CHURCH in AMERICA

J. Stanley Lemons

PUBLISHED BY THE CHARITABLE BAPTIST SOCIETY PROVIDENCE, RHODE ISLAND ©2001

CONTENTS

©2001 by J. Stanley Lemons

The First Baptist Church in America
75 North Main Street
Providence, Rhode Island 02903
401 454.3418
www.FBCIA.org

Lemons, J. Stanley
First: The First Baptist Church in America
ISBN 0-9708793-0-X

DESIGN Murphy & Murphy
PRINTING Meridian Printing
JACKET PHOTOGRAPH Warren Jagger

DRAWING BEHIND TITLE PAGE This drawing, showing the framing of
the steeple, was made by Norman M. Isham for his book, *The Meeting House
of the First Baptist Church in Providence: A History of the Fabric* (1925).

PREVIOUS PAGE Photo by Warren Jagger (2001).

AUTHOR'S FORWARD

For me, writing a new version of the history of the First Baptist Church in America is like having lightning strike twice in the same place. I wrote an earlier version for the 350th anniversary of the founding of the church in 1638. All of the books were sold to visitors and members, and the church decided to have a new history written. I incorporated the material, minus some errors, from the first history and have written a much more comprehensive and expanded history. What was three chapters is now eight, including one devoted to Roger Williams, another to the General Six Principle Baptist phase of our history, and another to the place of FBCIA in the community in the nineteenth century. Much more material and evidence became available to me since 1988, especially on the Six Principle Baptists and on FBCIA and the Civil War. For example, Brown University acquired a cache of letters and documents by Samuel Winsor, the last Six Principle Baptist pastor of the FBC, and I found the association records of the General Six Principle Baptists. Some minute books of the Standing Committee were discovered in a cupboard, and a careful analysis of the membership for 1832, 1861, and 1890 produced insights unavailable in 1988.

The interpretation of the evidence is my own, but I have received sound suggestions and commentary from a number of people who read the manuscript along the way. These include Edwin Gaustad, Ronald Dufour, Paul and Violet Becker, Linda Bausserman, Ruth Macaulay, Anthony Carlino, Dawn Casey, and Kimberly Formby. The church created the History Book Committee to see this project to its conclusion, and it was enthusiastically chaired by William Miller. Other members were Paul Becker, Kimberlee Miller, Ruth Macaulay, and James Wynn. Paul Becker undertook the arduous task of preparing an index, without which a book is much less useful. Colin and Jennifer Murphy of Murphy & Murphy patiently and cheerfully designed and guided the book to its beautiful conclusion. The support of the church made it possible to engage Warren Jagger to take the remarkable photographs of the Meeting House that are interspersed in the text. The Rhode Island Historical Society, Brown University, Providence Public Library, and the *Providence Journal* have all granted permission to use various historic pictures.

J. Stanley Lemons
March 2001

CHAPTER 1

"The Prophet of Religious Freedom"

In Geneva, Switzerland, stands the International Monument to the Reformation with statues depicting its leading figures, such as Martin Luther, John Calvin, Gustavus Adolphus, and John Knox. One person represents the whole of North America — Roger Williams, who is described as the "Prophet of Religious Freedom." What a remarkable honor for a man who was repeatedly forced into exile and persecuted in his search for "soul liberty" and whose ideas were scorned in his lifetime. He fled to America and then was banished from Massachusetts because of the convictions of his conscience. The neighboring colonies pointed to Rhode Island as a good example of a bad colony. They regarded Williams' ideas as evil and anarchistic because he believed that one's conscience could not be coerced into belief and that church and state must be separated if true religion is to exist.

When he died in 1683, Williams was generally ignored outside of Providence, and even there the location of his grave was soon forgotten. Yet, in the twentieth century, he came to be seen by many historians as the quintessential American of his time. More books have been written about him than about any other seventeenth century American.[1] When the Religious Newswriters Association* made its list of the ten most significant people and events in the world of religion in the last 1000 years, Roger Williams was eighth on the list. His principles of religious liberty and separation of church and state became part of the general fabric of the United States and are "a beacon for the world."[2] He, not Thomas Jefferson, first used the metaphor of the high "wall of separation" between the garden of Christ (the church) and the wilderness of the world (the state). Historians commonly write that America's main contribution to religion is the theory and practice of religious liberty, and Roger Williams was the prophet of that doctrine.

In October 1635 Roger Williams was convicted of sedition and heresy and sentenced to banishment. Rather than be deported to England, he fled into the snows of February 1636 to the Narragansett Bay area and was sheltered by the Wampanoags. Peter Frederick Rothermel painted this dramatic picture, "The Banishment of Roger Williams," about 1850, depicting a resolute Williams, Bible in hand, entering the wilderness. Courtesy of the Rhode Island Historical Society (RHi x5 20).

In his spiritual pilgrimage Roger Williams gathered only one church — the First Baptist Church in America. Although Williams left the Baptists after a few months, this congregation still honors his search for religious freedom and holds "soul liberty" as its watchword. Soul liberty and separation of church and state became trademark ideas of the Baptists, though in recent years even some calling themselves Baptists have wavered and fallen away.[3] Roger Williams' congregation stands today firmly for the principle of religious freedom.

The First Baptist Church in America was one of the distant consequences of the Protestant Reformation that resulted directly from the spiritual struggles of Roger Williams and other immigrants to New England. The English phase of the Reformation produced a bewildering array of groups and sects, among which were the Baptists. The Baptist movement began in the Old World, but its seeds scattered and sprouted in Rhode Island and elsewhere in the New World within two decades. The Baptists grew out of the Puritan/Separatist movement in England. Various individuals and congregations, described as "Puritans," sought to cleanse the Church of England of its remaining vestiges of Roman Catholicism. Some, despairing of this possibility, separated themselves from the Church of England. Between 1593 and 1607 a number of these dissenters fled to Holland to escape the persecuting hand of the established church. There, some exiles, influenced by the Dutch Mennonites, adopted the crucial Anabaptist idea that the scriptural concept of baptism was believer's baptism. This meant that only persons mature enough to make their own commitment to the Christian faith would be baptized.[4]

John Smyth began an English Baptist church in Amsterdam about 1609, and Thomas Helwys and his followers returned to London in 1611 to found the first Baptist church in England. Helwys' demands for religious freedom were the first to be published in the English language, and he died in prison in 1616 for his beliefs. These first Baptists were General Baptists: that is, they held that every person had a chance for salvation, that none was predestined to be damned, that Christ had died to save any who would

* The Association is comprised of the journalists in the United States and Canada who regularly cover religion for the secular press.

ABOVE In 1636 Roger Williams and his companions established a settlement at a freshwater spring on the banks of the Great Salt Cove. Williams wrote, "I, . . . having a sense of God's merciful providence unto me in my distress, called the place Providence; I desired it be for a shelter for persons distressed of conscience." Engraving from Welcome Arnold Greene. *The Providence Plantations for Two Hundred and Fifty Years* (1886).

believe. The General Baptists had a positive view of human nature, but they believed that one could fall away from grace and salvation. They also drew their pastors and officers from the laity which made the General Baptists fairly egalitarian, but their untrained ministry was less influential in the larger world of Baptists.[5]

A generation later in the 1630s, another variety called Particular Baptists emerged among Puritan/Separatist congregations that had concluded that infant baptism lacked a Biblical foundation. But, these churches were staunch followers of the ideas of John Calvin who held that Christ's atonement was only for the "elect," those predestined by God to be saved. They regarded human nature to be utterly corrupt, redeemable only by God's sovereign will. They also believed in the "perseverance of the saints," which meant, "once saved, always saved."[6] When these new predestinarian Baptists began organizing, the original General Baptists were often called "Old" or "Ancient" Baptists. The General Baptist persuasion soon became a minority view among the English and American Baptists.

OPPOSITE On March 24, 1638, the chief Narragansett sachems, Canonicus (whose mark was a bow) and Miantonomi (whose mark was an arrow) signed this original deed to confirm their 1636 verbal land grant to Roger Williams. The original deed is in the Providence City Archives. Photograph by Norman S. Watson.

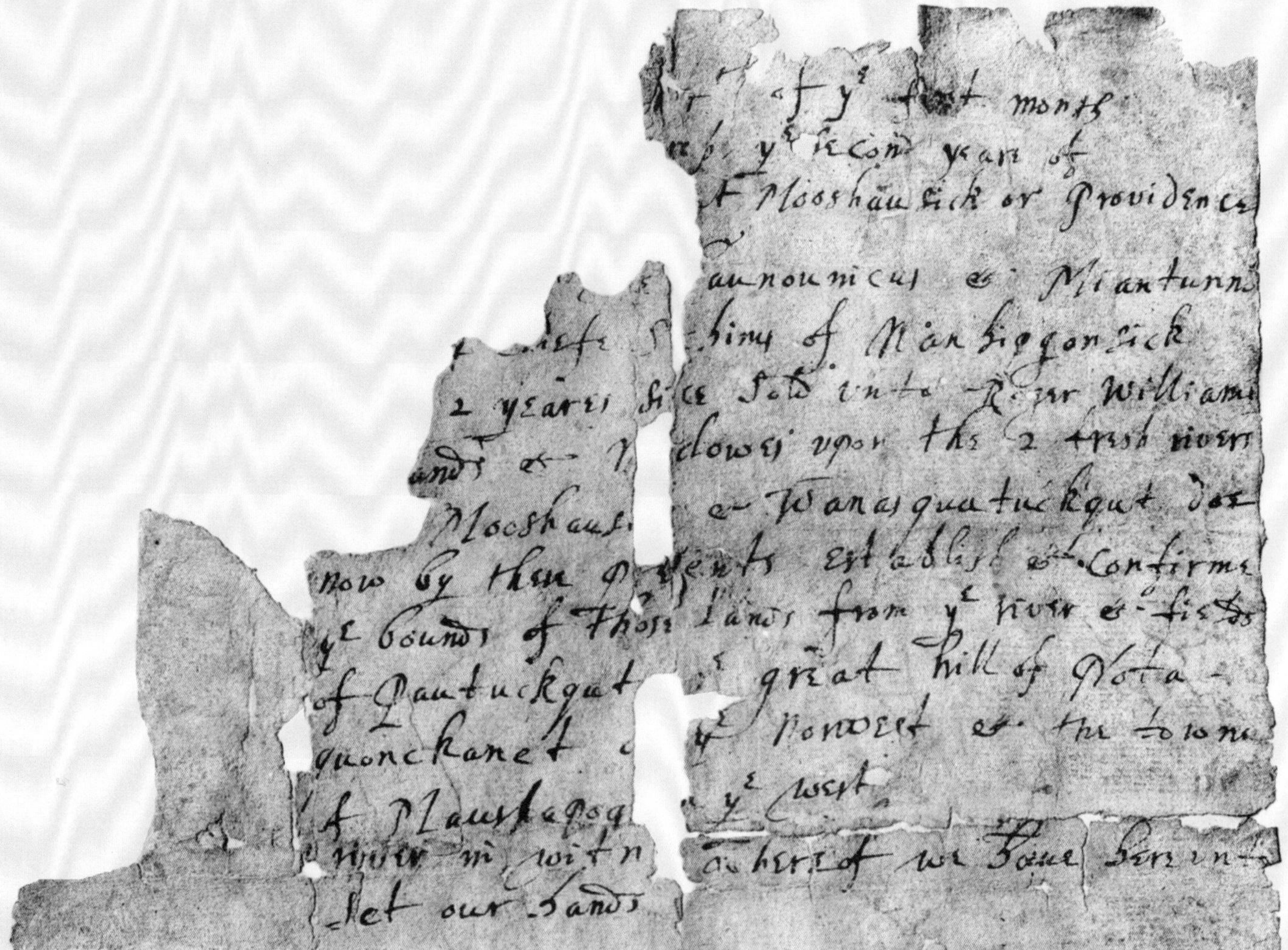
... of ye first month
... ye second year of
... Mooshausick or Providence
... aunnounicus & Miantunnomi
... Sachims of Nanhiggonsick
2 yeares since sold unto Roger Williams
... ands & meadowes upon the 2 fresh rivers
Mooshausick & Wanasquatucket doe
now by these presents establish & confirme
ye bounds of those lands from ye river & fields
of Pautuckqut ... great hill of Nota-
quonckanet ... Nowest & the towne
of Maushapog ... ye west
...
... our hands
in ye presence of ... ye mke of ... Caunounicus
ye mke of Sotaash
ye mke of Miantunnomi
ye mks of Assotemewit
... Witness here
... Roger Williams
Benedict Arnold

The First Baptist Church in America was to be a General Baptist church for most of its first 130 years. Its founder, Roger Williams, was a Particular Baptist. He was an orthodox Calvinist in his belief in limited atonement and predestination, yet the church he started was soon dominated by General Baptists.

Roger Williams was one of thousands of Puritans who came to the New World in the 1630s to establish "godly communities."[7] Williams studied for the ministry at Pembroke College, Cambridge University, where he adopted Puritan principles. Although ordained as an Anglican priest, his Puritan conscience prevented him from swearing an oath to obey the bishops of the Church of England, so he was denied his Master's degree from Cambridge in 1628. Instead he became the private chaplain to the family of Sir William Masham, one of the leading members of the Puritan landowning gentry in England. As such, Williams was involved in the discussions in 1629 which led to the great

> *He attacked the colony's laws that sought to enforce religious conformity. He denied the right of the civil magistrates to punish breaches of religious discipline, to force religious beliefs, or to compel people to attend church.*

migration of Puritans to Massachusetts Bay the following year. He and his wife Mary were not among the first wave that came in 1630, but sailed on the supply ship *Lyon* which arrived in February 1631.

The Boston Puritans welcomed him because he was personally known to many of the leaders and had a reputation for religious zeal; therefore, they offered him the assistant ministership of the Boston church. He stunned them by declining the position unless their church cut its ties with the Church of England. Since the Puritan founders had no intention of becoming Separatists but were seeking to create a godly society based on a *purified* Church of England, they rejected Williams' demand. After tarrying briefly in Salem, Williams departed for the Old Colony, Plymouth, to live among the Separatist Pilgrims.[8]

In Plymouth he assisted the minister of the church while earning a living by farming and trading with the Native Americans within the colony and around Narragansett Bay. A natural linguist, he learned the Indian tongues of the region, and he made firm friendships with the native peoples, moving freely among them even though the various tribes warred against each other. These friendships later saved his life and brought him a haven and home when he fled from religious persecution in Massachusetts Bay.

After two years in Plymouth, Williams resigned from the Plymouth church because he felt that it, too, was insufficiently separated from the Church of England. He learned that some members of the Plymouth congregation had attended Anglican services when they returned to England for a visit. When the Plymouth church did not reprimand them, Williams returned to Salem in late 1633. The Plymouth authorities were not entirely unhappy to see him leave, as Governor William Bradford wrote in his diary that Williams was "a man godly and zealous, having many precious parts but very unsettled in his judgment."[9] At that time

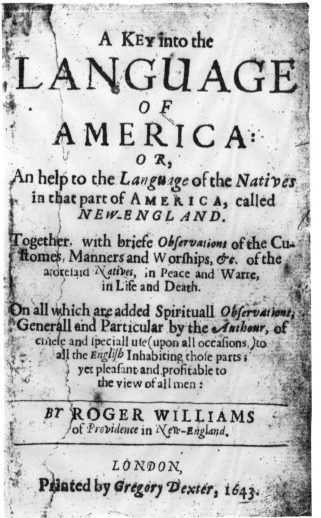

A KEY into the
LANGUAGE
OF
AMERICA:
OR,
An help to the *Language* of the *Natives* in that part of AMERICA, called
NEW-ENGLAND.

Together, with briefe *Observations* of the Customes, Manners and Worships, &c. of the aforesaid *Natives*, in Peace and Warre, in Life and Death.

On all which are added Spirituall *Observations*, Generall and Particular by the *Authour*, of chiefe and speciall use (upon all occasions,)to all the *English* Inhabiting those parts; yet pleasant and profitable to the view of all men:

BY ROGER WILLIAMS
of *Providence* in *New-England.*

LONDON,
Printed by *Gregory Dexter*, 1643.

Roger Williams returned to England in 1643 to seek a charter for the beleaguered Narragansett Bay towns, and while there, he published *A Key into the Language of America*, the first English-language dictionary of any Native American people. More than a dictionary, this work was ethnographic in nature and remains a valuable source of information about the Narragansetts. The printer, Gregory Dexter, accompanied Williams to Providence and in 1654 became the fifth pastor of the Baptist church. Courtesy of the Rhode Island Historical Society (RHi x3 19).

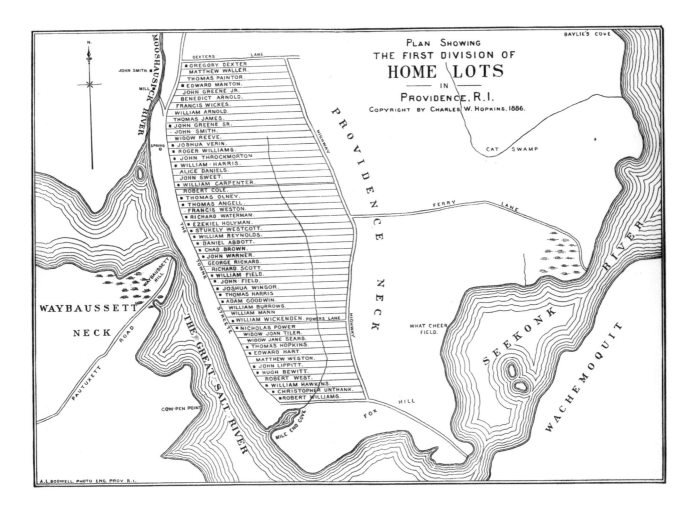

PLAN SHOWING
THE FIRST DIVISION OF
HOME LOTS
IN
PROVIDENCE, R.I.
COPYRIGHT BY CHARLES W. HOPKINS. 1886.

Elder William Brewster predicted that Williams "would run the same course of rigid separatism and Anabaptistry which Mr. John Smyth the Sebaptist of Amsterdam had done."[10] (Since Smyth had concluded that no one had a valid spiritual warrant to baptize, he baptized himself — thus the tag of "Se-baptist.")

Because Williams was engaged as the assistant minister for the Salem church, his return to Massachusetts Bay was a matter of concern to the civil authorities. They forced him to burn a manuscript in which he had questioned the right of the King to grant land to the colonists without first buying it from the Native Americans. The old minister in Salem soon died, and in August 1634 Williams was invited to be the pastor. Now, his ideas on religious freedom and the rights of the Native Americans had a platform. His favorite topic was liberty of conscience.[11]

He attacked the colony's laws that sought to enforce religious conformity. He denied the right of the civil magistrates to punish breaches of religious discipline, to force religious beliefs, or to compel people to attend church. The law required every person to attend the established church, regardless of whether he or she was a member. Williams declared that "forced worship stinks in the nostrils of God." He argued that merging church and state made the government the final arbiter of truth. That was dangerous to truth and religious purity because the state would most likely punish and persecute true religion. He wrote, "The civil sword may make a nation of hypocrites and anti-Christians, but not one Christian." He condemned interference by the government in church matters, saying that it rendered "the garden and spouse of Christ a filthy dunghill and whorehouse of rotten stinking whores and hypocrites." He argued that the church and the state derived from incompatible principles: the church was based on love, the state was based upon the sword. When the state became involved in religious matters, religion was corrupted. Religious liberty, he thought, was the only Christian way to preserve peace in the world and to advance true religion. He lived in an age when rivers of blood were being shed in the name of Christ, as Catholics and Protestants massacred each other in the terrible wars of religion.

Such ideas threatened the religious and political basis of the Puritan colony, but Williams went further. His attacks upon the Christian character of the King of England and his declaration that the King's charter was invalid threatened the colony's legal and economic basis. From the beginning enemies in England had sought to have the Massachusetts Bay charter revoked, and Williams' attacks caused the magistrates to fear that his insults to the monarch would be used to void the charter.

After failing to get Williams to recant, the magistrates forced the Salem church to withdraw its support from him so they could bring him to trial. In October 1635 the General Court found him guilty of having "preached and divulged divers new and dangerous opinions against the authority of magistrates."[12] His sentence was banishment to

ABOVE The original settlers of Providence received their home lots from Roger Williams in 1636 and 1637. The village had one street with nearly all the houses strung out along it. Roger Williams' lot is across from the spring, and next door was Joshua Verin. Map from Charles Wyman Hopkins, *The Home Lots of the Early Settlers of the Providence Plantations* (1886).

ABOVE Here Roger Williams is depicted as a "Cavalier," complete with long hair to his shoulders, a Van Dyke beard and mustache, a dandified plumed hat, and fancy frogs to button his coat. This mid-nineteenth century painting by Alonzo Chappel is "The Landing of Roger Williams." Courtesy of The Museum of Art, Rhode Island School Design, Museum Works of Art Fund, photography by Cathy Carver.

England. As he was ill and winter was approaching, the court stayed the banishment order until spring on condition that Williams stop talking about separation of church and state. Since he could not stop this free-flowing fountain, they decided to ship him out when the supply vessel came in February. Williams later claimed that his old friend John Winthrop, one of the judges of the court that had condemned him, warned him of the impending action. Hastily leaving his wife and home, he slipped away in the snows of January and set out from Salem for Narragansett Bay. After wandering in the wilderness for several weeks, he was rescued by Wampanoags and spent the rest of the winter in the wigwams of Massasoit at present-day Bristol, Rhode Island.

Several of his parishioners from Salem joined him in the Indian camp; and when spring came, Massasoit gave them land in present-day East Providence where they started to plant crops and build houses. But, an emissary from Governor Edward Winslow of Plymouth shortly arrived to tell Williams that he was still within the land grant of Plymouth and that Plymouth might be forced to extradite him to Massachusetts. Consequently, in May or June 1636, Williams led his little band across the Seekonk River, paddled around Fox Point to a fresh water spring on the banks of the Great Salt Cove, and established the first town in Rhode Island. The land was given to him by his good friends, Canonicus and Miantonomi, grand sachems of the Narragansetts. He wrote, "I, having made covenants of peaceable neighborhood with all the sachems and natives round about us, and having a sense of God's merciful providence unto me in my distress, called the place Providence; I desired it be for a shelter for persons distressed of conscience."[13]

Roger Williams
a study from the Bust in the Hall of Fame, by McNeil

His settlement began with five or six families. While they had no constitution or compact, Williams got them to agree that "no man should be molested for his conscience." Indeed, they signed a statement to subject themselves to such

TOP No one knows what Roger Williams looked like, so artists have invented images of him. This completely anachronistic engraving was done by F. Halpin in 1847. Williams is dressed in late 18th century clothing and is wearing a white, powdered wig. Halpin probably took an engraving of President John Adams and put a new face on it. Courtesy of the Rhode Island Historical Society (RHi x3 19).

MIDDLE Since the 1880s, some images of Roger Williams have used a male descendent of Williams as the model. This picture, drawn by C. Dodge in 1936, from a study of the bust of Roger Williams by McNeil in the Hall of Fame, presents Williams more accurately as a Puritan, with plain clothes and a "Roundhead" haircut. Photo from the archives of the First Baptist Church in America.

BOTTOM Another likeness of Williams, a charcoal portrait by the Providence artist Huseyin Halit, was given by the Student Government Association of Pembroke College, Brown University, to Pembroke College, Cambridge, in 1964. Closely resembling the 1936 C. Dodge drawing of Williams, it was probably based on the same source. Photo from *Pembroke Alumna*, (July 1964). Courtesy of Brown University Archives.

"orders and agreements as shall be made for the public good of the body in an orderly way by the major consent" (majority vote of the heads of households), but "only in civil things."[14] In a word, matters of religion and conscience were to be left to the individual. That proved to be easier said than done.

Providence was founded, as Williams said, "for such as were destitute, especially for Conscience sake." He gathered his little flock in 1636 and commenced worship services in his home. Living next door to Williams were Joshua and Jane Verin, who had followed him from Salem. Jane faithfully attended the services, which included not only Sunday preaching but prayer, Bible reading and personal testimonials in lengthy meetings during the week.[15] Eventually Joshua tried to prevent Jane from attending services because he thought it took too much of her time. He beat her so badly that the neighbors heard her screams, and Williams wrote that "she went in danger of her life." In May 1638 Joshua was brought before the town meeting and charged with infringing upon his wife's freedom of conscience. He replied that she was breaking God's commandment requiring "the subjection of wives to their husbands." The town meeting, however, stripped him of the right to vote until he agreed to permit her to worship freely. Consequently, he packed up his wife and his possessions and returned to Salem, where he could make her obey.[16]

Others took Verin's place, especially when the Antinomian controversy boiled over in Massachusetts. Among the newcomers were carriers of Baptist ideas. The Antinomians, a substantial group that gathered around the dynamic figure of Anne Hutchinson, became a theological and political threat to the established order in Massachusetts. They held that the Puritan stress upon obedience to the laws of the church and state led to an emphasis upon salvation by works rather than salvation by faith. They sought to elect members of their persuasion to the government and refused to serve in the war against the Pequots unless the chaplain was from their party. In November 1637 the magistrates disarmed, disenfranchised, and forced the Antinominans into exile. One of them, John Clarke, learned from Roger Williams that Aquidneck Island could be purchased, and Williams arranged to buy it from Canonicus and Miantonomi. The Antinomian refugees began arriving in Rhode Island in the spring of 1638. While most of them established the town of Portsmouth, some came to Providence. John Winthrop wrote in his diary that the "Anabaptists" among the Antinomians went to Providence.[17] ("Anabaptist" was a derogatory label commonly used in the seventeenth century to slander Baptists by trying to tie them to the wild, bizarre excesses of the Anabaptists who seized the German city of Munster a century before in 1534-1535.)

These new settlers included Richard and Catherine Scott. Governor Winthrop wrote: "At Providence things grew still worse; for a sister of Mrs. [Anne] Hutchinson, the wife of one Scott, being infected with Anabaptistry, and going last year to live at Providence, Mr. Williams was taken (or rather emboldened) by her to make open profession thereof. . . ." After joining Williams' congregation, Catherine helped to convince him that only believer's baptism was based on Scripture. As a result, Williams became a Baptist; and in the fall of 1638, he and about twenty other men and women were baptized.[18] Williams deputized Ezekiel Holliman to baptize him, and he in turn baptized the rest. Thus, began the first Baptist church in America. Williams and his congregation believed in congregational polity, that is, they rejected any church hierarchy and authority outside the congregation itself; they affirmed believer's baptism; and they held to "soul liberty," uncoerced freedom of conscience, which required separation of church and state.

Providence attracted the distressed of conscience and the land hungry, and Ezekiel Holliman was both. He arrived in Providence in 1638 and joined Williams' band of believers. Yet, Holliman was one of those who pressured Williams to grant extra land in the Pawtuxet area (present-day Cranston) to the original settlers, and in his search for more land, Holliman finally settled in Shawomet (present-day Warwick) in 1647. Although he was to be one of the original proprietors of Warwick, Holliman first moved to Aquidneck Island and began proselytizing, and, according to a recent historian, "was, in 1640, the only Baptist on the island."[19] This was four years before John Clarke established a Baptist church in Newport.

Despite having gathered the first Baptist congregation, Williams' spiritual migration did not end here. As Richard Scott said of Williams, "I walked with him in the Baptist way about three or four months, in which time he broke with the society and declared at large the grounds and reason for it — that their baptism could not be right because it was not administered by an apostle."[20] Williams, who was so radical in matters of conscience and separation of church and state, was quite conventional in his adherence to the traditional concept of apostolic succession. His concern for apostolic authority caused him to doubt the validity of his baptism. How could he be baptized by someone who had not been properly baptized? He concluded that the true church, true articles and ordinances, and the true succession had been lost since the fourth century when the Roman emperors designated Christianity as the state religion. "Christianity was

In the 19th and 20th centuries Roger Williams'
name and image were appropriated for everything
from the city seal of Providence to commercial
enterprises including a bank, a bottling company,
a flour mill, a brewery, livery stables, a dairy, a
brand of tobacco, a paint company, a silverware
manufacturer, the city park, street names, and
various pieces of sheet music. This late 19th
century advertising card for the Roger Williams
Insurance Company used the image of Williams
from the city seal of Providence.

THE

BLOVDY TENENT,

of Persecution, for caufe of
Conscience, difcuffed, in

A Conference *betweene*

TRVTH and PEACE.

VVho,

In all tender Affection, prefent to the High
Court of *Parliament,* (as the *Refult* of
their *Difcourfe*) thefe, (amongft other
Paffages) of *higheft confideration.*

Printed in the Year 1644.

eclipsed," said Williams, "and the professors of it fell asleep." He felt that the rites and articles of belief since then were mere "inventions of men," and the only hope of a true church was in the coming of a new apostleship from God.[21] He believed in the imminent return of Christ and admonished all to be prepared for it. Williams, therefore, separated from the church that he had gathered and remained an unaffiliated preacher until his death in 1683.

Williams' subsequent career and activities involved him deeply in politics to defend his haven for the "distressed of conscience." The neighboring colonies of Massachusetts

ABOVE *The Bloudy Tenent of Persecution, for cause of Conscience* has become Roger Williams' most famous book. Published in 1644 while he was in London to secure a charter for his threatened colony, it was his vigorous defense of religious freedom. Mincing no words, he wrote that "it is the will and command of God that . . . a permission of the most *Paganish, Jewish,* Turkish or anti-Christian consciences and worships be granted to *all* men of all nations." Courtesy of the Rhode Island Historical Society (RHi x3 1411).

Bay, Connecticut, and Plymouth formed the United Colonies, a military alliance which pointedly excluded the towns around Narragansett Bay, and they attempted to extend their jurisdiction over Rhode Island. Williams rushed to England in 1643 and secured a charter from Parliament for "Providence Plantations in Narragansett Bay in New England." This grant provided for a government that would unite the four towns (Providence, Warwick, Portsmouth, and Newport), but it took until 1647 to persuade Newport and Portsmouth to cooperate. Under this charter Williams was Chief Officer from September 1644 to May 1647. When William Coddington of Newport obtained a patent that made him governor for life over Newport and Portsmouth, Williams and his friend John Clarke sailed to England in 1651 to get Coddington's commission revoked. Having succeeded, Williams returned home, leaving Clarke in London to represent the interests of the colony. In the restored government, Williams served as governor from September 1654 to May 1657.

Through it all, Williams laid down the principles of religious freedom that Rhode Islanders came to accept. While many settlers dissented from the orthodoxy of the Puritan colonies, most wanted to mix church and state, but Williams' principles won out. The religious diversity of Rhode Island became so great that they agreed that acceptance of religious freedom was a minimum requirement for civil peace. When the restored monarchy in England voided the old charter, Clarke wrote the principle of religious liberty into the Charter of 1663, saying that the people wished

*to hold forth a lively experiment, that a most
flourishing civil state may stand and best be
maintained . . . with a full liberty in religious
concernments . . . no person within the said colony
at any time hereafter shall be in anywise molested,
punished, disquieted or called in question, for any
difference in opinion in matters of religion. . . .
All and every person. . . freely and fully have
and enjoy his own judgements and conscience
in matters of religious discernments.*[22]

Subsequently, similar language was included in the new charters for New Jersey, the Carolinas, and Pennsylvania.[23]

Roger Williams

In the 1640s and 1650s Williams plunged headlong into the religious debates in England and America.[24] Not the least was the publication of his vigorous defense of soul liberty and the attack upon religious persecution in *The Bloudy Tenent of Persecution, for the Cause of Conscience*, published in 1644. On the second page of his tract he boldly wrote, "It is the will and command of God that . . . a permission of the most *Paganish*, *Jewish*, Turkish or anti-Christian conscience and worships be granted to *all* men, in all nations and countries . . . ."[25] Soul liberty meant that everyone must be free to follow his conscience.

After he resigned from the Baptist church, he maintained an interest in Baptist doctrine and activities. In 1649 he observed that the practice of immersion which John Clarke and Mark Lukar were using in baptizing converts "comes nearer the first practice of our great Founder Christ than other practices of religion do. . . ."[26] When Clarke, Obadiah Holmes and John Crandall were arrested in Massachusetts in 1651 for violating the law against Baptists, Holmes was given thirty lashes well laid on. Williams responded with a furious letter to Governor William Endecott: "The Maker and Searcher of our hearts knows with what bitterness I write. . . ." He warned Endecott that punishing dissenters might cause him to persecute Christ himself. "It is a dreadful voice from the King of Kings and Lord of Lords: 'Endecott, Endecott, why huntest thou me? Why imprisonest thou me? why finest? why so bloodily whippest? why wouldest thou . . . hang & burn me?' " Williams said that when one fights against the human conscience, one eventually fights against God.[27]

Williams' final decades were troubled by bitter controversies with greedy, land-hungry settlers who sought to steal the Narragansetts' lands, endless boundary disputes with Connecticut and Massachusetts which continued to press claims over Rhode Island, and the descent of New England into the worst Indian war in American history which saw Providence (including Williams' own house) burned to the ground. He outlived nearly every one of his contemporaries and died sometime in early 1683.

Roger Williams never wavered in his defense of soul liberty, but his example was rejected outside of Rhode Island. He was generally forgotten for the next seventy years. Then, when mid-eighteenth century Baptists of New England battled against ecclesiastical taxes, they rediscovered Roger Williams. In the early nineteenth century, all of the states and the United States were inventing their histories, and Williams, the founder of Rhode Island, suddenly found several biographers. His reputation has continued to rise since then, leading the historian Edwin Gaustad to write in 1999, "The cause of one lonely prophet in the seventeenth century has become, on the eve of the twenty-first century, the cause of humankind."[28]

ABOVE This is Roger Williams' signature from his letter to the town of Providence on December 8, 1680. Courtesy of the Rhode Island Historical Society (RHi x3 1444).

CHAPTER 2

"The Ancient Baptist Church of Providence"[1]

Until 1755 the First Baptist Church did not keep a "book of records" of its members and transactions, but by then this lack was "attended with great inconveniences."[2] Consequently a clerk was elected and minutes and membership lists written down. This means that the details of the congregation for much of its first 120 years are sketchy. Enough is known from early accounts, manuscript collections, and family histories, however, to show the church persisting, growing, and being the leader of the General Six Principle Baptists in southern New England.

Its story reflected the great religious movements of the day as well as the political and economic climate of Rhode Island. The Providence Baptist church survived the resignation of its founder and leader, an early schism in its body, the destruction of the entire town during King Philip's War, and the arrival of substantial religious competition. The congregation erected the first church edifice in Providence and grew as the town surged in size and prosperity after 1700.

With the departure of Roger Williams, leadership in the church passed to a series of lay elders, drawn from the congregation itself. In fact, the Providence church did not have a college-educated pastor from 1639 until the coming of James Manning in 1771. In the seventeenth century most Baptists, including Roger Williams, rejected the idea of a "hireling ministry."[3] Beginning with Chad Brown and ending with Samuel Winsor, Jr., these lay pastors exhorted the faithful on the Sabbath, carried out other pastoral functions, but earned a livelihood in secular occupations. They received no remuneration from the church as most considered any payment as committing the sin of simony. Samuel Winsor, Sr., so wanted to avoid even the appearance of simony that he refused to accept invitations to Sunday dinner with his church members.[4] The unpaid ministry ended with the calling of Manning, who insisted upon a salary.[5]

OPPOSITE After many years of concern and planning, in 2000 the organ was rebuilt by the Foley-Baker Organ Company. The Meeting House had no organ until 1834 when Nicholas Brown donated the instrument which was built by the E. & G.G. Hook Co. of Boston. In 1884 Hilborn T. Roosevelt rebuilt and enlarged the organ, and then about 1927 the Skinner Organ Company rebuilt part of it again. A major reworking by the Wicks Organ Company occurred during the restoration of the building in 1957-58, but aspects of that organ began to fail by the late 1970s. Photo by Warren Jagger (2001).

In the years after Williams resigned, Chad Brown, Thomas Olney, William Wickenden, Gregory Dexter, and Pardon Tillinghast held simultaneous or overlapping terms as pastor. Of these, only Olney was among the original flock baptized by Williams — and he would lead a splinter group out of the church in 1652. Isaac Backus, the eighteenth century Baptist historian, stated that Olney succeeded Williams as the pastor, but Chad Brown is traditionally regarded as the second pastor of the church. Brown later ordained William Wickenden.[6] Wickenden became less involved in the Providence church in the 1650s and went to New Netherlands [New York] in late 1656 to proselytize among the settlers there. The Dutch authorities arrested and imprisoned him for four months and then expelled him. He was described as "a cobble from Rhode Island" who "stated that he was commissioned by Christ. He began to preach at Vlissingen [Flushing] and then went with the people into the river and dipped them."[7]

Gregory Dexter joined the church in 1644 after accompanying Roger Williams back to Rhode Island from England. They met in London while Williams was securing a charter to protect Rhode Island from its hostile neighbors, Massachusetts Bay, Connecticut, and Plymouth. Williams persuaded Dexter, a printer by trade, to publish his first books, *A Key into the Language of America* and *The Bloudy Tenent of Persecution for the Cause of Conscience*. Dexter, already a General Baptist and a preacher, provoked the displeasure of the English authorities by his activities.[8] As a result he emigrated when Williams sailed home and soon became a leader in the church in Providence. Dexter was typical of the sort of Baptists who were coming to Rhode Island: an austere General Baptist.[9] An old account said he "was never observed to laugh and seldom to smile. So earnest was he in the ministry, that he could hardly forbear preaching when he came into a house, or met a number of persons in the street."[10] He served as one of the elders until his death in 1700 at age ninety. By then, Pardon Tillinghast had become the sixth minister of the church.

From 1638 until the beginning of the eighteenth century, Baptists were the only organized body of worshipers in Providence. But, the dissenting impulse that has resulted in

TIMELINE

1652	Schism in FBC; Particular Baptists seceded
1654	FBC Elders helped establish the 2d Baptist Church of Newport
1692	General Six Principle Baptist Association began
1700	First meetinghouse erected
1726	Second meetinghouse built
1727-32	Joseph Jenckes, Governor of Rhode Island
1754-63	French and Indian War
1764	Rhode Island College (Brown) chartered
1767	Warren Baptist Association began
1770	Rhode Island College relocated to Providence
1771	Schism in FBC; Six Principle Baptists seceded
1774	Six Principle Baptists formed the Baptist Yearly Meeting

at least sixty Baptist denominations in the United States today was already at work in the seventeenth century, even in the thin ranks of that first Baptist church. After 1652 when the church divided over the ritual of laying-on-of-hands and differences of theology, there were two Baptist congregations.[11] That impulse was even stronger in the Baptist church in Newport which split into three kinds of Baptists between 1644 and 1671.[12]

The theology of Roger Williams had been Calvinist, but by 1652 the majority in Providence had become General Six Principle Baptists. As General Baptists, they held that Christ died that all may have a chance to gain salvation. As Six Principle Baptists, they believed that Hebrews 6: 1-2 listed six principles of Christ, among which was the ceremonial laying-on-of-hands. In the seventeenth century all varieties of Baptists generally practiced the rite of laying-on-of-hands in addition to baptism, the Lord's Supper, dedication of children, right hand of fellowship, the kiss of charity, love feast, foot washing, and anointing with oil.[13] However, the Six Principle Baptists emphasized the ritual of hands, making it equal to baptism and communion. They also banished congregational singing from their services because they considered it to be a desecration of worship. Thomas Olney opposed the requirement of laying-on-of-hands and withdrew in 1652 with a Calvinist minority. Until his death in 1682, he served as their pastor. Olney's son seems to have

taken over when the father died, but the break-away group, including the son, had drifted back into the original church by 1718.

Laying-on-of-hands, which tends to be reserved today to the ordaining of clergy and deacons, was for the Six Principle Baptists a manifestation of an egalitarian understanding of the "priesthood of all believers." All believers, not just pastors, had to go "under hands" which emphasized the spiritual equality of church members. The rite of hands for all members diminished a special role for clergy and marked the acceptance by Six Principle Baptists of the laity's preaching, prophesying, and performing baptisms.[14] Since the Six Principle Baptists preferred unschooled ministers, they held that "all Christian believers received the promise of the Holy Spirit by the act."[15] By eliminating a professional ministry, the Six Principle Baptists greatly reduced clerical domination. Furthermore, women seem to have had equal voting rights and permission to speak in Six Principle Baptist church meetings.[16]

One must be careful not to overemphasize the divisions among Baptists because a rather fluid relationship existed between the different varieties.[17] Members and ministers moved back and forth between congregations or they changed their doctrines; however, the issue of laying-on-of-hands probably was more divisive in Rhode Island than elsewhere. It eventually became the cardinal distinctive for Six Principle Baptists. This issue produced tension within First Baptist and within the larger Six Principle Baptist denomination for many years. The eighth pastor, James Brown, and Governor Joseph Jenckes (brother of Ebenezer Jenckes, the seventh pastor) sought to relax the ritual of imposing hands in 1730-1731 by attempting to bring in a co-pastor who did not hold to the necessity of laying-on-of-hands. Governor Jenckes also thought that the minister ought to be paid.[18] This effort was vigorously opposed by Deacon Samuel Winsor, Sr., and a schism threatened. Winsor declared, ". . . all those who took anything for preaching were like Simon Magus."[19] In a showdown in May 1732, Winsor carried the day, and the Providence church adopted a policy of closing its communion to anyone not "under hands." This practice of closed communion subsequently spread through the Six Principle churches.

When Elder Brown died in October, Winsor was elected to succeed him as pastor. Winsor represented the traditional, rural Baptists while Brown and Jenckes reflected the urban and urbane trend in the developing commercial seaports of New England.[20] Baptists in the major seaports, particularly Boston and Newport, were being affected by a kind of "iron law of creeping respectability." They wanted greater acceptance and respect from other denominations, and this desire manifested itself in their imitating Congregationalist decorum and practices. Winsor's victory in 1732 postponed the

Laying-on-of-hands, which tends to be reserved today to the ordaining of clergy and deacons, was for the Six Principle Baptists a manifestation of an egalitarian understanding of the "priesthood of all believers."

---

day when the forces of respectability would triumph in Providence.

By 1771 the rigid Six Principle believers found themselves in the minority, so they seceded from the Providence church and followed their pastor, Samuel Winsor, Jr., to Johnston to establish another church. Although the issue would arise from time to time, the matter was essentially settled in the Providence church in August 1791 when the congregation voted to eliminate laying-on-of-hands as a requirement for membership.[21] The Six Principle Baptists retreated from the commercial seaports of Rhode Island into the back country where they declined in the first decades of the nineteenth century. One issue was always how rigidly they would maintain their peculiar rites.[22] After 1815 they rapidly lost ground to the Freewill Baptists who also believed in general atonement and generally favored uneducated ministers, but practiced open communion, readily accepted members from other denominations, and enjoyed congregational singing.[23] While churches all over New England struggled to develop congregational singing, the Six Principle Baptists would have none of it.[24]

The Providence church was the founding church of the General Six Principle Baptists in New England. Not only was it the first of its kind here, two of its pastors, Gregory Dexter and William Wickenden, went to Newport to install the Second Baptist Church in Newport in 1656.[25] Then Baptists from Providence helped the Swansea church get established after 1680.[26] Furthermore, members of First Baptist spread out in the countryside around Providence and founded other churches in Smithfield, Glocester, Cranston, and Johnston. Jonathan Sprague, ordained by the Providence church in 1685, began preaching in Smithfield, and in 1706 John Hawkins, another member from Providence, gathered a congregation in Smithfield and was ordained by them to be their pastor. Hawkins' church was

subsequently pastored by still another member from First Baptist, Joshua Winsor, from 1741 to 1757.[27] When the Richmond Six Principle Baptist church organized in 1732, Daniel Averitt of First Baptist was its first pastor.[28] Later, Thomas Burlingame, the 10th pastor of First Baptist, helped to establish a church in Cranston and was called to be their first pastor in 1764.[29]

By 1692 the Six Principle churches began to gather yearly to associate and share concerns, making it the first Baptist association in America.[30] They called upon each other to settle disputes and to ordain new pastors and deacons. By 1739 the Six Principle Baptist Association included twelve churches, led by the Providence church. Finally in 1764 they decided to have each church send three delegates who would assemble in Providence each May. Two years later they voted to rotate the annual meetings between Providence, Newport, and Swansea, the three dominant churches in the association. Even after the split in the Providence church in 1771 when most of the Six Principle believers seceded, First Baptist remained active in the Six Principle Baptist Association. James Manning preached the opening sermon at the September 1773 meeting of the association in Swansea, and delegates from First Baptist attended the annual meetings for several years until the association became extinct. Manning was one of the ministers who ordained Benjamin Mason of Swansea in September 1784 at the annual association meeting at Newport.[31] This event is noteworthy in that the Providence church had finally joined the Warren Association in 1782, ending its formal ties to the Six Principle Baptist Association. On the other hand, James Manning, the president of a struggling Baptist college which sought support in all directions, tried to maintain cordial relations with all kinds of Baptists.

Providence Baptists were a modest group in a small town until the eighteenth century. The community was just a

ABOVE Joseph Jenckes (1656-1740), governor from 1727 to 1732, was the first Providence man to serve in that office under the royal charter of 1663. His brother, Ebenezer Jenckes, was pastor of First Baptist Church from 1719-1726. The Jenckes's favored relaxing the ritual of laying-on-of-hands, and Joseph wanted his church to become more sophisticated and respectable by having a college-educated, paid minister. Courtesy of the Rhode Island Historical Society (RHi x3 595).

James Manning (1738-1791) was the twelfth pastor of the church and the first
since Roger Williams to have a college education. Initially he came to Rhode
Island to found a college in 1764, which became Brown University. After the
college moved to Providence, Manning was called in 1771 to the pastorate of
the church, and he resigned just months before his death in 1791. A large
man, he was 32 years old when the Scottish immigrant Cosmo Alexander
painted this portrait in 1770. Manning's attire, wearing a wig, black coat and
Geneva bands like the Congregationalist ministers, reflected the new formality
and sophistication that urban Baptists desired. Courtesy of Brown University.

farming village, stretched along a single dirt lane before King Philip's War (1675-1676) left the town in ruins and all its people scattered. When that terrifying and devastating war hit New England, Newport was untouched; but the Native Americans swept away everything on the west side of Narragansett Bay. They laid waste to the whole of the Providence Plantations so that by April 1676 not a single English family remained from Point Judith to Providence. However, after the complete defeat of the Indians, the settlers returned and began rebuilding. A few local figures turned from farming to seafaring with other colonies and the West Indies. One of these, Pardon Tillinghast, built a storehouse and the first wharf in Providence in 1680 and became a man of substantial means. As the town prospered, its population grew, new streets were laid out, and various public buildings erected. The town built its first jail in 1699, and Tillinghast erected the first religious meetinghouse in 1700.[32]

Until that time, the Baptists had worshipped in homes or out-of-doors in pleasant weather. Tillinghast built on his property at his own expense a tiny meetinghouse — described as having a roof in the shape of a haycap.[33] In the middle of the room was a firepit, and the smoke escaped through an opening in the roof. While the place might seem grim and smoky to moderns, it was heated, which is more than can be said of many of the larger meetinghouses of the eighteenth century, including the present Meeting House when it was built seventy-five years later. This little edifice was located on a 30-by-30 foot lot on North Main Street at the bottom of present-day Star Street, and the deed indicated that it was a Six Principle Baptist church. Tillinghast deeded the property to the church in 1711.[34]

The eighteenth century ushered in a period of expansion for Providence. With the Native American threat gone, settlers moved into the outlying areas so that the territory that once was the town of Providence—the whole northern third of the colony—began to be subdivided into new towns, beginning in 1731 with Glocester, Smithfield and Scituate. New growth and people brought additional religious activity, and soon the Baptists had plenty of competition from other denominations. During the first thirty years of the new century, Quakers, Congregationalists, and Anglicans all erected meetinghouses and churches, and the Baptists replaced their little building with a larger one.

The other denominations first appeared in Newport, which was by far the most prosperous and dynamic part of the colony until the 1730s. While Providence was still a struggling, back-water, agricultural community, Newport, through oceanic commerce, became one of the leading towns in British North America. Even on the eve of the American Revolution, by which time Providence was swiftly catching up, Newport still had more than twice the population of

Nicholas Brown and Daniel Jenckes were wealthy, cosmopolitan merchants who, like many urban Baptists, desired greater respectability and formality. Establishing the college was part of this effort. Especially they wanted an educated minister, instead of the usual "illiterate" preachers who made up the ranks of the Six Principle elders.

Providence. Nevertheless, overseas trade had produced a merchant elite in Providence that shaped political, economic, and religious affairs in the second half of the eighteenth century.

The Quakers who arrived in Newport in 1656 dominated Aquidneck Island from the 1660s. By then they had begun to attract people in Providence; in fact, Richard and Catherine Scott are often regarded as the first Providence converts to the Quakers. The first non-Baptist meetinghouse to be erected in the whole, undivided Providence was a Quaker meetinghouse in present-day Saylesville in Lincoln in 1703-1704. By 1718 a mission group was meeting in Providence proper, and in 1725 the members built a meetinghouse on Stamper's Hill, on present-day University Heights.

Quaker efforts in Providence were paralleled by those of the Congregationalists and Anglicans. Indeed, it appears that an element of competition and rivalry spurred some of this activity. In October 1721 three Congregational ministers from Massachusetts sent a letter to the leading men of Providence asking for their support in starting a church and inviting these gentlemen to build a pew in a meetinghouse that might be erected. They hoped that "ancient matters, that had acrimony in them, may be buried in oblivion." Those "ancient matters," of course, were the persecution of Baptists and other dissenters in Massachusetts. Their letter was answered by Jonathan Sprague, an elder in the Baptist church, who denounced them as wolves in sheep's clothing and described their letter as "the voice of false prophets."[35] He noted that the persecution of dissenters still continued in Massachusetts, that constables in Attleborough and Mendon had recently seized the property of Baptists who refused to pay taxes that were levied to support Congregational ministers and meetinghouses.[36] Undeterred, the Congregationalists bought a lot on the corner of Benefit and College streets and erected a meetinghouse in 1723. The activities of the Congregationalists stirred the Anglicans to establish a church in Providence. A smattering of Anglicans already lived there, and in 1722 they organized King's

Church and erected a building at the corner of Howland and North Main Street.[37] (King's Church was renamed St. John's after the American Revolution.)

With all their competitors building meetinghouses in the 1720s, and their membership increasing, is it surprising that the Baptists felt the need for a new edifice? And, so, on May 30, 1726, they raised a new meetinghouse on the lot beside their little haycap building. (It stood on the site where the office building at One Smith Hill now stands.) This meetinghouse was 40 by 40 feet; inside, it had backless benches instead of pews and a raised pulpit on the western end of the room. At high tide the water of the Great Salt Cove nearly came up to that side of the building. This served as the meetinghouse until the erection of the present structure in 1774-1775. After that, it was used successively as a sugar refinery, a rag depository, a paper mill, and storehouse before being torn down in the nineteenth century.[38]

John Howland, who worked in Benjamin Gladding's barber shop in 1770, left a description of the services at "Elder Winsor's meeting." He noted that the worship was led by elders rather than by trained clergymen, as was the case with the Congregationalists and Anglicans. These elders were often farmers who had no salary or other means of support except their own labor. They preached in any place where there was a gathering, and the congregation did not know who would preach until one began. When more than one elder was present and the first had exhausted himself, he would declare, "There is time and space left if anyone has further to offer." Then, one after another, the elders would get up and preach; so a church service had no set time for its end.[39]

Samuel Winsor, Jr., was the leading elder of the Providence church until the arrival of the Rev. Dr. James Manning. Manning had come to Rhode Island to establish a Baptist college for which he had received a charter from the General Assembly in 1764. He became the pastor of the Baptist Church in Warren and opened a Latin School for prospective scholars. A contest ensued between Providence and Newport to see which would become the permanent home of the new college. Despite the manifest advantages in size, wealth, and sophistication that Newport seemed to hold, Providence won the prize. Through the efforts of its merchant elite and Governor Stephen Hopkins, the college relocated to Providence in 1770.[40]

The Rev. Ezra Stiles, a Newport Congregationalist minister and future president of Yale, wrote in his diary on May 3, 1770, that the Baptist college had recently voted to remove to Providence and "the Browns and Jenckes intend to turn off Elder Windsor [sic] & put in President Manning for their minister."[41] Nicholas Brown and Daniel Jenckes were wealthy, cosmopolitan merchants who, like many urban Baptists, desired greater respectability and formality.

Establishing the college was part of this effort. Especially they wanted an educated minister, instead of the usual "illiterate" preachers who made up the ranks of the Six Principle elders. ("Illiterate" meant that they could not read Greek or Latin, that they were not college-educated.) The effort to exclude "illiterate" preachers was such that Elder Nathan Young of Smithfield complained in early 1770 "that it had got so far already as scarcely to do for a common Illiterate Minister to preach in the baptist meeting at Providence."[42]

Manning immediately associated himself with the "Elder Winsor's meeting" and was invited to preach. Ironically, Winsor gave Manning the opening. By 1770 Winsor was making repeated complaints to the church that his duties were too heavy for him, particularly since he lived several miles away in Johnston. Not only was he preaching in Providence, he held other services for the growing number of members who lived in the country. In fact, in 1761 those backcountry Baptists began trying to build a meetinghouse in Johnston.[43] Winsor urged the church to provide help for him in the ministry, and James Manning seemed to be the answer.[44] But, Manning was a Calvinist who did not insist on the laying-on-of-hands as a requirement for church membership, and he favored congregational singing, something which Winsor felt was "very disgustful."[45] An impressive speaker and personality, Manning soon had the majority on his side. When Manning applied for membership, Winsor opposed it, but when the vote was taken, Manning won. Women made up a majority of the membership and they mostly sided with Manning.[46] Winsor was so upset at this turn of events that he appealed to the next meeting of the Six Principle Association "whether the Sisters had a right to vote in Church Meetings." The association replied that each church determined its own practices.[47] Having failed to prevent Manning from being admitted, in May 1771 Winsor withdrew along with eighty-six others who clung to the strict practices of the Six Principle Baptists.[48] In July the church elected Manning as its twelfth pastor.

Winsor and his folk regrouped, beginning with a church meeting at the home of Nedabiah Angell in North Providence on June 21, 1771, at which time they elected Winsor as Moderator and Job Olney as Clerk. John Dyer, one of the first three deacons of record in the Providence church, continued that role in the secessionist church, and he was joined in November by Nicholas Easton, another of the original three deacons. Easton's views on the laying-on-of-hands were soft, but he was admitted "by his acknowledgment and promise that he would not make any more difficulty about the fourth principle of the church."[49] In some measure, the decision to leave was a family matter because many of the secessionists were related by blood and marriage. For example, seventeen of them were related to Samuel Winsor, including his mother, three sisters and their

Propositions made to the Church at Providence Baptist
1 by James Manning that notwithstanding
Manning holds to a free communion with
those Baptist Churches not under hands
though under it himself that this Church
would admit him to communicate therein
that is to say sit down with them
At the Lords table so long as his moral
character and conduct are agreeable to the gospel
2 that the church allow James Manning
to appoint a lecture on the afternoon
of the Lords day after the usual time of
publick worship here or at any other
time not interfearing with the before
stated times of publick worship in
this Church And that he be allowed
liberty to sing in publick worship

husbands and children, assorted cousins, and various others as the links ramified through the Olney, Whipple, Potter, and Williams families. In addition seven Dyers, eight Carpenters and Spragues, four Fenners, four Watermans, four Kings, and bunches of Eddys, Burlingames, Jenckes, Higgenbottoms, and Dexters all left to form a new Six Principle Baptist Church in Johnston.[50]

As circumstances would have it, the annual meeting of the Six Principle Baptist Association took place in Providence that September. The major question facing the association was whether "those members of the Baptist Church in Providence which meet together to worship God in the Town or those which meet together to worship God out of Town be reckoned and adjudged to be the Church of Providence." The delegates from Providence were President Manning, Daniel Jenckes (the third wealthiest man in Providence and a justice of the Rhode Island Supreme Court), and Arthur Fenner, Esq. No one represented Winsor's new church in Johnston. The Rehoboth church withdrew from the association, and the rest voted to recognize the in-town congregation as the "Church of Providence."[51]

These events led to the disintegration of the original Six Principle Baptist Association, as all of the churches except Providence, Newport, and Swansea resigned in the next four years. In 1774 the rural Six Principle churches formed a new association, called the Baptist Yearly Meeting, which met for the first time in Samuel Winsor's new meetinghouse in Johnston.[52] The rising tide of respectability, decorum, and sophisticated formality had driven the Ancient Baptists out of Providence. The take-over of the Providence church by James Manning was a sign that First Baptist was moving from the small arena of the Six Principle Baptists into the national denomination of Baptists.

ABOVE James Manning asked the Providence church for permission to "sit down . . . at the Lord's Table" with any Baptist "not under hands. . . so long as his moral character and conduct are agreeable to the gospel." Furthermore he wanted to "appoint a Lecture [to preach] on the afternoon of the Lord's day after the usual time of publick worship. . . . And that he be allowed Liberty to sing in publick worship together with those that are free to join with him." Despite Samuel Winsor's strong opposition, the congregation granted Manning's motion, leading to a schism in May-June of 1771. From the Samuel Winsor papers, courtesy of Brown University Special Collections.

CHAPTER 3

Becoming Regular Baptists

The ministry of James Manning ushered in a new era for First Baptist. His coming signified the triumph of a more sophisticated and formal style of church than the rustic Six Principle Baptists allowed. Beginning with Boston and then Newport in the 1720s, Baptists in the growing seaport towns of New England sought greater acceptance and respectability by adopting educated, paid ministers, pew rents, congregational singing, more decorum and better order. The latter included keeping minutes of meetings, lists of members, regular celebration of the Lord's Supper, elimination of lesser rituals, such as footwashing, anointing with oil, and the kiss of charity, and a diminished role for women.[1] The desire for an educated clergy underlay the support for the new Baptist college. Manning demanded and was paid a salary. He introduced congregational singing, discontinued the exclusive ritual of laying-on-of-hands, and oversaw the erection of a large, formal meetinghouse. No longer were the ministers to be homegrown laymen plucked from the local congregation. Instead First Baptist now called its ministers from other states, used the developing network of Baptist colleges to find pastors, and plunged into the activities of the larger denomination.

Manning's arrival in Rhode Island was a consequence of the Great Awakening, a profound religious revival that swept the American colonies. It was the first common, inter-colonial experience for the British colonies in America and was one of those elements which helped to produce an American nationalism that led to the War for Independence. Small revivals began in the middle colonies in the 1720s and in New England in the 1730s, but the Great Awakening was consolidated and spread from Massachusetts to Georgia in the 1740s by the remarkable itinerant preacher George Whitefield.[2]

In addition to gathering in many unchurched people, the revivals split the established denominations. The Congregationalists divided into New Light and Old Light factions, and the Presbyterians and Dutch Reformed had New Side and Old Side elements. Even the Baptists experienced a division over revivalism. The Regular Baptists

frowned on evangelical emotionalism while the Separate Baptists believed that the excitement was God's work. While this division was particularly significant in the South, in New England the Regular and Separate Baptists soon blended into a single denomination by the end of the eighteenth century and were all called Regular Baptists.[3]

Before the Great Awakening, Baptists had been few in number and lacked weight in general colonial matters. In 1700 (sixty-two years after the founding of the first Baptist church in America) New England had only ten small Baptist churches with about 300 members altogether.[4] Indeed, only fourteen Baptist churches existed from Maine to South Carolina; in addition to the ten New England congregations, there were three in the Philadelphia area and one in Charleston. This last was principally composed of Baptists who had fled from Puritan persecution in Kittery, Maine. Moreover, those ten New England Baptist churches came in three different varieties.[5] Six of the ten were General Six Principle Baptist, all members of America's first Baptist association. In 1707 five Particular Baptist churches in the Philadelphia area formed the Philadelphia Baptist Association. This association would have a great impact in that it sent out energetic missionaries to the South and West to establish more Baptist churches and associations, adopted the Philadelphia Confession of Faith (1742), and caused the founding of the Baptist college in Rhode Island.

The coming of the Great Awakening substantially increased Baptist activity. Ironically, the Old Baptist churches of New England were feeble in their evangelism. Although they believed that salvation was possible for all people, the General Six Principle Baptists preferred intimate, communal congregations and were suspicious of innovations, including revivalism. On the other hand, the great expansion of Baptists in the eighteenth century came through the Particular (Regular) Baptists and was a consequence of the fervor of the Great Awakening — which was a revival of Calvinist beliefs. While the Particular Baptists held that Christ had died only for those predestined by God to be saved, they were energetic in their evangelism. Eventually most New England Baptists were transformed by the Great Awakening into the Particular (Regular) variety.

Photo by Warren Jagger (2000).

Another result of the Great Awakening was the establishment of new colleges by the various denominations in order to produce educated ministers for their churches.

TIMELINE

1773	Boston Tea Party
1774	First Continental Congress met in Philadelphia
1774-75	**Present meetinghouse erected**
1775-83	The American Revolution
1776	Declaration of Independence
1782	**FBC joined the Warren Baptist Association**
1784	Rhode Island passed a gradual emancipation law
1789	James Manning and others formed the Abolition Society
1789	U.S. Constitution ratified; George Washington elected President
1790	Rhode Island ratified U.S. Constitution
1791	Slater Mill began operating in Pawtucket
1792	**Crystal chandelier installed in the Meeting House**
1793	The Baptist foreign mission effort launched in England.

The Baptists were a major beneficiary of the Great Awakening as many congregations separated from the state churches and reorganized as Separate Baptist churches.[6] In addition, energetic Baptist preachers created congregations where none had existed. The great Baptist evangelist, Isaac Backus of Massachusetts, carefully counted the number of Baptist churches of New England. In 1734 there had been only fifteen Baptist churches of all varieties (Particular, Six Principle, and Seventh-Day), while by 1795 the Particular Baptist churches alone numbered 325, with an estimated membership of over 21,000.[7] In the whole United States by 1790 there were now at least 868 Baptist churches with nearly 65,000 members.[8] Baptists had ceased to be a marginal sect; they now constituted a significant denomination.

Another result of the Great Awakening was the establishment of new colleges by the various denominations in order to produce educated ministers for their churches. New Side Presbyterians established Princeton (1746), New Side Dutch Reformed started Rutgers (1766), and New Light Congregationalists founded Dartmouth (1769). In this movement to establish colleges, the Philadelphia Baptist Association sent James Manning, a 25-year old graduate of Princeton, to start a Baptist college and to help draw New England Baptists into an association to support the college.[9] These efforts led to the founding of Rhode Island College in

1764 and the Warren Association in 1767. Once Manning added the pastorship of the Providence church to his positions as president of Rhode Island College (renamed Brown University in 1804) and leader of the Warren Association, the church, college, and association became major promoters of the Baptist movement in New England.

The principal agency in advancing and consolidating Baptist efforts in New England was the Warren Association.[10] While none of the delegates to the founding meetings objected to the association's being limited to Particular Baptists, the very idea of an association touched the anti-institutional, anti-hierarchical fears of most. As a result, only four churches were willing to join in September 1767. However, Manning rewrote the constitution of the association to state clearly that "such an association is consistent with the independency and power of particular churches because it pretends to no other than an advisory council, utterly disclaiming superiority, jurisdiction, coercive right and infallibility."[11] With this assurance, the Warren Association began to grow. By 1777 it had thirty-one member churches, mostly from Massachusetts and primarily because of the influence of Isaac Backus. Most Rhode Island Baptists were already part of the Six Principle Baptist Association and refused to cooperate. When Manning first came to Rhode Island, the Warren church was invited to join the Six Principle Association, but in 1766 they reversed the call when they realized that "none of [their] members are under the laying on of hands."[12] It took Manning until 1782 to persuade the Providence church to join the Warren Association. (At that, First Baptist was only the second Rhode Island church to join, the first being Warren, which was Manning's previous pastorate.)[13] Soon, however, other associations began to form so that by 1804 New England had thirteen Baptist associations.[14]

The Warren Association did many things to advance the Baptist movement, but the greatest of these was its work on behalf of religious liberty in America. The association engaged Isaac Backus as its agent, and he became the principal spokesman for Baptists trying to bring about the disestablishment of the Congregational church in New England. He was a tireless evangelist who preached 9,828 sermons and travelled 67,600 miles outside his own parish in his 60-year ministerial career.[15] In words that echoed Roger Williams, Backus declared that "God has appointed two different kinds of government in the world which are different in their nature and ought never to be confounded together; one of which is called civil, the other ecclesiastical government." When they are mixed, he said, God's people are deprived of liberty of conscience.[16]

Backus and the Baptists began the rediscovery and rehabilitation of Roger Williams. Almost forgotten because his ideas were so unacceptable and because his colony was gen-

James Gibbs sketched four designs for the steeple of the Church of St.
Martin's-in-the-Fields in London, one of which was chosen and used in 1726.
The other three appeared in Gibbs' *Book of Architecture* (1728), and Joseph
Brown, architect for the Meeting House, picked the middle one for the
Meeting House. Photo from Norman M. Isham, *The Meeting House of the
First Baptist Church in Providence: A History of the Fabric* (1925), written to
commemorate the 150th anniversary of the dedication of the Meeting House.

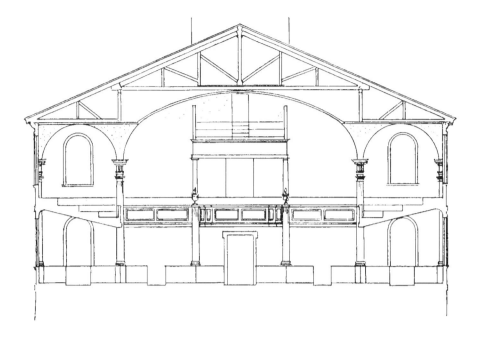

erally regarded as the "Isle of Errors" and "Rogues Island," Williams languished in general obscurity until the middle of the eighteenth century when the growing Baptist movement in Massachusetts and Connecticut began its struggle against the state churches of those colonies. They re-emphasized Williams' dedication to religious liberty, and Backus wrote that no other person in New England "acted so consistently and steadily upon right principles about government and liberty, as Mr. Williams did."[17]

The Warren Association reached beyond New England in pressing the cause, even sending Manning and Backus to present the Baptist case for religious liberty to the Continental Congress in Philadelphia in 1774. At the time, the attempt was a political mistake because it created the impression that the Baptists were Loyalists who opposed the movement toward independence.[18] John Adams, a Massachusetts delegate to Congress, believed that the plea for religious liberty was actually a ploy to break up the Continental Congress.[19] Ezra Stiles, pastor of the Second Congregational Church in Newport, wrote: "In truth, the Baptists intend to avail themselves of this opportunity to complain to England of Persecution—because they hate Congregationists who they know are hated by the King's Ministry & Parliament. They will leave the general Defence of American Liberty to the Congregationists to the Northward and Episcopalians to the Southward. . . ."[20] It took Baptists some time to overcome this impression, but the long-term crusade for religious liberty ended in victory. Stiles never forgave Manning, and his diary was sprinkled with sour comments belittling him.

John Leland was a leader among Baptists who fought to disestablish the Anglican church in Virginia and supported the need for a specific guarantee of religious liberty in the new Constitution.[21] After his conversion in the Great Awakening in Connecticut, Leland moved to Virginia in 1776. There he served for fourteen years as the pastor of the

Orange Baptist Church, Culpeper County, and he became a friend and supporter of Thomas Jefferson and James Madison. These philosophical liberals received strong support from evangelical Baptists to break the church-state connection and to have a "free church in a free state."[22] And so there appeared in the first lines of the First Amendment: "Congress shall make no law respecting an establishment of religion, or prohibiting the free exercise thereof. . . ."

Both James Manning and Isaac Backus favored ratification of the Constitution when it was presented to the states.[23] Manning travelled to Boston during the Massachusetts convention in order to convince antifederalist Baptist delegates to vote for ratification. In 1789, Providence supporters of the Constitution held a service of thanksgiving at the Meeting House upon learning of its adoption and prayed that Rhode Island would soon follow suit.[24] However, Rhode Island was the last of the original thirteen states to ratify. It might be noted that while religious liberty was embedded in the United States Constitution through the Bill of Rights in 1791, complete disestablishment of the Congregational church in Connecticut and Massachusetts was not accomplished until 1817 and 1833 respectively.

With James Manning as its leader, the Baptist church of Providence stepped into the widening stream of the Baptist movement. The new college and the old church were linked not only in the fact that the president and pastor were the same person from 1771 to 1791, but also through a magnificent new meetinghouse which became the place of graduation for Brown students, and has remained so until today. The new Warren Association and the Providence Baptist Church worked together in the years ahead, as Manning continued his leadership role in the association and drew the church into it.

After Samuel Winsor's secession in 1771, the church was left with only 118 members on the roll. However, the church's new style soon added another hundred members. That number does not include an additional, substantial group of "hearers." These people faithfully attended, contributed, owned pews, but did not become members for a variety of reasons. One obstacle was the conversion experience to which one had to testify before the Standing

ABOVE Cross section of the Meeting House, looking west to the rear of the auditorium as it was originally constructed, showing the second balcony, which was removed to make way for an organ in 1834. Drawing from Norman M. Isham, *The Meeting House of the First Baptist Church in Providence: A History of the Fabric* (1925).

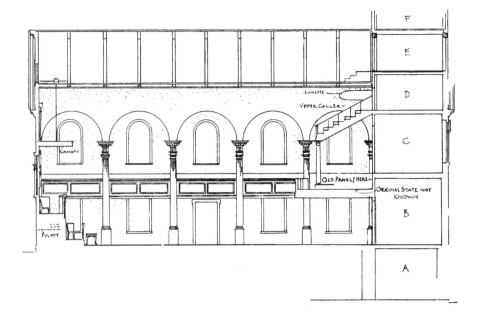

ABOVE The lengthwise section of the auditorium looking south as it was until 1834, showing the second balcony, where people of color were forced to sit. William J. Brown called it a "pigeon hole," as "all the churches at that time had some obscure place for the colored people to sit in." Drawing from Norman M. Isham, *The Meeting House of the First Baptist Church in Providence: A History of the Fabric* (1925).

Committee (composed of the deacons, the pastor, and seven men elected at large). One was expected to detail the workings of the Holy Spirit in his or her life and to be able to pinpoint the moment when the miracle of conversion had occurred. Any number of earnest and upright individuals who failed to have such an experience were never admitted to the membership list.

Notable among the "hearers" were John and Nicholas Brown, two of the most powerful, wealthy men in Providence. Nicholas' son, also named Nicholas, never joined the church even though he was one of its greatest benefactors. Among other things, he gave $2000 to buy a lot and build a parsonage in 1792, and he donated the pipe organ in 1834. Through the years he was a multiple pew-owner, holding sixteen pews in 1832.[25] He served as moderator of the Charitable Baptist Society for thirty-two years, including the entire period from 1811 to his death in 1841. Indeed, he was so generous in his bequests that Brown University was named in his honor. His sister, Hope Brown Ives, who donated the grand chandelier that has hung in the Meeting House since 1792,[26] did not become a member of the church until July 1840 when she was sixty-eight years old. In fact, of the twelve-man committee in charge of the construction of the Meeting House, only one was a member of the church when they began in 1774; and only one of the nine men who pledged the largest amounts to the project was a member![27] So, to take only the membership list is to underestimate the true strength of the congregation. This goes far to explain how a church with so few members could erect a meetinghouse that was among the largest in colonial America in 1774 and 1775.

The old meetinghouse was too small for the congregation by 1774, and Manning chafed at the fact that commencements of Rhode Island College were being held in the Second Congregational meetinghouse (1770-1774) because it had more space. In February 1774, some of the leading men associated with the church created the Charitable Baptist Society to handle financial and real estate matters, and the Society petitioned and received a charter of incorporation from the Rhode Island General Assembly.[28] Nicholas Brown was elected the Society's first moderator. His brother Joseph was appointed as the principal architect, and brother John was made "the Committee man for carrying on the building." In addition to deciding what sort of building they wanted, the Society had to acquire the desired land. Their problem was that the main parcel was owned by John Angell, who despised the Baptists. So, an Anglican friend, William Russell, purchased the Angell property and sold it to the Charitable Baptist Society.[29] Although it took until July 28, 1774, to complete the property transactions, construction had begun on June 3.

To aid in the fund-raising effort, the General Assembly granted the Charitable Baptist Society the right to hold a lottery, a common way in that period to raise money for large undertakings. For example, in 1767 the General Assembly had authorized the Warren Baptists to hold a lottery to build a parsonage for James Manning, president of Rhode Island College.[30] However, most of the cost of the meetinghouse was met by monetary pledges. Those who could not give money donated labor and materials. For example, Jonathan Hammond, Comfort Wheaton, and Martin Simmons pledged £12 each, to be paid in "work upon the House." Likewise, Daniel Hawkins pledged £6 "to be paid in Timber & bords," and John Pettis pledged £9 "to be paid in Stones." The expenses of the undertaking included wages paid to workmen and costs of lumber, nails, stone, doors, windows, and so on. The expense accounts also record: "Licker at Raiseings & at other times...£22."[31] The acceptance of lotteries and liquor indicates that eighteenth century Baptists held some different attitudes from those that would dominate most Baptists after the revivals in the nineteenth century.

The Meeting House itself represented a dramatic departure for Baptists in New England. Previously their buildings had been almost Quaker-like in their plainness. This was the first Baptist meetinghouse to have a steeple, and the spire is

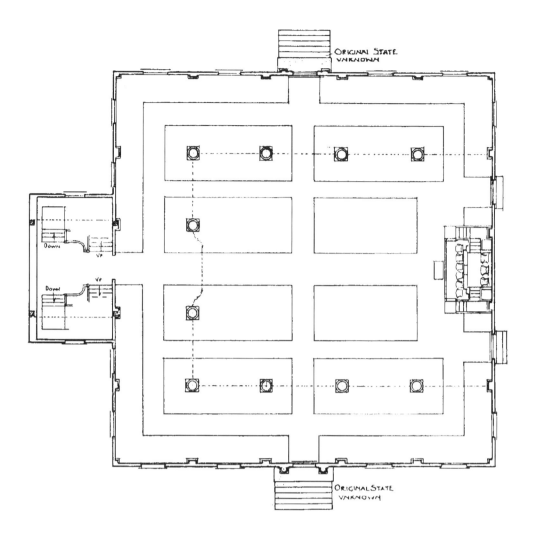

a copy of one which James Gibbs proposed in 1726 for St. Martin's-in-the-Fields in London.[32] The building is dignified in its restrained ornamentation, but the classical details were standard pattern-book designs, common to Georgian-style buildings of the eighteenth century. While the building derived some of its form from Anglican churches, it retained at least three major elements of the New England meeting-house style. First, it was square, 80 x 80 feet. Second, it lacked iconography: no stained glass, no statues, not even a cross. The Baptists were quite conscientious in their exclusion of religious symbols, including the cross itself. The Puritans were thorough iconoclasts, and the Baptists of Rhode Island maintained that tradition even as they constructed an elegant building. Third, the high pulpit was placed against the wall and centered in order to emphasize the preaching of the Word and to banish the idea of an altar. Yet, the aisle and pew arrangement provoked some controversy in the congregation. Originally a center aisle ran from back to front. Some people could almost imagine a procession of priests parading down that center aisle. To overcome the difficulty, the cross aisle from the side doors became the way that most entered the building. Entering there, no one was confronted by a hint of an altar or processing prelates.

When the Meeting House was being erected in 1774 and 1775, it was the biggest building project in New England. Here was a structure that would seat 1200 people in a town of 4321. It was the largest building in town and had a steeple taller than even the Anglican church. This great size reflected the faith and optimism of its builders. As Baptists, they had seen their ranks increase through the Great Awakening,

and they expected their congregation to continue its growth. As president of Rhode Island College, Manning expected the college to prosper and to need a large hall as the graduating classes became bigger. Here also was a building that matched the booster spirit of the leading men of the town. By then Providence was beginning to challenge Newport to become the premier town in Rhode Island.

Between 1760 and 1820, Providence rose from having less than half the population of Newport to having more than twice as many people. While Newport sank under the blows of war, weather, and economic change, Providence took the lead in oceanic commerce and industrialization.[33] During the period, the town fathers erected a series of large structures—homes, warehouses, a market building, and impressive church edifices.[34] The Meeting House of the First Baptist Church was the first of these new church buildings which replaced the old, plain structures erected earlier in the century. Next came the First Congregational Church in 1795. This "monumental work" was destroyed by fire in 1814, and the present structure, now the Unitarian church, was built and dedicated in 1816. While the Unitarian church was slightly smaller than the Baptist meetinghouse, its steeple

ABOVE The floor plan of the Meeting House in 1775 had a center aisle and a cross aisle connecting the side entrances. The chandelier which Hope Brown Ives gave to the church in 1792 in memory of her father, Nicholas Brown, hung at the intersection of the main aisles. The pews were the square, high-backed sort and were owned or rented by members of the congregation. This floor plan was considerably changed by the remodeling of 1832. Drawing from Norman M. Isham, *The Meeting House of the First Baptist Church in Providence: A History of the Fabric* (1925).

was five feet taller. The Second Congregational Church became the Beneficent Society in 1795 and erected a new meetinghouse in 1809-1810. Finally, the Episcopalians built a new church in 1810.

The construction of the Baptist meetinghouse also benefited from the growing tension between the American colonies and Great Britain. In December 1773 the Boston Tea Party took place, and the following spring the British Parliament responded with the Coercive Acts which abolished the Massachusetts legislature and closed the port of Boston until the perpetrators of the tea party were surrendered to British justice. Just as those penalties fell on Massachusetts, the Meeting House was begun in Rhode Island. Many of the skilled craftsmen who worked on the structure were carpenters and shipwrights who were put out of work when the port of Boston was closed.[35] The construction went forward so rapidly that in a year the building was completed enough to permit its dedication and use. The first service was held May 28, 1775. Two weeks later, the *Providence Gazette* of Saturday, June 10, reported, "Last Tuesday the Raising of the Steeple, which lasted three Days and an Half, was finished. . . 'tis thought it will be a most elegant Piece of Architecture."[36] And, the builders did their work well, because the building has survived the hurricanes since then. While the steeples of other churches in Providence have been destroyed by various causes, the 185-foot steeple of the First Baptist Meeting House has stood through the years.

The creation of the Charitable Baptist Society also constituted a way that respectability was advanced in the Baptist church. Only pew owners could be members of the Society, and many of these people were not members of the church. While the church's rolls included women, Native-Americans, African-Americans, sailors, and laborers, none of these was admitted to the Society whose ranks were filled with professors, lawyers, physicians, merchants, and entrepreneurs. The Society owned the new meetinghouse and paid the minister, sexton, and organist (when an organ was finally acquired about half a century later). The Society was virtually a men's club, beyond the reach of the discipline of the predominantly female membership of the church itself. While the pastor was a member of the Charitable Baptist Society, the organization was, in fact, run and dominated by laymen.

The Meeting House was a physical sign of the vitality and spirit of Baptists in the community, and their vigor was not entirely religious. Members and "hearers" of the congregation played major roles in town and state affairs, and some of Rhode Island's leaders in the American Revolution sat in the pews. John Brown was probably the principal figure in the Patriot cause in Providence. He organized and led the attack which burned *H.M.S. Gaspee* on June 9, 1772. Then in 1775 his sloop *Katy* was sent to Philadelphia to be recommissioned *Providence*, becoming the first ship in the new Continental Navy. The Hope furnaces of the Browns manufactured cannons for the Revolutionary army, and John was later elected to both the Congress of the Confederation and the United States Congress. Another member, Arthur Fenner, was appointed to the Providence Committee of Safety and Inspection in December 1774 to enforce the decree of the Continental Congress that all imports from England should cease. Later, Fenner was the Governor of Rhode Island from 1790 to 1805.

Many of the skilled craftsmen who worked on the structure were carpenters and shipwrights who were put out of work when the port of Boston was closed. The construction went forward so rapidly that in a year the building was completed enough to permit its dedication and use.

Ironically, the canard that Baptists were really Loyalists was lodged against the pastor of the church. Ezra Stiles accused Manning of withholding prayers for Congress and the success of the Revolutionary army until George Washington once attended the Providence church.[37] Stiles wrote, "He is a Baptist Tory. . . an Enemy to the Revolution here, altho' afterwds he trim'd about. . . ." [38] Manning did deplore the war, but he wrote, "I think I can say that I never in one instance doubted the justice of our cause. . . ."[39] He might well deplore the war if only for the effect it had upon Baptist concerns: Rhode Island College was nearly destroyed and many of his church members were scattered by the upheaval.[40] Few joined and many departed or disappeared—so much so that Manning wrote in 1783 that at least fifty members could not be accounted for.[41] Nevertheless, when the Declaration of Independence arrived in Providence in July 1776, it was read from the front steps of the Meeting House, and Manning later served in the Congress of the Confederation in 1785 and 1786.

The congregation was touched by the anti-slavery currents of the era, and found itself in some disagreement over slavery. Ten percent of the church's members were African-Americans, but a leading proponent of the slave trade in Rhode Island was John Brown. The Quakers were first to move toward emancipation, and the Great Awakening stirred an anti-slavery impulse among other Protestants. In addition, the spirit of liberty engendered by the Revolution brought various elements in Rhode Island together to attack the African slave trade and slavery itself. The opponents of the slave trade gained their first victory in 1774 when the General Assembly prohibited the further importation of slaves into Rhode Island. In 1778 Manning (who had freed his only slave in 1770) joined with Moses Brown, a Quaker since his conversion in 1773, and Stephen Hopkins, a disfellowshipped Quaker and signer of the Declaration of Independence, to agitate for the abolition of slavery. They won a gradual emancipation act in 1784 and another law in 1787 to fine the Rhode Island owners of any vessel engaging in the slave trade. In 1789, with some others, they founded the Providence Society for Abolishing the Slave Trade.[42] Their efforts resulted in John Brown's angrily resigning from the Charitable Baptist Society.

When John Brown started to outfit a slaving ship in 1790 despite the law and forced one of his slaves to board it, the Abolition Society filed charges against him. He agreed to free the slave if they dropped the prosecution.[43] Unable to retaliate against the Abolition Society itself, Brown quit the Charitable Baptist Society because some, such as Manning and ex-Congressman David Howell (the moderator of the

Charitable Baptist Society in 1790), and Governor Arthur Fenner, were prominent in both organizations.[44] He wrote that he was resigning because "of a molishous lawsuit against me" whose principal promoters were

> *several members of the [Baptist] Society who have lately opposed me in so unchristian, ungentelman & unfriendly a manner. . . in their late conduct in depriving me of the benefit of my slaves. . . I can not sitt at woship of the Supreme being till they purge themselves of their unheard of wickedness. I am with purfect respect and esteeme to every member of the Society but those Abommonable abolitioners.*[45]

In 1796 the Abolition Society again brought suit against John Brown when one of his slave ships was caught. In this case, however, a sympathetic jury in Newport (the center of slave trading in Rhode Island) rendered an odd split decision—they found the elderly patriot innocent but condemned his ship.[46]

Meanwhile, by the mid-1780s Manning had become almost too busy to carry out his pastoral duties. He was increasingly absorbed in the Warren Association, Congress of the Confederation, the college, and town affairs. He had even become a member of a Providence school committee urging the establishment of free public schools supported by compulsory taxation.[47] Therefore, in 1788 the church called John Stanford, an Englishman, to become co-pastor. The calling of Stanford illustrated the new connections of First Baptist. He was assisting John Gano, pastor of the Baptist church in New York City, and Gano was a brother-in-law of Manning. Unfortunately, in the following year an anonymous letter arrived from New York which charged "that Mr. John Stanford was tried in the Court of King's Bench in Westminster, and convicted of sodomical practices, and fled his country."[48] He was dismissed after serving twenty months. The charges were actually false as Stanford routed his tormentors in a libel action in 1802 when they tried to ruin him again. He went on to have a distinguished ministerial career in New York.[49]

Manning's services were only intermittent in his last years, but he did not formally resign as pastor until April 1791. He died from a stroke in July 1791. The church turned immediately to a brilliant young preacher who was a member of the church. Jonathan Maxcy was the 1787 valedictorian of Rhode Island College. Maxcy was licensed to preach by First Baptist in 1790 and ordained as its minister in September 1791. He was also the first professor of divinity and a trustee of the college; so despite his being only twenty-four, he became the second president of the Baptist college.[50] He resigned as pastor of the church on September 8, 1792, after only one year of service, and was replaced by Stephen Gano who led the church for thirty-six years until his death in 1828. Gano's election reinforced the new connections: he was John Gano's son and nephew of James Manning.[51]

Gano had intended to study at the college under his uncle, but the American Revolution interfered. Instead, he studied medicine with another uncle in New Jersey, and in 1779, at age seventeen he was appointed surgeon's mate in the Continental Army. He resigned within a year and enlisted on a privateer. Captured by the British, he was confined to one of their terrible prison ships. After the war he prac-

ticed medicine until being ordained in his father's church in 1786. During a trip to visit family members, on January 20, 1790, he organized the first Baptist church in the Northwest Territory at Columbia, Ohio, within present-day Cincinnati.[52]

During Gano's long pastorate at First Baptist in Providence, the congregation experienced a series of revivals and in 1820 reached a size that would not be equalled again until 1901.[53] He served one of the longest tenures in the church's history and saw his congregation grow into one of the largest Baptist churches in the nation. His advice and counsel were in constant demand, and he travelled widely to evangelize and to settle church disputes. During his time First Baptist entered the home and foreign mission movements, the Sunday school movement, and the Bible and tract societies. First Baptist helped to establish four new churches during Gano's pastorate. He was one of four New England delegates to the Philadelphia gathering in 1814 which created the "General Missionary Convention of the Baptist Denomination in the United States of America for Foreign Missions." This came to be known as the Triennial Convention and was the first national organization of Baptists in the United States. Locally, Gano served as moderator of the Warren Association from 1805 to 1824, and in 1825 he was a founder and first president of the Rhode Island Baptist State Convention.[54] He was finally stopped only when he died of congestive heart failure in August 1828.

As distinguished as he was in the world at large, he once had a serious problem in his own home. Gano was the subject of the most bizarre episode in the entire history of the Providence church. This occurred in 1803 when his fourth wife, Joanna, denounced him and seven others for being Freemasons. Following the death in December 1800 of his third wife Mary (a daughter of Joseph Brown), Gano had remarried in October 1801 to Mrs. Joanna Latting of Hillsdale, New York, where he had once been pastor. In mid-1803, Joanna threw the church into turmoil by accusing her husband and the others of worshiping idols and perverting the Scriptures.[55] She had discovered that her husband was a Mason, and like many rural and small-town Baptists of her time, she regarded membership in the Freemasons to be incompatible with Christianity.[56] She denounced the Masonic Society as the "Mystery of Iniquity," a "Covenant with Death and agreement with Hell."

In a series of meetings, one lasting six hours, the church examined these charges against its pastor and the other men. Indicative of the new order of things in church meetings, Joanna was not allowed to speak, and her two-hour indictment was read by her husband! In the end Stephen demanded a vote as to whether "he was guilty of the horrid charges his wife had brought against him [and] whether he was unworthy [of] a place in the church of God, much less of the Pastoral Office. . . ."

In response they unanimously voted "that they will still hold in their fellowship those brethren who are Free Masons," and acquitted Gano and the others of all charges. Finally, the church excommunicated Joanna.[57] Although she continued to live separately in the town, Gano never spoke to her again.[58]

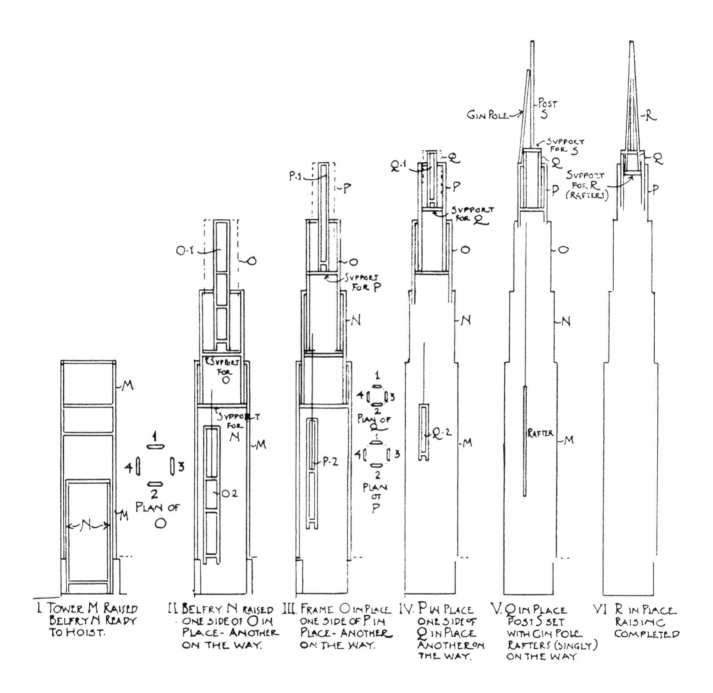

ABOVE These figures illustrate how the steeple was erected in only three and a half days in early June 1775. The sections were framed on the ground and then hoisted up inside the tower, each higher section being pulled up through the lower ones, like a telescope. The tower stands 185 feet from base to weather vane. Drawing from Norman M. Isham, The Meeting House of the First Baptist Church in Providence: A History of the Fabric (1925).

CHAPTER 4

The Second Great Awakening

Stephen Gano pastored the First Baptist Church into the nineteenth century and saw it respond to new religious currents. Some of these ideas, such as foreign missions and the Sunday school, came from Great Britain, and they worked themselves out in the local situation in Rhode Island and in the larger context of the Second Great Awakening. The religious surge in the first decades of the nineteenth century dwarfed the eighteenth century awakening both in size and impact. Beginning in frontier camp meetings in Kentucky at the turn of the century, revival fires flared repeatedly until the eve of the Civil War. While a major achievement of this awakening was to Christianize the newly settled areas of the frontier, the revival movement also swept the cities on the eastern seaboard, and Providence was shaken along with the rest of New England. The Great Awakening increased congregations, multiplied denominations, founded colleges and seminaries, changed concepts of moral behavior and stimulated reform.[1] Baptists and Methodists, minor denominations in 1750, were the preeminent evangelists of the Second Awakening and, thus, became the largest Protestant denominations by the Civil War.[2]

The Sunday school movement, home and foreign missions, and the Bible and tract societies were all energized by and became part of the Second Great Awakening. Each was an element in the "ferment of reform" which swept over the nation as a result of the recurrent revivals. As people were called to repent their personal sins, they turned to attack the evils of society. The result was a blizzard of new societies and organizations to reform everything. They redefined personal morality to banish the use of alcoholic drinks, tobacco, and even coffee, and they called upon the nation to eradicate the evil of slavery.

For its part, Providence grew steadily, beginning the nineteenth century with 7,614 people, reaching 50,666 by 1860 and ending with 175,597 in 1900.[2] Urban growth produced both problems and opportunities for the religious institutions of Providence, and First Baptist was one of the foremost of the churches. The industrial neighborhoods and mill villages constituted an urban frontier which alarmed the religious community because it thought the people in those areas to be ignorant and heathen. Missions and Sunday schools sought to bring education and Christianity to the industrial masses.[4]

In Providence Stephen Gano presided over four major revivals. In 1805-6 he added 186 members to the church (153 by baptism); in 1812 another 112 (110 by baptism), in 1816 another 114 (94 by baptism), and in 1820 another 157 (147 by baptism). By 1821 the First Baptist Church counted 648 members and was one of the largest in the nation, despite having transferred over 100 members to launch four new churches between 1805 and 1821.[5] The revival spirit in Providence was deeply felt, especially by young people who committed themselves to missions and personal evangelism. Some of them immersed themselves in starting Sunday schools.

The Sunday school movement that had its genesis in the British industrial revolution came to America in the 1790s.[6] Slater's Mill in Pawtucket in 1791 had the first water-powered spinning machines in America, and by 1815 Rhode Island had 100 textile mills. Most of the workers in those early factories were children, and religious people found them to be virtual heathens. Initially Sunday schools were aimed at these children, and a major effort was made to teach them reading and writing as well as religion on their one day off from the factory. Samuel Slater hired teachers and began a school on Sunday for the children of his Pawtucket mill in 1796. But, Slater's teachers taught only secular subjects until Rev. David Benedict was put in charge of the school in 1805. He added Bible reading and religious instruction to the curriculum.[7]

Sunday schools in Providence did not begin until after the War of 1812. They arose through the independent efforts of women from several churches, aided by young men from

ABOVE Stephen Gano (1762-1828) served as pastor from 1792 until his death in 1828. His ministry was marked by the greatest growth in the history of First Baptist Church, and he presided over several major revivals and the planting of four daughter churches. A national Baptist leader, he travelled widely to mediate problems and to encourage new congregations and missions. He was one of the founders of the Triennial Convention and a founder and first president of the Rhode Island Baptist State Convention. Under him First Baptist entered into the home and foreign missionary movements, the Sunday school movement, and the Bible and tract societies. Courtesy of the Rhode Island Historical Society (RHi x3 4455).

By 1821 the First Baptist Church counted 648 members and was one of the largest in the nation, despite having transferred over 100 members to launch four new churches between 1805 and 1821.

Brown University. Eventually these became parish Sunday schools.[8] In 1816 members of St. John's Episcopal Church began instruction in three different locations, one of which was for African-American children. The next year St. John's Sunday School was opened, becoming the first church school in Providence.[9] In that same year a Congregationalist woman collected her nieces and nephews for study and started a school on Eddy Street. She placed the superintendency of her school into the hands of a fellow member, Allen Brown. (He subsequently joined First Baptist, where he was licensed to the ministry in 1819 and then became the first pastor of Third Baptist Church in 1820.) The Eddy Street school moved in 1818 into the vestry of Beneficent Congregational Church. It continued as a non-denominational Sunday school under the sponsorship of Beneficent Congregational, Richmond Street Congregational, and Second Baptist Church until 1828 when it became the parish Sunday school of Beneficent.[10]

The third Sunday school belonged to First Baptist Church.[11] In 1815, Maria Gano, recently baptized by her father Stephen, started a school for African-American women and children in a house on Olney Street. She was soon joined in her effort by other young women and a couple of university students. In 1818 they met in Stephen Gano's study at the suggestion of Henry Jackson, who was to become a Baptist minister himself and marry Maria. The result was the creation of the Union Sunday School which met at noon in the old Town House, where the present-day Providence County Court House stands. Finally, they decided that a church Sunday school was needed, so they organized the First Baptist Sunday School on May 30, 1819.

It was a young people's movement (all fifteen of the teachers, ten women and five men, were under twenty-one), and the whole project was regarded with apprehension by their elders. Only a few, including Stephen Gano, encouraged their efforts. When they applied to use the basement for a Sunday school, the church agreed after considerable hesitation: "Upon the whole, they consented to grant the request, on condition that the applicants pay the expense of the occasion." As amazing as it may seem today, the older members thought that the teaching of school on Sunday would encroach on "sacred time" and cause "a falling off of parental instruction" and produce a "decline in family religion."[12]

The growth of the Sunday school led to the complete transformation of the basement of the Meeting House. Until 1802 the primitive and unfinished lower region had been rented out to local businessmen, was a practice room for an incipient church choir, and had been used to store the hearse which the Charitable Baptist Society had imported from England in 1791.[13] Then it was improved to create a meeting room, but it was still dim and damp when the Sunday school began in 1819. A desk sat in a small level area on the west side in front of the basement doors.[14] The floor then sloped sharply upward to the walls like an amphitheater and seats were fixed in rows on the sloping floor and were divided by a number of steep aisles. The school began with forty students, but during the great city-wide religious revival in 1820, the average attendance jumped to 120.[15] Within the decade the number of students exceeded 200.[16] This necessitated creating rooms for different classes; for example, in 1833 a room was made in the southeast corner for the Infant Class as it came to have 100 children in it. The next year a room was constructed in the northeast corner to accommodate an adult Bible class, paid for by the members of the class themselves. The floor was leveled in 1837; and finally, after years of debate, the whole lower region was excavated and reconstructed in 1857 to accommodate the Sunday school.

Since the Sunday school was not, at first, regarded as an organic part of the church, it had to be self-supporting and self-governing. Those who wished to have a school at First Baptist created in 1820 the Sunday School Society. It was composed of members of the church and congregation who made annual contributions to defray the cost of the Sunday school. Their reports were made not to the church but to the Rhode Island Sunday School Union (formed in 1824). In the mid-1820s several of the men of the congregation established a library of several hundred books for the Sunday school—a significant matter at a time when no public library existed.[17] By the 1830s Sunday schools were common in most churches, but many of them reported to the Sunday School Union. Convocations and annual gatherings of the union were frequently held at the Meeting House where the number in attendance reached 1000 to 1400 children and adults.[18]

Not until 1844 was the Sunday school made a part of the church under its care and control.[19] By then they had 400 enrolled and averaged over 250 in attendance. Now, the health of a church began to be measured by the strength of its Sunday school, and what had been regarded as a threat became a necessity. In fact, First Baptist not only ran its own school, but operated a number of missions and outposts elsewhere which helped to establish at least three more Baptist churches in industrial neighborhoods.

In what may seem amazing and even appalling to today's educators, the emphasis was upon rote memorization of hymns and Scripture verses. A Providence paper on August 10, 1819, reported that students at the Baptist Sunday school in the last session had learned 22,499 verses and 4,398 hymns. One boy of twelve years had memorized 2,421 verses and had recited 640 of them on one Sabbath. It was later said that one student memorized the entire New Testament in fourteen months and could recite fifteen chapters at a time.[20] This approach changed in 1827-1828, when rote memorizing gave way to the study and exposition of passages of the Bible each week. This required the teachers to prepare lessons, and to this end they met each Monday evening for a study and prayer meeting. Whether it was due to these changes or revivalism, baptisms among the youth of the Sunday school increased. From 1832 to 1842 fifteen teachers and 128 students were baptized. In 1869 the Sunday school superintendent was able to report that over the years 285 members of the school had been added to the church by baptism.[21] In addition, the Sunday school gener-

ated many organizations within the church, including the Young Ladies' Association (1832), the First Baptist Knitting Society (1835), a sewing school for the poor (1837), a young women's weekly prayer meeting with an average attendance of 50 by 1858, the Young Ladies' Missionary Association (1866), and the Young Ladies' Improvement Society (1885). In fact, the Sunday school became the heart of the home and foreign mission efforts of the church.

While they built a Sunday school in the church itself, some of the young people created branch or mission schools elsewhere. The Sunday school at the African Union Meeting was almost entirely supported by contributions from the First Baptist Sunday School from 1819 to 1840; and for a number of years many of the teachers of the "African School" were young people from First Baptist.[22] Another Sunday school, called the "round house sabbath school," was across the Cove Basin near the state prison in a working class neighborhood next to the new railroad yards.[23] Another mission school in 1837 was run by Durlin Brayton, who was ordained by First Baptist that year and later became a missionary to Burma.[24] The young women organized a sewing school for this mission and taught the girls to sew while instructing them in Christianity. In the 1860s First Baptist established and ran at least three more schools, one in the Woodville section of North Providence, another on Smith Street, and a third on Eddy Street—all in working class neighborhoods.[25] Another, more significant sewing school resulted from the revival of 1858, and it included singing, prayers, recitations, and Bible lessons along with sewing for the girls who were described as coming "almost entirely from the ranks of those who are growing up in ignorance and sin, who from their earliest years are familiar with nearly every form of vice, and from whom bigotry and superstition have but too effectually shut out the true light."[26] This sewing school met on Saturday afternoons in the Meeting House and enrolled nearly 400 children by 1867.[27]

After the great revival of 1820, the most significant activity in the church was occurring down in the Sunday school; upstairs the church seemed to be resting following the excitement. After baptizing 147 in 1820, Gano counted only nineteen more baptisms in the next eight years.[28] Moreover, decreases due to death, letters of dismissal, and expulsions caused the total membership to decline by 150 by the time Gano died in 1828. Eighteen more months passed before the thirty-year old Robert Pattison began his pastorate, but the whole institution was ready for great changes. In Pattison, the church had an able, energetic man whose "influence was magnetic and irresistible."[29]

Nearly fifty years later, the *Christian Standard* (Chicago) described Pattison's ministry in Providence: "His people cherish his memory with an affectionate interest unsurpassed by that pertaining to any pastor which that most

favored church has had. It was not merely pulpit power. . . but social and personal influence which bound him so strongly to the hearts of his people. They trusted him and sought his counsel in secular as well as spiritual matters."[30] In 1877, Samuel Caldwell, the nineteenth pastor, recalled the impact that Pattison had made on him back in the 1830s: "He was a man to make immediate, incisive impressions.... He had singular power in reaching men's consciences."[31] Through these talents, he invigorated the church. He oversaw major changes in the auditorium, including new pews, a new pulpit, and the installation of an organ, but more, the church experienced a new burst of growth. Clearly benefitting from another city-wide awakening in 1831-1832, the church brought in 125 members (97 by baptism). During Pattison's first stint as pastor (1830-1836), he added 278 members and promoted the Sunday school.

Another of the currents that gathered strength in the 1790s and early nineteenth century was the home mission movement. Since the First Great Awakening, Baptists had worked the frontier settlements with lay pastors and itinerant preachers, so the home mission movement represented an effort to institutionalize frontier evangelism.[32] British Baptists began their Home Mission Society in 1797, and the mission-society concept spread quickly to the United States. In 1798 Massachusetts Baptists set up a fund to send missionaries to the newly settled parts of New England, and in 1802 they founded the Massachusetts Baptist Mission Society. In 1806 Gano's daughter Margaret and her friend, Eliza Pitman, daughter of the Rev. John Pitman, a former clerk of the church, visited Salem where they learned about the work of the local missionary society. Inspired, they returned and founded the Female Mite Society, the first missionary group in Rhode Island. Members paid a penny a

After the great revival of 1820, the most significant activity in the church was occurring down in the Sunday school; upstairs the church seemed to be resting following the excitement.

ABOVE Providence was a growing commercial and industrial city by the 1830s, which prompted considerable concern among the local churches about the souls of the working class. The recurrent revivals of the Second Great Awakening brought many converts and saw the planting of new churches in the new neighborhoods. This pen and ink drawing of Market Square, 1835, by E. L. Peckham shows the Meeting House in the background, behind some commercial shops and buildings. Courtesy of the Rhode Island Historical Society (RHi x3 955).

Another of the currents that gathered strength in the 1790s and early nineteenth century was the home mission movement. Since the First Great Awakening, Baptists had worked the frontier settlements with lay pastors and itinerant preachers, so the home mission movement represented an effort to institutionalize frontier evangelism.

week to home missions, and the funds were sent to the Massachusetts Baptist Mission Society. Female Mite Societies quickly spread to other Rhode Island churches. In 1812 the Female Mite Societies decided to use their money for missionaries right in Rhode Island and employed them directly from 1812 to 1825. These efforts led straight to the formation of the Rhode Island Baptist State Convention in August 1825 in the Meeting House. Stephen Gano was elected president and his son-in-law, David Benedict, was chosen as secretary.[33]

First Baptist had a hand in producing one of the great leaders in American Baptist home missions and education. Jonathan Going entered Brown University in September 1805. Although he came from a religiously indifferent family, he was converted in a revival during his freshman year and was baptized by Stephen Gano in April 1806. Called to

ABOVE As Providence developed industrially, it became the home of America's leading silverware maker, the Gorham Mfg. Co. Jabez Gorham (1792-1869), after apprenticing with Nehemiah Dodge, opened his own shop on the corner of North Main and Steeple streets in 1813. In time the factory occupied the entire block across the street from the Meeting House (which is visible at the left). When the company moved to a huge plant on Reservoir Avenue in 1890, it was one of Providence's "Five Industrial Wonders of the World." Jabez Gorham, a descendent of the church's fifth pastor, Gregory Dexter, was a pew owner in the Meeting House, and his daughters Amy and Susan joined by baptism in 1841. Engraving of the Gorham Manufacturing Plant from Welcome Arnold Greene, *The Providence Plantations for Two Hundred and Fifty Years* (1886).

the ministry, he was licensed to preach by First Baptist in 1809, and after graduating from Brown that year, he continued his theological studies under President Asa Messer. He returned to his native Vermont, having been "sent out by the First Baptist Church of Providence as a missionary to the Indians and other heathens in Vermont." The Cavendish Baptist Church ordained him on May 9, 1811, when he became their pastor after they promised him "$100 and keep for self and horse."[34] He was the only college-educated Baptist minister in the state. In 1815 he began a sixteen-year pastorate at the First Baptist Church of Worcester, Massachusetts, building a weak congregation into a powerful church and founding the Worcester Baptist Association. His tremendous interest in Baptist education led to the establishment of Worcester Academy and in 1825 the Newton Theological Institution, the first Baptist seminary in America.[35] Furthermore, his efforts on behalf of weaker churches contributed to the organization of the Massachusetts Baptist State Convention in 1824.

In 1826 John Mason Peck, the champion of home missions, spent a night in Going's home in Worcester, and subsequently they maintained a correspondence. In the summer of 1831, Going was given leave by his church to make an extensive tour of Kentucky, Indiana, Illinois, and Missouri with Peck to investigate the state of spiritual destitution in the West. Greatly inspired by the need, Going returned east, convinced leading individuals and organizations to support the idea of a home mission society, and issued a call through Baptist papers to a meeting. As a result, the American Baptist Home Mission Society was organized on April 27, 1832, and Going was elected as its corresponding secretary. He resigned his pastorate in Worcester and moved to Brooklyn, New York, where he served as secretary from 1832 to 1837.

During his 1831 trip to the West, Going helped in the formation of the Ohio Baptist Education Society and was a founder of the Granville Literary and Theological Institution. He wrote the by-laws for the new institute which was soon called Granville College and eventually Denison University. In November 1837, he accepted the presidency of Granville College and served there until his death in 1844.[36] Through Going's conversion, baptism, licensing, and commission, First Baptist Church of Providence played an important part in the creation of one of the Baptist leaders in the Second Great Awakening.

In the order of things, home missions and the establishment of state conventions came later than the national organization of Baptists; still, the principal impetus in either case was the grand, exciting idea of evangelizing the world. The Baptist foreign mission movement had its beginning in England too. The author of that idea was William Carey, who challenged a Baptist gathering in Northampton, England, with the question, "Have the churches of Christ done all they ought to have done for heathen nations?" The chairman of the meeting rebuked him, "Young man, sit down! When God pleases to convert the heathen world, he will do it without your help or mine either!"[37] But, Carey kept up his agitation until 1792, when the Baptist Society for Propagating the Gospel among the Heathens was created; and the next year he sailed to India where he served until his death in 1834. Carey's example galvanized British Congregationalists and Wesleyan Methodists into beginning foreign mission stations in India and Africa, and the idea began spreading among Baptists and Congregationalists in the United States. By 1799 American Congregationalists counted at least five local foreign missionary societies, and after 1802 the Massachusetts Baptist Mission Society sought to raise funds for foreign missions as well.

In this period Congregationalism was wracked by the trinitarian-unitarian struggle. Most Unitarians held that God was too good to condemn pagans to Hell, so missionaries were not needed. When in 1805 an avowed Unitarian became the Professor of Divinity at Harvard, trinitarian Congregationalists fought back by founding Andover Theological Seminary. Andover became the breeding ground for the foreign mission crusade in America, and one of its converts was Adoniram Judson.

Judson was the son of a Congregationalist minister from Massachusetts. Graduating first in his class at Brown in 1807, he delivered the class-day oration from the pulpit of the Baptist Meeting House. His father had hoped the pious character of Brown would bolster his son's faith, but Judson, unlike fellow student Jonathan Going, lost his religion while at college and went off to New York after graduation to become a playwright. A series of experiences brought a religious conversion; and he enrolled at Andover, was ordained a Congregationalist minister, and caught the spirit of the missionary movement. Andover students spread this spirit all over Massachusetts; and as a result, in 1810, Congregationalists established the American Board of Commissioners for Foreign Missions. Adoniram and Ann Judson and Luther Rice, another Andover graduate, were among the first missionaries commissioned by the American Board; and in 1812 they sailed for India.

En route to India, they studied the Scriptures and concluded that believer's baptism was the only form that the New Testament supported. Re-baptized in India, they resigned from the American Board, thus losing their financial support. In addition, they had arrived during the War of 1812, so they were unwelcome, both as Americans and because the British East India Company feared that Christian missionaries were bad for business. As a result, they were forced out. The Judsons went on to Burma, and Rice returned to the United States to try to generate support among the Baptists for the work of the Judsons. Rice began in Boston and preached up and down the seaboard states on behalf of missions.

Baptists were up to the task. In May 1814 they created the Triennial Convention, which in turn established the Baptist Board of Foreign Missions to commission missionaries and to oversee the foreign mission effort on a continuous basis. Since no general meeting of Baptists in America had occurred before, one may say that foreign missions made Baptists into a national denomination.[38] The First Baptist Church of Providence had a direct hand in this because Stephen Gano was there at the creation of the Triennial Convention and was one of the committee that drafted its constitution. Support of missions and participation in the mission enterprise became a major theme in First Baptist from then on.

Another young man inspired to evangelize in foreign lands was Barnas Sears, whose work began the Baptist missionary effort in Germany. Sears joined First Baptist in 1822, graduated from Brown in 1825 and later went to Germany to pursue his theological education. On April 22, 1834, he baptized six German converts in the Elbe River in the dark of night to evade the police, leading to the establishment of the first Baptist church in Germany.[39] Sears eventually served as Brown's fifth president from 1855 to 1867. Solomon Peck,

In 1830 only a small band of people espoused abolitionism, but antislavery sentiment swept across the North as a consequence of the Second Great Awakening. In the 1840s the number of antislavery societies rose into the thousands, and religious people could no longer evade the issue.

baptized by Gano in 1818, licensed and ordained for the ministry by First Baptist, served as corresponding secretary for the Board of Foreign Missions from 1835 to 1855.[40] Horace Love, after joining First Baptist in May 1836, went to Greece in December to help found the Baptist mission there.[41] Replacing Love in Greece in 1844 was Albert Arnold, who had been baptized at age seventeen at First Baptist in 1831. The mission at Corfu was nearly dead when he arrived, but he preached both to Greeks and the British garrison on the island until 1851. After working in Athens until August 1855, he returned to the United States, and the Greek mission was closed in 1857.[42] Altogether, from the 1840s to the beginning of the twentieth century, twenty-two members of First Baptist Church went to the foreign mission fields. At least two died: Alfred B. Satterlee in Burma and Charles Hartsock in Africa. Fifteen more became home missionaries while still others served as members and officers on the various home and foreign mission boards over the years.[43]

Founded as an instrument of national Baptist support for foreign missions, the Triennial Convention foundered on the rocks of the slavery controversy. Brown University president, Francis Wayland, a member of First Baptist since 1828,

ABOVE This picture, taken in 1854, is the earliest known photograph of the interior of the Meeting House. It shows the pulpit arrangement for the period 1832 to 1876. The original high pulpit was removed in 1832 and replaced by the dark, Empire-style pulpit. The Palladian window behind the pulpit was plastered over in 1846, and gas lights and chandeliers were added in 1848. The original pews gave way to those shown here in 1832, and the organ (not shown) was installed in the rear gallery in 1834. Photo from the archives of the First Baptist Church in America.

ABOVE Present appearance of the auditorium. Photo by Warren Jagger (2001).

was the president of the Triennial Convention when the issue of slavery ruptured the national unity of Baptists. Wayland was a national figure among Baptists, but his efforts to keep the slavery issue from fracturing the denomination provoked the wrath of abolitionists.

In 1830 only a small band of people espoused abolitionism, but antislavery sentiment swept across the North as a consequence of the Second Great Awakening. In the 1840s the number of antislavery societies rose into the thousands, and religious people could no longer evade the issue. Many Baptists in the North began to question whether it was moral to commission missionaries who were slaveowners. As a result, an increasing number of individuals and missionary societies began withholding their contributions from the Triennial Convention because they believed it was immoral to mix their funds with those coming from slaveowners.[44] A leader in this movement was Robert Pattison, who twice pastored the First Baptist Church (January 1830 to August 1836 and September 1840 to March 1842). He resigned the second time to join Solomon Peck as corresponding secretary for the Board of Foreign Missions, serving there from March 1842 to May 1845 during the final split of northern and southern Baptists. As editor of the *Christian Reflector* in 1840, he wrote that he would vote against the appointment of a slaveowner and called on his colleagues to join him in his stand.[45] Wayland, trying to hold the denomination together, declined to denounce slavery as a sin, but referred to it as a "moral evil" and sought to be a

pacifier and reconciler on the issue. The abolitionist paper, *Herald of Freedom,* slashed at Wayland, charging that he owned slaves on a Cuban plantation and calling him a "great champion of slavery for the North."[46]

On the other side, by 1840 various southern state conventions threatened to withhold funds and to organize their own boards. After the American Baptist Home Mission Society voted against considering a slaveowning candidate, in December 1844 the Alabama Baptist State Convention demanded to know if the Foreign Mission Society would commission a slaveholder. Despite the fact that the 1841 and 1844 meetings of the Triennial Convention had sought to take a neutral stance, the Acting Board of Foreign Missions responded in February 1845 that "if any one should offer himself as a missionary having slaves, and should insist on retaining them as his property, they could not appoint him. One thing is certain, we can never be a party to any arrangement which would imply approbation of slavery."[47]

The final steps leading to the break-up of the Triennial Convention occurred in the Meeting House.[48] The thirty-first annual meeting of the American Baptist Board of Foreign Missions gathered at First Baptist during the last week of April 1845. As was the custom, the annual meetings of the American and Foreign Bible Society, the American Baptist Publication Society, and the American Baptist Home Mission Society were held there as well. On April 28, a special committee of the Home Mission Society adopted a resolution which declared that it would be more expedient if separate organizations in the North and South carried on the work.[49] Then on May 1, the Board of Foreign

Missions ratified the decision of the Acting Board not to appoint any slaveowner; exactly one week later delegates meeting at Augusta, Georgia, formed the Southern Baptist Convention.[50] With the exodus of its southern members, the Triennial Convention reorganized itself at a special convention in November 1845 and began operation in May 1846 as the American Baptist Missionary Union. It should be noted that Wayland now clearly emerged as an antislavery advocate.[51]

The most important reform movement of the pre-Civil War era was the abolition of slavery, and First Baptist was drawn deeply into it. When paid agents of the American Anti-Slavery Society began touring the state in 1835, some of the wealthiest and most influential citizens sought to rally opposition against the antislavery movement. Among the thirty-six men who called the meeting in Providence on November 2, 1835, were three associated with First Baptist. Former Governor James Fenner, Nicholas Brown, and his nephew Moses Brown Ives, were wealthy pew owners; and Brown and Ives were members of the Charitable Baptist Society. The group declared, "All coercive measures for the abolition of slavery are in violation of the sacred rights of property, and of the fundamental provisions of the national compact." They maintained that slavery was a local matter and that abolitionism would produce greater evils than slavery.[52] Many of these "gentlemen of property and standing" were textile manufacturers whose companies produced a large volume of "negro cloth," a coarse cloth used to make clothes for Southern slaves.[53]

Nicholas Brown was the moderator of the Charitable Baptist Society which paid the minister's salary and provided the parsonage. However, Brown's pastor in 1835 was Robert Pattison, who became convinced of the utter iniquity of slavery. Moreover, sitting up the aisle from Brown in pew #44 was a leader of the abolitionist effort, Joseph Bogman, a convert in the revival of 1812. Bogman was the wealthiest man to sign the call for a state antislavery convention in January 1836.[54] Another abolitionist parishioner was Brown's cousin, Hugh Hall Brown, a convert in the 1820 revival and Sunday school superintendent from 1821–1827.[55] And, William Drowne, a young merchant, was the recording secretary of the antislavery convention.[56] One occupant of the pew connecting Nicholas Brown's front pew was young Phebe Jackson, a radical abolitionist.[57] In fact, had Brown looked around him, he would have found at least a dozen people who were openly abolitionist. So, the division in First Baptist was strikingly visible.

In the 1830s, antislavery circles generally regarded First Baptist Church as an unfriendly place. They viewed Francis Wayland as the church's spokesman when he preached against radical abolitionist ministers in the Warren Association in March 1836.[58] When the Rev. Basil Manly of

The most important reform movement of the pre-Civil War era was the abolition of slavery, and First Baptist was drawn deeply into it.

South Carolina, a slaveholder, preached at First Baptist in November, an antislavery spokesmen charged that an abolitionist minister would never be allowed pulpit privileges there. However, a Pawtuxet minister said that "not one in a hundred in First Baptist Church knew at the time that Mr. Manly was a slave holder. . . ." Furthermore, a deacon declared that had he known that Manly was a slave owner, "he should not have been willing to hear him."[59] Although the anti-abolitionists tried to prevent antislavery agents from speaking in Rhode Island, when the famous abolitionists Angelina and Sarah Grimke lectured in Providence on April 23 and 24, 1838, on "the sin of slavery," some members of First Baptist went to hear them.[60] In the 1840s the antislavery side gained greater acceptance,[61] and a small indication of the church's awareness of the pain of slavery is revealed in an entry in the Church Treasurer's report of 1852 which read, "Subscription for Rev. E. Kelly to aid him in procuring [the] release of his family from slavery."[62]

None of these events dampened the ardor of First Baptist Church for foreign or home missions. Richard E. Eddy, a deacon and superintendent of the Sunday school for a decade, was the treasurer of the American Baptist Missionary Union from 1846 to 1855. Four members of the church would serve as president of the Missionary Union, three others as chairmen of the Board of Managers. Furthermore, the eighteenth pastor of the church, James Nathaniel Granger, was absent from the pulpit from October 1852 to May 1854 as one of an official visiting team to the mission stations in India. (There he contracted a disease which caused his death in 1857.)[63] During Granger's tenure, the church sent three more of its own to the mission field in Burma. In the post-Civil War era, another twelve went abroad.[64]

The cause of missions so inspired Sarah Durfee that she devoted most of her life to it. In 1866 she organized the Young Ladies' Missionary Association at the church and served as its president from 1866 to 1905. (When they were no longer young ladies, the group changed its name to the Woman's Foreign Missionary Association.) In 1871 when Baptist women across the nation established their own missionary organization, the Woman's American Baptist Foreign Mission Society, the First Baptist missionary society became an auxiliary. Durfee was the national president for fifteen years, and in recognition of her support, a school in

Himeji, Japan, was named for her.[65] Later, Sarah Faunce, wife of Brown President William H.P. Faunce, and Mary A. Greene were national vice presidents of the Woman's American Baptist Foreign Mission Society.

Still another movement which involved the church was the effort to print and spread Bibles and tracts. This idea, too, came from England, where Bible and tract societies sprang up in the 1790s. By the first decade of the nineteenth century similar organizations appeared in America, culminating in the creation of the American Bible Society in 1816. The Bible Society printed Bibles in many languages, helped the missions of all denominations, and was a major contributor to the Triennial Convention until the 1830s. The Rhode Island Bible Society was organized on September 3, 1813, in the Meeting House of the First Baptist Church. One of the major efforts of the Bible Society throughout the century was to supply the local Sunday schools with Bibles and other religious literature. While it was a non-denominational group, several of its officers were Baptists, and Stephen Gano offered the prayer for the new organization. Nicholas Brown was president of the Bible Society from 1823 until his death in 1841. Later, long-time church member Professor William Gammell served as the Rhode Island Bible Society president from 1869 to 1884.[66]

In the first half of the nineteenth century First Baptist and other Protestant churches in Providence evolved toward a common definition of piety and faith. This evolution was the result of the recurrent revivals and the common responses of the churches to the social problems of a rapidly growing city. City-wide religious enthusiasm erupted in Providence in 1805-6, 1812, 1816, 1820, 1831-2, 1834, 1838, and 1857-8. The great revivalist Charles Grandison Finney preached twice in Providence, including a three-week meeting in the fall of 1831. He later wrote, "There was a great shaking among the dry bones in different churches."[67] All the churches in town grew, especially those in the newer sections; and they were all being moved by the same evangelical spirit.

Initially, the Second Great Awakening intensified the sectarian spirit, but by the time of the revival of 1857-8, American Protestantism had been transformed in substantial respects. A major casualty was Calvinism, with its doctrine of particular or limited atonement. When the century began, Particular Baptists like those at First Baptist regarded Freewill Baptists as utterly wrong; and embracing Freewill ideas led to expulsion from the church. Freewill Baptist churches were excluded from association with the Regular Baptists, and at one point in the 1820s three of the four Baptist churches in Providence were outside the Warren Association.[68] But, by the late 1850s, this hostility had faded substantially as American Protestants in general moved toward the Freewill idea. The Calvinist notion that only a

predetermined few could be saved was felt to be incompatible with the revivalist and missionary impulses. Calvinism in First Baptist had largely evaporated by the 1850s.

The Freewill Baptists represented an anti-Calvinist tide that eventually swept Calvinism out of most Baptist churches in Rhode Island, regardless of their origins. Most of the new Baptist churches being organized in the rural areas of Rhode Island after 1820 were of the Freewill variety, and some new Providence congregations were also Freewill Baptists, beginning with Fourth Baptist. In addition, the Second and Third Baptist Churches became embroiled with Freewill doctrines in the 1820s. Like every other church in Providence, Second Baptist was swept by a revival in 1820, but by September it was expelled from the Warren Association for having "embraced Unitarianism."[69] In 1824 the association expelled Third Baptist because it had adopted the Freewill belief in general atonement. However, in the

ABOVE Robert Everett Pattison (1800-1874) twice served as pastor of First Baptist Church (1830-36, 1840-42), in addition to pastorates in Salem, Massachusetts, and St. Louis, Missouri. He was twice called to the presidency of Waterville College, now Colby College (1836-39, 1854-57), in addition to being president of the Western Baptist Theological Institution at Covington, Kentucky (1845-1848). He was also chairman of the Department of Christian Theology at Newton Theological Institution (1848-1854) and professor of theology at Shurtleff College in Alton, Illinois (1864-1870). He became an abolitionist, and as the Corresponding Secretary of the Home Department of the American Board of Foreign Missions (1842-1845), he urged the mission boards to refuse to commission any slave owners as missionaries. This very issue brought the Baptist denomination to its breaking point in 1845. This photograph of the elderly and frail Dr. Pattison was taken in 1871-1872 while he was acting president of the Theological Seminary of the West in Chicago. Courtesy of Colby College Special Collections.

The Second Great Awakening ultimately softened the hard edge of sectarianism and promoted a mutual respect among most Protestant denominations.

1830s all would be in the Regular ranks, but Freewill Baptist ideas had undermined the doctrines of limited atonement and closed communion. By then First Baptist church no longer expelled members who wanted to join a Freewill Baptist church.

The Second Great Awakening saw a change in the way individuals gained entry into the First Baptist Church. Previously, one had to be able to testify to a definite and profound conversion experience. Such a stringent requirement prevented any number of individuals, such as Nicholas Brown, from ever being baptized into the church. Such persons might live righteous, upright lives and believe the tenets of Christianity, but never undergo the existential experience of conversion.[70] Ho7wever, by the 1840s some began to gain admission by affirming the beliefs of the church, not by testifying to a conversion. It is possible that the sixty-eight-year-old Hope Brown Ives was admitted, at last, as a result of this basic change.

A spokesman for this trend in American Protestantism was Horace Bushnell, a Congregationalist minister in Hartford, Connecticut, who argued in his book, *Christian Nurture* (1847), that one could become a Christian without an emotional experience of conversion. He said, "The child is to grow up a Christian and never know himself as being otherwise."[71] He felt that a child reared in a Christian home could know the spirit of God as naturally as he would learn ethics and morality from his parents. As such ideas gained strength, so did the importance of Christian education. At First Baptist the Sunday school came to be regarded as more important than revivalism in winning souls.

Hostility to Universalism also waned. Universalism went beyond free will by saying that not only did everyone have a chance to be saved, but that everyone *would* be saved. When this idea was introduced into America from England in the 1770s, Baptists regarded it as unabashed heresy and excommunicated anyone who adopted it. First Baptist expelled a member as late as 1857 for holding that view; but by the twentieth century, it would cooperate in summer union services with a group of churches which included the Universalists.[72]

The Second Great Awakening ultimately softened the hard edge of sectarianism and promoted a mutual respect among most Protestant denominations. For example, at the begin-

ning of the nineteenth century, First Baptist simply condemned and expelled anyone found to be attending the churches or espousing the doctrines, of other denominations. However, in 1837 the church adopted a standard letter of dismissal to any other Baptist church and in 1838 began issuing a "certificate of good standing" to individuals leaving to join non-Baptist churches.[73] By the late nineteenth century, it routinely issued letters of transfer to non-Baptist denominations and moved toward "open communion." Open communion involved the taking of communion with people who had not been baptized by immersion. The Freewill Baptists held this view, and it came to be practiced in Baptist churches throughout Rhode Island by World War I. In fact, the Freewill Baptist denomination merged with the Northern Baptist Convention in 1911, signaling the end to that old division and marking the acceptance of the Freewill concept of general atonement by Northern Baptists.[74]

One of the consequences was the blurring of denominational lines and a growing cooperation among Protestants in combating the perceived evils of the nation. From the 1820s to the Civil War, one increasingly saw the appearance of non-sectarian organizations to confront the problems of alcohol, tobacco, ignorance, slavery, prostitution, unhealthy diets, sexual misbehavior, Sabbath breaking, mental illness, prisons, marriage and the family, domestic servants, and industrialism. A host of cooperative agencies, organizations, and societies constituted a kind of "righteous empire." An example was the work of Rev. William Douglas, a member of First Baptist, who was hired in 1838 by the Providence Female Domestic Missionary Society to be a city missionary to the poor. In addition to handing out tracts and Bibles, Douglas distributed coal, wood, soap, flour, stoves, clothing and shoes. He tried to find work for the unemployed, and he held services in "destitute neighborhoods." He regularly preached at the Dexter Asylum, the State Prison, and the Seaman's Home.[75] While he definitely sought to minister to the poor, he worked for a non-sectarian organization. Even the last great revival of the pre-Civil War era had a non-denominational character about it.

The *annus mirablis*, the miracle year of 1858, was the culmination of the nation-wide religious revival of 1857-1858, which was itself the final wave of the Second Great Awakening in the United States. Perhaps more than any of the previous eruptions of revivalism, this last revival hit the northern urban areas of America with great effect.[76] The revivalist impulse seemed to have waned in the 1840s, and the Protestant establishment sought to institutionalize itself, but then the revival fires burst out again in the midst of a nation coming apart in the late 1850s.

The revival had a greater play in the North which was suffering through the depression of 1857 and 1858, and the revivalist fervor was at its peak during the spring of 1858 when the United States Senate debated the infamous, pro-slavery Lecompton Constitution for Kansas. Political and economic tensions mounted in the nation, and the revival surge probably related to those general conditions. In Providence at least 4000 men were unemployed in the winter of 1857-1858, and the prayer meetings in working class churches were thronged by men and women alike.[77] At the same time, businessmen met each day at noon at the Franklin Hall on Westminster Street for prayer meetings. A number of the major churches, including First Baptist, held other prayer meetings in the mornings and evenings. For example, First Baptist held a prayer meeting in the vestry at five o'clock several days a week, and the *Providence Daily Journal* reported on March 23 that the vestry of the Meeting House was too small for the crowd, and on Saturday afternoon the meeting was held upstairs in the auditorium. "The body of the large edifice was entirely filled, and many occupied the galleries."[78] Another thing that distinguished the 1858 revival from the earlier eruptions of the Second Great Awakening was its calmness and lack of exuberance. Observers commented approvingly that it was a quiet revival and that the "work was free from excitement and evidently the fruit of 'the still, small voice.'"[79]

First Baptist experienced a surge in 1858, adding sixty-three new members, including forty-seven by baptism, the most to join the church since a revival in 1838. Significantly, more men than women were baptized in the *annus mirablis*. In most Baptist churches women generally out-numbered the men by two to one, but the revival in Providence in 1858 manifested itself in prayer meetings of businessmen and conversions of young men.[80] An interesting phenomenon was that fifteen young men, aged 16 to 23, were baptized into First Baptist in the revival, and all but one later served in the armed forces in the Civil War.

First Baptist Church grew along with the city of Providence and the Baptist denomination in the nineteenth century. Responding to the currents of the Second Great Awakening and to the opportunities and problems of growth, it became a leader in Baptist activities, as well as cooperating with other denominations in local religious efforts. It planted new churches in Providence and sent members to the home and foreign mission fields in order to evangelize the world. First Baptist was affected by many of the reform currents in the ante-bellum era, and although at first it felt some ambivalence about the abolitionist crusade, the church grew in stature in the community.

ABOVE A highly successful merchant-industrialist, Nicholas Brown (1769-1841) was probably the richest man in Rhode Island when this portrait was made. He showed great liberality to those institutions dear to his heart, but he was politically and socially conservative. The Baptist college was named for him in 1804. He provided it with its first endowment, donated Hope College and Manning Hall, and was the university treasurer for twenty-nine years. He was generous to his family church as well, giving the new organ in 1834, providing land and a parsonage for the minister, donating the clock that still hangs in the auditorium, owning multiple pews in the Meeting House, and serving as moderator of the Charitable Baptist Society for thirty years. His sister, Hope, gave the grand chandelier to the church in 1792 in memory of their father, also named Nicholas. On the other hand, he was a leading opponent of the abolitionist movement in Rhode Island in the 1830s, fearing that the effects of abolitionism were worse than the evils of slavery. Courtesy of the Rhode Island Historical Society (RHi x3 4004).

THE
FIRST BAPTIST
CHURCH
FOUNDED BY
ROGER WILLIAMS
A.D. 1638
THE OLDEST BAPTIST CHURCH
IN AMERICA
THIS PRESENT CHURCH ERECTED
THIS MEETING HOUSE BUILT
A.D. 1775

CHAPTER 5

A Pillar of the Community

In 1984 Edwin Gaustad published an article entitled, "WHERE ARE THE LIONS . . . when we really need them?"[1] He argued that the distinctive Baptist identity had resulted from being a persecuted minority. What happens when Baptists become the majority or a respected part of the establishment? What happens when they are regarded as one of the pillars of the community instead of the pariah? Gaustad was commenting on the fact that in the late twentieth century Baptists were at risk of losing their identity because they were now comfortably part of the establishment.

The path of First Baptist Church showed that its identity was evolving in the nineteenth century. The effects of the "iron law of creeping respectability" reached its full force in that period as the church overcame its rural backwardness about church music and installed the finest organ in the city in the 1830s, chose its ministers only from the college and seminary ranks, struggled to impose order and decorum in the worship services, and disciplined the moral and social behavior of its members. From being a sect once persecuted by government outside of Rhode Island, Baptists, led by First Baptist, now declared it to be a Christian obligation to support the government.

From the last quarter of the eighteenth century and into the twentieth century, First Baptist Church had an important place in the life of Providence. Respectability was wedded to a sense of responsibility and to the church's growing influence in religious circles and in secular events. As the intertwined institutions of First Baptist and Brown University moved through the nineteenth century, they received increasing esteem and respect from the wider community. What would Roger Williams have thought had he been present that Sunday morning in June 1861 when the Second Regiment of Rhode Island Volunteers packed the church and heard the pastor give them a patriotic send-off, saying that they were doing God's work? What had happened to the high wall that separated Christ's garden from the wilderness of the world? The irony was that Roger Williams' congregation had become an ally of the state.

For many years the auditorium of the Meeting House was the largest public space in the city. When it was altered to seat 1400 in 1832, it increased its seating capacity over any other structure. This, plus the church's central role in the city and university, made it the principal site for large convocations and commemorations. Practically every major civic celebration or event involved the Meeting House in some respect. Whether the occasion was to hail the ratification of the Constitution in 1789, to send off a Civil War regiment in 1861, or to celebrate the 250th anniversary of the founding of Providence in 1886, the Meeting House marked these and other major public events.[2] Many a Fourth of July oration was delivered from the pulpit of the Meeting House.[3] Sometimes the entire spectacle occurred in the auditorium; other times the celebrants stopped at the Meeting House for a service as they wound their way through the city. For example, in 1836 when the city celebrated the 200th anniversary of the founding of Providence, a grand procession moved through the streets, stopping at First Baptist Church for prayers and music before crossing the river to the Weybosset side. The day ended with a public dinner at the Franklin House and fireworks at the Cove.[4]

In the 1830s the building underwent substantial changes that represented an evolution toward greater formality. Alterations that had been long under discussion now were carried out. First, the old square pews were torn out, and the cross aisle which ran from the side doors was eliminated.[5] The present long pews were installed and auctioned in September 1832 for $32,000.[6] Equally dramatic was the removal of the high pulpit and its sounding-board. As Henry Melville King described it in his 1900 Historical Discourse, ". . . the lofty pulpit was brought down nearer to the people and the minister humbled from his high elevation. . . ."[7]

The second balcony on the west end of the auditorium was also taken down in anticipation of the organ which the church finally acquired in 1834. That upper gallery had been "set apart" for people of color, and one pious account explained that it was not to isolate them but "to recognize that in this notable house of worship a place for them, too, should be provided."[8] William J. Brown, who had to sit in that gallery when he attended the Meeting House, had quite

OPPOSITE Photo by Warren Jagger (2000).

TIMELINE

1800	State memorial service for Washington in the Meeting House
1820	Missouri Compromise
1832	**Pews, pulpit, and aisles altered to present configuration**
1834	**The organ was installed**
1838	**A baptistry installed in the Meeting House**
1842	The Dorr Rebellion in Rhode Island
1843	The 1663 Charter replaced by a state constitution
1846-48	The Mexican War
1857	**Completion of excavation of lower level of the building**
1859	**First hymnals at FBC**
1861-65	Civil War
1876	Telephone invented
1880	Practical electric lights developed
1884	**New baptistry addition to Meeting House; organ rebuilt; auditorium decor was Victorianized**
1895	**Individual communion cups introduced**
1901	State memorial service for Wm. McKinley at Meeting House

a different feeling about segregation. He noted that many blacks did not attend any church because "they were opposed to going to churches and sitting in pigeon holes, as all the churches at that time had some obscure place for the colored people to sit in."[9] The exodus of African-Americans to establish the African Union Meeting after 1820 meant that fewer blacks attended any of the white churches and made it easier for First Baptist to eliminate its "pigeon hole."

The installation of the organ climaxed the sixty-year evolution of the Providence Baptist Church from its Six Principle rejection even of congregational singing. The organ of 1834 was a statement as bold as the steeple of 1775, completing a transformation in the church. Elder Winsor had resigned with fourscore members in 1771 because "singing in public worship was very disgustful to him."[10] In the next three decades the church had struggled to develop congregational singing, including establishing a choir to lead. At the turn of the century the church prevailed upon George Teel to take charge of the choir; but then in 1803, he was expelled for drunkenness.[11] In 1804 a bass viol was introduced to accompany the singing despite the objection of one oppo-

nent who declared that "to use a fiddle in the house of God would be a base violation of the sacredness of worship."[12] Then in 1807 the Charitable Baptist Society voted to raise a subscription to support a "singing school," but the money was used to pay for candles and fuel, not singers or a director. Congregational singing continued to be a problem, and the first professional musicians were hired to play and sing in the 1820s. The final step was the installation of the organ. Nicholas Brown had first introduced the idea in 1817, but it remained a dream for seventeen years. Instead of importing an organ from England, they engaged E. & G.G. Hook of Boston to build an instrument. With that, the Meeting House became a center of musical performance, with concerts and recitals as standard fare.[13]

Still, over the years the leaders fretted about the lack of decorum that accompanied the worship service. Perhaps it was a consequence of large numbers of new, unsophisticated members, but matters of when to sit, when to stand, and how to stand all led to official resolutions and church votes. One effect of not having a singing tradition prior to 1770 and having no hymnals until 1859 was that the congregation had to learn everything by ear. That is why "choristers" and a "singing school" were introduced. The balcony at the back of the auditorium, where the organ was placed, was fitted for the choir, and for some years the congregation stood, turned, and faced the choir to sing the songs. Evidently, as time passed, some stood to sing, some remained seated, and many, without singing, turned to watch the choir. To address this disorder, in 1847 a resolution declared, ". . .the proprieties of public worship and the comfort & edification of the worshippers themselves, requires *uniformity* in the practice of a Christian Congregation . . . inasmuch as the want of such uniformity necessarily tends to promote confusion and to diminish the solemnity of the service." They specifically attacked the practice of merely looking at the choir. This, they felt, injured "the devotion of the Congregation, besides subjecting the Choir to unnecessary Embarrassment."[14]

Evidently congregational singing was itself such an embarrassment that it was discontinued, because a decade later the church voted to create a committee "to take into consideration the subject of introducing congregational singing in our

public worship." The committee recommended that congregational singing be introduced "as soon as suitable arrangements can be made."[15] Two more years passed before the church adopted a hymnal, but they agreed that the choir be discontinued on the grounds that it discouraged congregational singing.[16] However, over time the congregation again became confused about when to stand or sit for hymns and prayers, and the quality of the singing continued to be a problem. In 1863 another committee examined congregational singing, and created another "singing school."[17] The music committee attempted to reestablish a choir in 1865, but that prompted 108 leading women to sign a petition protesting against "falling back to choir singing . . . ." They declared, "The history of our church, we think, will show that the introduction of a choir has ever been detrimental to congregational singing. And our own experience must convince us that when the music centers in the orchestra, the voices cease below." They asked that the voices that had been gathered in the choristers' seats in the balcony be returned to the floor, "leaving only the leader and the organist in the orchestra."[18]

The controversy surrounding choristers, choir, and congregational singing disappeared by the 1870s, and in 1871 the church adopted a new hymnal compiled by its own minister, Samuel Caldwell, and Adoniram Judson Gordon.[19] The music program was under the jurisdiction of a committee of the Charitable Baptist Society since it hired the organist and any professional musicians. In 1888 the paid musicians consisted of the organist and a vocal quartet, and the program for the 250th anniversary of the church listed the same singers "assisted by a volunteer chorus, and Mr. Bowen R. Church, *Cornetist*."[20] By then, the level of music in the Meeting House "was excellent for the period."[21]

If the music continued to be a problem, how the church selected its ministers was not. As noted in a previous chapter, the coming of James Manning altered who and from where First Baptist Church called its pastors. No longer were they uneducated laymen picked from the congregation as preaching elders. From 1770 on, all the ministers were to be drawn from the ranks of educated, ordained clergymen in the wider world of Baptists. First Baptist Church and Brown

University were linked in this new arrangement as the church nourished the college which provided the contacts to ministers around the country. Brown's first two presidents were pastors of First Baptist, and all the rest in the nineteenth century were members. Brown's fourth president, Francis Wayland, filled the pulpit at one point for over a year, though he declined to accept the church's call to become the permanent pastor.[22]

Wayland was a central figure in determining the ministerial leadership of First Baptist from 1828, when he first joined the church. He had been a member of the church only three months when he was placed on the pulpit committee to find a replacement for the dying Stephen Gano.[23] Wayland's presence on the committee meant that First Baptist now sought only college- and seminary-educated ministers, and the search used the developing network of Baptist colleges, seminaries, and denominational societies, such as the Foreign Mission Society or the Home Mission Society. The change that had begun with James Manning's election was completed.

ABOVE Francis Wayland (1796-1865) was a leader in Baptist circles in the nation and a significant figure in public affairs in Rhode Island. He was president of Brown University from 1827 to 1855, overseeing the reform and expansion of the college and pulling it through a major financial crisis. A popular and influential member of First Baptist Church, he served as Acting Pastor in 1857-1858 after the death of James Granger. Despite repeated entreaties from the church to him, he declined to become the permanent minister. He was president of the Triennial Convention when the slavery controversy split the Baptist denomination in 1845, and he oversaw the creation of the American Baptist Missionary Union. Engraving from a photograph from *A Memoir of the Life and Labors of Francis Wayland,* Vol. I (1867). Courtesy of the Rhode Island Historical Society (RHi x3 4584).

Gano's successor, Robert E. Pattison, was an 1826 graduate of Amherst College, a tutor at Columbian College in Washington, DC in 1827-1828, then a professor of mathematics and natural philosophy at Waterville College (now Colby College), in 1828-1829. Pattison later served two stints as president of Waterville, was president of two seminaries in the West, and was professor at Newton Theological Institution and at Shurtleff College in Alton, Illinois. In fact, Pattison resigned his pastorate at First Baptist in August 1836 to assume the presidency of Waterville College.[24]

When Pattison resigned, the church appointed a three-man pulpit committee: Wayland and deacons Nathaniel Bump and Varnum Bates. They voted to call William Hague on December 1, 1836. First Baptist had invited Hague to become its pastor in 1829 to replace Gano, but he declined. A graduate of Hamilton College in New York (another Baptist college) in 1826, Hague studied at Princeton Theological Seminary and graduated from Newton Theological Institution in 1829. He took a church in Utica, New York, before becoming a professor of Greek and Latin at Georgetown College in Kentucky. Then, in 1831 he became the pastor of the First Baptist Church of Boston with Francis Wayland preaching the installation sermon. Not surprisingly, Wayland urgently pressed Hague to accept the call to Providence, but at first he declined. Wayland persisted, and Hague became the pastor in June 1837.[25]

When Hague resigned in August 1840, the church again appointed the pulpit committee of Wayland, Bump & Bates. Wayland prevailed upon Pattison to return, and the church voted to call him just one month after Hague left. This was not well received by some, and the motion passed after

lengthy debate 54-9.[26] Pattison remained only two years before becoming the corresponding secretary for the American Baptist Board of Foreign Missions. So, the church appointed a pulpit committee: again, Wayland, Bump & Bates.

By November 1842, Wayland had used the Baptist network to find James Granger, a twenty-eight year old graduate of Hamilton Literary and Theological Institution.[27] When Granger died in 1857, Wayland filled the pulpit for a year and was instrumental in getting Samuel Caldwell to come to Providence in 1858. Caldwell graduated from Waterville College in 1839 and Newton Theological Institution in 1845.[28] He pastored the church until 1873. Since Wayland died in 1865, his selection of ministers ended with Caldwell; however, the pattern had been set. Every pastor would be a college graduate. They would be tied into the network of Baptist seminaries and often taught in colleges and seminaries, if not before, then after they left First Baptist. For each search for a new pastor, the church formed a pulpit committee, invariably including Brown University professors. All of the clergymen who led the church were eminently respectable.

ABOVE This picture shows how the auditorium appeared from 1877 to 1884. The large pulpit of 1832 gave way to this small, but ornate Victorian podium and furniture. The stage was flanked by large semi-urns standing on half pedestals, and the area within the pilasters and keystoned arch was papered with a fleur-de-lis design. This stage furniture especially suited Edward G. Taylor, the twentieth pastor, who preached with an energetic, evangelistic style. One of his suggestions was rejected, however; he wanted the pews removed and replaced with theater seats. Photo from the archives of the First Baptist Church in America.

It must be pointed out that prior to the Second Great Awakening the United States was the "Alcoholic Republic." People drank hard liquor at all occasions—weddings, births, elections, militia parades, even ordinations and church raisings. The seriousness of the drinking problem in the United States goes far to explaining why one of the moral crusades of the Second Great Awakening was against any drinking.

First Baptist Church, like all churches in earlier times, examined and regulated the behavior of its members, and it was a high and narrow standard. In addition to theological and doctrinal issues, personal morality and public decorum were also scrutinized. Each church member was supposed to act properly in and out of church, and being quarrelsome in church or misbehaving in public led to discipline.

The church expelled individuals for "lewd and unchristian conduct," "gross immorality," homosexuality, adultery, "awful sin of fornication," "unchastity before marriage," divorce, remarriage while a former spouse was living, "lying and tattling," and being a "railer and profane person." Family disputes merited church attention as when Benjamin Jones was expelled for abusive language toward his father and brothers.[29] In October 1827 three sisters, Abigail, Mary, and Zilpha Chace were suspended "until they should become reconciled to each other," and they were not restored to membership until December 1829.[30]

Those who were argumentative or obstinate were often cited for "disorderly conduct," "disorderly walking," or "refusing to hear the church." The pastor's wife, Joanna Gano, was excluded on these grounds.[31] In 1808 David Martin, the last person who tried to insist on members "going under hands," was declared to be "disorderly," and he ceased attending.[32] The church excommunicated Harriet Fenner for lying and for "loose and disorderly conduct."[33] Altogether, from 1782 to 1855, more than fifty members were disciplined for "disorderly conduct" or "disorderly walking," most being severed from the church.[34] A substantial number of those disorderly cases involved public behavior and actions that were seen as bringing shame on the church.

A recurring phrase appearing in many cases was "the painful subject of the Open Reproach . . . brought on this Church."[35] In 1787 Henry Whipple was excluded for nearly a year for behaving "in a scandalous and reproachful manner" toward non-members Esek Hopkins and his wife.[36] Other examples of public misbehavior included John Whipple's "quarrelling and fighting with Wheeler Martin, Esq. in the Street," Stephen Thornton's "quarreling in a tavern," and young Gustavus Field's "visiting a house of ill-fame."[37] Abigail Carr kept "in her house persons of infamous character and both bedded and boarded with a certain white man, by the name of Simeon Anderson, and hath also been guilty of drinking to excess."[38] Stephen Randall, M.D., sold a lot to "a woman of bad character" who built "a house of ill fame thereon . . . but after it was sold [he] could not see that it was wrong to continue to sell adjoining lots to the same character."[39] Various others were excommunicated for committing crimes, including forgery, theft, counterfeiting, larceny, stealing, prostitution, bigamy, and embezzlement.[40]

In 1795 the church concluded that it was improper to attend a theater, saying that "the Theatre is productive of many disadvantages to Civil Society, as well as tends to create undue levity. . . . "[41] Circuses were added to the list of forbidden amusements in 1827 because they were "sources of dissipation."[42] Henry A. Anthony was expelled from the church in 1826 for "repeatedly visiting the theatre," and in 1839 Leonard Marble was excluded for "repeatedly attending dancing school and cotillion parties."[43] With the revivals of the nineteenth century came an increased stress upon strict Sabbath observance, sobriety, and industriousness. In particular, First Baptist joined the crusade against alcohol.

It must be pointed out that prior to the Second Great Awakening the United States was the "Alcoholic Republic." People drank hard liquor at all occasions—weddings, births, elections, militia parades, even ordinations and church raisings. Workmen and artisans imbibed all through the day as did gentlemen and gentry. Baptist preachers were sometimes paid with whiskey. Since drunkenness was a common problem, when people were expelled from the membership for using alcohol, it is certain that they were heavy drinkers. Moreover, those were the ones who did not repent and receive forgiveness. The seriousness of the drinking problem in the United States goes far to explaining why one of the moral crusades of the Second Great Awakening was against any drinking.[44]

Temperance became prohibition. As one historian has said, ". . . believing that prohibition at its worst is better than licence at its best," reformers raised the standard to total abstinence.[45] The effect was clearly shown in the sharp increase in the number of members expelled from First

First Baptist Church, like all churches in earlier times, examined and regulated the behavior of its members, and it was a high and narrow standard. In addition to theological and doctrinal issues, personal morality and public decorum were also scrutinized.

Baptist for intemperance. From 1775 to 1812 a total of six individuals were removed for drunkenness; but from 1813 to 1835, as any drinking came to be regarded as sinful, twenty-six were excommunicated.[46] One of these was Deacon Thomas Northup, who was ejected in 1826. Northup experienced a conversion in a revival in 1831 and became one of the leaders of the temperance crusade in Providence afterwards.[47] Many other individuals were brought before the church, repented, and were forgiven. In 1832, the First Baptist Church adopted a temperance pledge that all members had to accept, and cases of intemperance became extremely rare.[48]

The church put a high premium upon internal order and harmony, and the minutes of the Standing Committee and the church itself are filled with the struggle to impose discipline. The Standing Committee (all men) was composed of the pastor, four deacons, and seven others who constituted an executive committee, handling most issues and business before they ever reached a church meeting. They often resolved matters, and these never came before the congregation. For example, the church acted against only one of six

ABOVE The climax of the process of Victorianizing the interior of the Meeting House came in 1884. A jut was added to the east end of the building and a baptistry installed, complete with dark mahogany wood and wine-colored drapes. The baptistry was topped with a cross, the first use of such iconography in the Meeting House. Above and behind was a stained glass window, which was a radical departure from the plain, Puritan meeting house style. The ceiling of the auditorium and gallery was painted with "blues, sage green, and other colors. . . ." The large gas chandeliers came down, but three and five-light gas fixtures were installed around the gallery. Photo from the archives of the First Baptist Church in America.

men who supported Thomas Dorr in 1842 because the cases of the other five were satisfactorily dealt with by the Standing Committee. The church took the responsibility to make respectable citizens of its members, and it sometimes had its hands full trying to assimilate and discipline new members who flooded in during the big revivals. For example, the great 1820 revival brought in 157 new members, but eventually 25 percent of these were dismissed. Of these, nine were expelled within two years for drunkenness, fornication, "gross immorality," and disorderly conduct. Charles Seaman's conversion lasted only four months before excommunication.[49]

The truth is that the members of the church were generally quite ordinary people; it was the pew owners (mostly nonmembers), members of the Charitable Baptist Society, and the visible, male leadership of the church that were prestigious. In 1832 the actual church members were two-thirds female, and one-fourth of these were widows.[50] Most of the widows were quite poor, having no taxable property, living in boarding houses, and often sharing rooms with other widows. Although twenty-two members (or their husbands) fell within the highest quintile of property taxpayers in Providence, 75 percent owned no taxable property at all.

ABOVE This view of the rear of the auditorium in 1884 shows the dramatic effect of the ceiling decoration. "The woodwork has all been painted ivory white, brightened here and there with gold; the walls are a warm yellowish buff. . . ." Gas lights were added all around the auditorium and the grand chandelier was now piped for gas. Some of the beauty of the chandelier was obscured by its being festooned with strings of glass balls. The organ was enlarged by additions on the sides while retaining the original case. Courtesy of Brown University Archives.

While the church had a number of small-business men, such as grocers, shoestore owners, merchants, and meat dealers, others were artisans, such as coopers, cabinet makers/undertakers, shoemakers, and carpenters, and still others were ordinary laborers, teamsters, and mariners.

On the other hand, the pew owners included the richest man in Rhode Island, Nicholas Brown, his brother-in-law, Thomas Poynton Ives, and nephew Moses Brown Ives.[51] The ranks of the pew owners included many merchants, bank officers, attorneys, a judge and clerk of the U.S. Circuit Court, former and future governors, Brown University professors and president, ship captains, and manufacturers. These men owned the most prominent pews and set a visible standard for the rest of the congregation. By 1832 only men could speak freely or vote in church meetings, and the elected leaders (Deacons, Clerk, and the Standing Committee) were all middle-class property owners. As the century progressed, the general wealth of the membership improved, but the ratio of men to women remained constantly two-thirds female. While African-American members still numbered thirty in 1832, none remained by 1890. Nevertheless, by 1890 a significant number of members of the church were immigrants or children of immigrants, mostly coming from northern Europe and Canada.[52]

Another way that First Baptist expressed its sense of responsibility in the community was by supporting struggling churches and major institutions in Providence. In addition to its contributions to the Rhode Island Baptist State Convention, which gave subsidies to "feeble churches," First Baptist gave direct assistance to many other churches in and

PEWS AND FLOOR
—OF THE—
FIRST BAPTIST MEETING HOUSE,
PROVIDENCE, R. I.

No.	Val.	Val.	No.
15	100	350	54
16	115	475	53
17	200	525	52
18	225	550	51
19	250	550	50
20	175	450	49
21	175	500	48
22	175	475	47
23	160	475	46
24	175	450	45
25	125	325	44
26	120	300	43
27	120	240	42
28	115	200	41
29	110	175	40
30	90	135	39
31	80	115	38
32	70	115	37
33	60	100	36
34	50	50	35

PULPIT.

No.	Val.	Val.	No.
55	750	750	90
56	775	775	89
57	800	800	88
58	800	800	87
59	800	800	86
60	800	800	85
61	775	775	84
62	775	775	83
63	700	700	82
64	625	625	81
65	550	550	80
66	425	425	79
67	325	325	78
68	225	225	77
69	150	150	76
70	155	155	75
71	100	100	74
72	50	50	73

No.	Val.	Val.	No.
91	350	100	130
92	475	115	129
93	525	200	128
94	550	225	127
95	550	250	126
96	450	175	125
97	590	175	124
98	475	175	123
99	475	160	122
100	450	175	121
101	325	125	120
102	300	120	119
103	240	120	118
104	200	115	117
105	175	110	116
106	135	90	115
107	115	80	114
108	115	70	113
109	100	60	112
110	50	50	111

EAST DOOR. EAST DOOR. NORTH DOOR. SOUTH DOOR. WEST DOOR.

ABOVE In 1878 the Charitable Baptist Society [CBS] issued this chart show-ing the assessed value of each pew. The CBS raised money to pay the pastor, sexton, organist, and to repair and maintain the building by levying taxes upon the pews. It worked exactly like a property tax. Each year the CBS set its budget, voted a "tax rate," and the amount owed depended upon the assessed value of the pew. And, just like the New England town financial meeting, only pew owners could vote on the budget and the tax rate. Begun when the Meeting House was built in 1774-1775, this system of financing was completely abandoned in the 1930s. Chart from *Charter and By-Laws of the Charitable Baptist Society in Providence, with the Amendments* (1878).

> *Suffrage reformers believed that the American Revolution validated the principle that government derived its legitimacy from the consent of the governed and that the people could exercise popular sovereignty to establish a new government.*

around Providence. For example, the Friendship Street Baptist Church (later Calvary Baptist) received $5000 in 1854 to erect a place of worship, and another gift was given in 1863 to help liquidate its debts.[53] Aid to struggling church-es was by no means confined to Providence or even to Rhode Island. In 1844 alone, aid was given to build meeting houses for the Cumberland Hill Baptist Church, Second Baptist of Hopkinton, and First Baptist of Westerly.[54] Frequent finan-cial help went to the Lime Rock and Albion churches, and gifts of money aided the Baptist Church on Block Island and the Knight Street Baptist Church in Pawtucket. When the Woonsocket Falls Baptist meetinghouse burned, First Baptist sent money to help to rebuild it.[55]

Aid and relief extended well beyond Rhode Island. The Baptist church in Camanche, Iowa, was destroyed by a tor-nado, so First Baptist contributed money for a new build-ing.[56] Money went to Baptist churches in Burlington and Iowa City, Iowa; Rock Island, Galesburg, and Joliet, Illinois; Middleburg, Indiana; Milwaukee and Oshkosh, Wisconsin; Salt Lake City, Vicksburg, Pittsburgh, Baltimore, and Washington, D.C.[57] Aid went to the starving in Ireland dur-ing the great potato famine in the 1850s and for the relief of the victims of the Great Chicago Fire in 1871.[58]

Community institutions found significant support at First Baptist. When Brown University experienced a serious finan-cial crisis in 1850 and sought to raise $125,000 to avert it, members of First Baptist Church gave $50,175 to that fund and another $8,000 to the university library.[59] Five years earlier, members of the congregation subscribed $38,222 to the campaign to establish the Rhode Island Asylum for the Insane (later called Butler Hospital).[60] When a subscription

drive was mounted in 1863-1864 to establish Rhode Island Hospital, twenty-five members of the congregation pledged $36,150.[61] So, scarcely a worthy cause escaped the attention and support of the members and congregation of Rhode Island's oldest church.

The reaction of First Baptist Church to the so-called "Dorr Rebellion" of 1842 revealed how much the church had become part of the established order of the state. This vest-pocket civil war was the culmination of several decades of agitation over voting rights and legislative representation in Rhode Island. In 1776 Rhode Island probably had been the most democratic state in the nation; but by 1830, owing to the restrictive property requirements for voting and malapportionment of the General Assembly, it was the least democratic.[62] This trend, accompanied by reform agitation since the 1790s, culminated in the Dorr Rebellion.

Suffrage reformers believed that the American Revolution validated the principle that government derived its legitimacy from the consent of the governed and that the people could exercise popular sovereignty to establish a new government. One of those who argued that the people could bypass the legislature and call a constitutional convention

ABOVE The struggle to expanded the voting franchise resulted in a People's Convention writing a People's Constitution which led to the election of Thomas W. Dorr as governor of Rhode Island. All of this was extra-legal and in 1842 led to the "Dorr Rebellion" when the sitting government invoked harsh penalties against the People's government. At least six members of First Baptist were identified as supporters of the suffrage movement and were called before the Standing Committee to explain themselves. In the aftermath, the church adopted a resolution which declared it to be "a *Christian duty*" to support the legitimate government. Used by permission from the broadside collection of the Rhode Island Historical Society.

was James David Knowles, a young member of First Baptist and student of the ministry. A convert in the revival of 1820, he was baptized, licensed to preach, and soon departed to attend seminary.[63] He said that when a government ceased to have popular consent, it could be replaced. The reformers regarded the present form of government in Rhode Island as having become illegitimate.

Another spokesman for reform, coming from the disenfranchised working class, was Seth Luther, a convert in the 1815 revival and fellow member with Knowles. However, in 1824 Luther was expelled for "disorderly walking."[64] A passionate, argumentative carpenter, Luther became a leader of the suffrage movement after 1833.[65] He argued that God had made everyone "of the same materials, and subject to the same laws of our common nature."[66] However, God's just order for the world had been perverted by avaricious mill owners and oppressors of the poor. They exploited the poor in the factories and denied them education and the vote.[67] When the state government failed to reform, the suffrage forces, led by Thomas Dorr, held the People's Convention, wrote the People's Constitution, saw it overwhelmingly approved in a popular referendum, and then elected the People's government — all of which was extralegal. After the legal government invoked harsh penalties against the People's government, Dorr led an unsuccessful attempt to overthrow the state government by force. One of the Dorrites was John Barton. In the aftermath and defeat of the suffragists, Barton was expelled from First Baptist for "sustaining the movement of Thomas Dorr in his late treasonable designs against this State."[68] Evidently, Barton's involvement also ruined his surveying business because after

Community institutions found significant support at First Baptist. When Brown University experienced a serious financial crisis in 1850 and sought to raise $125,000 to avert it, members of First Baptist Church gave $50,175 to that fund and another $8,000 to the university library. Five years earlier, members of the congregation subscribed $38,222 to the campaign to establish the Rhode Island Asylum for the Insane (later called Butler Hospital).

1842 his wealth plummeted to one tenth of its former amount.[69] He was reduced to being a guard at the railroad station and living in a boarding house on Benefit Street.[70]

Barton was one of six members identified as Dorrites by the church. He alone was punished, but he was the only one who refused to meet with the Standing Committee to answer the charges.[71] Stephen Barker, a grocer, first wrote a letter questioning the right of the church to inquire into his political beliefs, but after a session with the Standing Committee, he contritely appeared before a special church meeting. He had "upon reflection changed his mind with regard to the authority of the church to inquire into his conduct . . . ." He was forgiven, and then given permission to transfer his membership to the West Baptist Church, a more liberal congregation which favored abolitionism.[72] George Buffington, a 36-year old grocer, Horace Robbins, a 32-year old tin-worker, and Jonathan Sisson, a young gardener and laborer, all received forgiveness after explaining that they had never intended or supported violence. They admitted that they had marched in a parade supporting the People's Constitution and Thomas Dorr, but they "did not mean to encourage any treasonable design . . . [and] they wholly disapproved the resort to arms. . . ."[73] The sixth man was the elderly Daniel V. Ross, also a grocer and member of the church since 1797, and his case was simply dropped after being visited by a member of the Standing Committee.[74]

After Barton's expulsion, the church adopted a resolution introduced by Professor William Gammell, which stated that "as a Church and as individuals we hold allegiance to the civic government to be a *Christian duty* enforced by many precepts, and sanctioned by the *whole* spirit of the *Gospel*." It regarded anyone who had supported "the insurrectionary movements in this state as having *grievously erred*," and required them to repent, confess, and renounce their error.[75]

Gammell's resolution was the first instance in First Baptist records of the view that allegiance to the state was a Christian duty. After the Dorr War several other Baptist churches wrote this idea into their "Articles of Faith and Practice."[76] It is noteworthy that those Baptist churches that subsequently adopted this article had strong links to First Baptist. These included Third Baptist and Brown Street Baptist (both daughter churches of First), Mt. Pleasant Baptist (sometimes called the "First Baptist mission"), and the Central Baptist Church of Newport whose pastor was Henry Jackson from Providence's First Baptist Church.

OPPOSITE Interior view of the southwest side, 2001. Photo by Warren Jagger (2001).

ABOVE This interior view of the northeast side, about 1908, clearly shows the 1884 style of decorating the ceiling of the auditorium and the groined arches of the balcony. Photo from the archives of the First Baptist Church in America.

Thomas Dorr was convicted of high treason and sentenced to life imprisonment in May 1844. The following April the Liberation party, headed by Charles Jackson, won the state elections, campaigning on the issue of freeing Dorr from prison. Dorr was pardoned and released from prison. Jackson, now governor, was the owner of the center-front pew #90.[77] His abolitionist sister, Phebe, and his wife, also named Phebe, were members of First Baptist. The man that Jackson replaced as governor in 1845 was the elderly James Fenner, a "hearer" and pew owner in the Meeting House for nearly half a century.

When the Civil War broke out, the alliance of church and state was manifested in the vigorous support given by First Baptist to the Union cause. Pastor Samuel Caldwell, Brown University president Barnas Sears, and past president Frances Wayland used their influence and prestige to advance the war effort. Their patriotic speeches around the city on behalf of the Union cause inspired men to enlist. As noted in the previous chapter, nearly the entire cohort of

ABOVE The most controversial departure from the "New England meeting-house style" in the new addition to the auditorium in 1884 was the insertion of a memorial stained glass window, crafted in Boston. The grandchildren of Hope Brown Ives donated this window, depicting the baptism of Jesus by John the Baptist. Because the window was so out of keeping with the Meeting House's design, it was shuttered over. Photo from the archives of the First Baptist Church in America.

young men baptized in the revival of 1858 went off to war, and Brown University students flocked to the colors.[78] The unique relationship between the church and the university meant that the young men heard the same message from the same leaders in both places. Caldwell spoke at Brown convocations and Sears, Wayland, and various Brown professors were leaders down the hill at the Meeting House.[79]

A clear example of First Baptist's endorsement of the war effort was the blessing that Samuel Caldwell gave to the men of the Second Regiment when they attended Sunday morning services on June 9, 1861, prior to departure for Washington, D.C. That the "wilderness of the world" had invaded the "garden of Christ" was evident in the newspaper description: "The pulpit and the wall above it were tastefully adorned with national banners . . . . Most of the pews in the body of the house were required for the soldiers. But every inch of space left in the aisles and galleries were occupied." Also in attendance were Governor William Sprague, "a large number of our prominent citizens," and local United States military officials.[80]

Dr. Caldwell told the soldiers: "Blessed indeed is the army which carries with it the benediction of religion, and sets up its banners in the name of God." He continued, saying, "[God] consents, nay, demands, to be served sometimes by the soldier as well as the priest. . . . The musket of the soldier may be a vessel of the Lord, executing the powers ordained of Him, speaking for Him to men who are deaf to other arguments. You may serve God, even as a priest unto Him, with as clear a sense of duty, with a conscience as loyal to Him, in smiting rebellion, as in supporting His worship. Powder may be sanctified by the word of God and prayer, as well as your daily bread." What God required in return was that the soldier remain faithful to God, to walk uprightly and morally. "The sword, the pen, the plough, the hammer, alike you may make vessels of the Lord, by the spirit in which you use them." Therefore, he preached, "Be ye clean that bear the vessels of the Lord. . . . Let Holiness to the Lord be written on their very guns, out of whose smoking mouths this cause of God and humanity is looking for its pure and immortal victory."[81]

There before Caldwell in the ranks of the regiment were Edward and William, two sons of president Barnas Sears, both captains of their companies and both to give distinguished service in the war. Seated there also was Pvt. John Nicholson, a servant to Miss Martha Barney. He was killed

at Bull Run on July 21. The conflict also saw past-president Wayland's son, H. Lincoln, serve as a chaplain for ʼe years with the 7th Connecticut Regiment; future president Alexis Caswell's son, Thomas, entered the Navy in 1861 and became a career officer, rising to the rank of admiral by the 1890s. Caldwell's own two sons were just children, but George James Whipple, his servant, joined the U.S. Navy in 1862. Over the course of the war at least fifty-seven members or relatives of members went off to war. Many other members dwelt in homes where someone from that household fought in the war, so that it was hardly possible to escape close and personal involvement. While no active member died in the service, death claimed several others, including Miss Barney's servant. Disease was the principal killer of men in the Civil War. Gustavus Field, one of the cohort of 1858, (but expelled from the church in 1861 for visiting a prostitute) died in a hospital in New Orleans in 1865. Mary Carr's son Thomas became so ill that he was discharged in late December 1862 and died at home on January 2, 1863.

Sgt. William Martin was severely wounded at Antietam in September 1862 and was discharged from the army on a "surgeon's certificate." Mrs. Rosamond Hopkins' son Stephen lost a foot in the blundering assaults at Fredericksburg on December 13, 1863. Discharged, he returned home, but died before the end of the war. Andrew T. MacMillan was wounded at Malvern Hill in July 1862 and captured at Cedar Creek in August 1864. George Porter, a surgeon in the regular army, was captured in 1862 and wounded in 1863. Altogether, only five men suffered wounds that appeared on their official records. Six became prisoners of war, but were paroled or exchanged by the Confederates. James Lowry, the sexton of the church in 1861, enlisted twice and was sent home both times because he became too sick. He spent most of both stints in the hospital, first in South Carolina and then in Louisiana. Mrs. Hannah Thornton suffered the ultimate embarrassment when her son Jesse deserted at Harrison's Landing, Virginia, June 20, 1864, and never returned to Rhode Island.[82]

Perhaps the most interesting and saddest story of a First Baptist soldier was that of William Henry Smith, the only African-American of military age in the church. Blacks were not allowed to enlist until the summer of 1863, but Smith enrolled in Company A in August when Rhode Island began recruiting the 14th R.I. Heavy Artillery Regiment. In

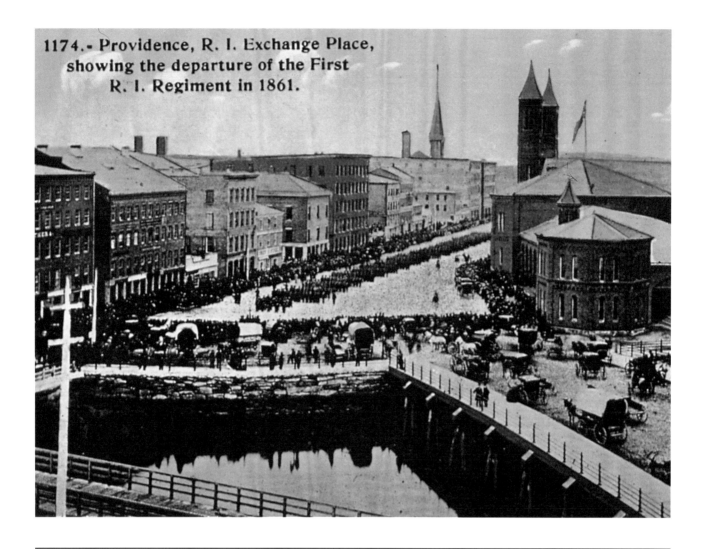

1174.- Providence, R. I. Exchange Place, showing the departure of the First R. I. Regiment in 1861.

As noted in the previous chapter, nearly the entire cohort of young men baptized in the revival of 1858 went off to war, and Brown University students flocked to the colors. The unique relationship between the church and the university meant that the young men heard the same message from the same leaders in both places.

December he married a widow with three children just two weeks before the regiment shipped out to the Gulf Coast of Texas. The 14th Regiment spent its entire time doing garrison duty on Matagorda Island, Texas, and then in the swampy lands south of New Orleans. The conditions were extremely unhealthy, and the regiment lost as many men to disease as other regiments lost in heated combat. To make matters worse, the soldiers were often abused by their officers and paid less than white soldiers. This led to the famous protest of the 54th Massachusetts Regiment, which refused to accept any pay until it was equalized. A smaller protest erupted in the 14th R.I. Regiment, when three companies (out of nine), including Smith's own Company A, refused to accept the unequal pay. All the sergeants and corporals of the three companies and some twenty privates,

ABOVE On June 20, 1861, the R.I. Second Regiment departed for the South and their baptism by fire at the Battle of Bull Run on July 21 where they suffered 114 casualties, including 28 killed. The entire regiment had attended church at the Meeting House on June 9 to receive a patriotic blessing from Samuel Caldwell, the nineteenth pastor of the church. As this postcard indicates, this scene is generally misidentified as a picture of the departure of the R.I. First Regiment.

including Smith, were arrested. Before that matter was resolved, about two weeks later Smith involved himself in an incident that landed him in prison. All officers of black regiments were white, and a lieutenant wantonly shot one of Smith's comrades in the back of the head. Smith rushed to the scene, ripped off his jacket, and declared that "we did not come down here to be shot down like dogs for nothing by Union men or officers."[83] He was arrested for "mutinous conduct," convicted in a court-martial on April 22, 1864, and sentenced to five years hard labor at Fort Jefferson, Florida.[84] He was stripped of all pay and considerations, which meant that his wife, back in Rhode Island, lost her $4 weekly allotment as a soldier's wife. As a result she deserted him and married another man. Released in May 1866, Smith returned to Providence where he became a janitor at the Franklin House for many years. Sadly for Smith, the Congress passed a law to equalize the salary in June, just weeks after his conviction. He paid a terrible price: he was jailed, lost his wife, and was later refused a Civil War pension.

It is interesting to note that nothing about the war appeared in church minutes until September 1862, when the struggle was going badly for the North.[85] At its annual meeting, the church voted to accept the recommendation of the Warren Baptist Association to observe the third Thursday in October "as a day of fasting and prayer with special reference to the present distracted condition of our country."[86] Then in November they voted to make every fourth Sunday evening a time for "a special concert of prayer. . . with special reference to the condition of our country, and to ask the blessing of God on the men composing our army."[87] Subsequently in 1863 and 1864, the church observed various days of humiliation, thanksgiving, or fasting with respect to the war.[88] Finally in 1865 the church wrote the Warren Association saying, "We desire to unite with you in devout thanks to Almighty God that . . . the Great Rebellion has been suppressed and Freedom given to millions of a down trodden and much abused race among us. . . . This baptism of blood" has ended the evil of slavery.[89]

The end of the war did not eliminate the reminders of what had happened. Not only did the church's men return, but additional veterans joined in the following decades. They brought with them the visible evidence of the horrors of war. For example, William Spencer, who came to study for the ministry at Brown, had lost his right leg in battle in 1862. And, later, when Professor Benjamin Andrews arrived to teach at Brown and then to become its president (1889-1898), he brought a fearsome countenance due to the loss of an eye at Petersburg in 1864.

In the 1880s, the appearance of the auditorium increasingly took on "high church" aspects. The characteristics of the New England meetinghouse style came under direct assault in 1884 as the white walls were painted a "warm yellowish buff," the woodwork became "ivory white," and the

By the end of the nineteenth century, First Baptist was clearly one of the venerable institutions in the city. By then, the church was 250 years old. Beginning with the 100th anniversary of the dedication of the Meeting House in 1875, a series of celebrations found the speakers emphasizing the unique history and glory of the Providence church.

ABOVE Thomas W. Fry was William Henry Smith's captain in the R.I. Fourteenth Heavy Artillery Regiment when Smith was arrested and court-martialled for "mutinous conduct." The two men might have known each other before the war because Fry's sister, Annie Fry, was baptized into the church during the same religious revival in 1857 that saw Smith's baptism. The Frys were English immigrants, and Thomas was a jeweller in Providence when the Civil War began. Fry was an experienced officer, having served with the R.I. Third Heavy Artillery from 1861 to 1863 before accepting a commission in Rhode Island's only black regiment. Photo from William Chenery, *The Fourteenth Regiment: Rhode Island Heavy Artillery (Colored), in the War to Preserve the Union, 1861-1865* (1898).

ceilings of the auditorium and gallery were painted in large panels with "blues, sage green, and other colors. . . ."[90] An addition to the east end of the Meeting House accommodated a new, grand baptistry and a stained glass window. Made of dark mahogany with wine-colored drapes, the baptistry was topped by a cross, the first use of such iconography in the auditorium. The dark wood of the baptistry was matched by the gift of an "elegant pulpit and its rich furniture."[91] In the rear of the addition was the stained glass window, the only one in the Meeting House. The grandchildren of Hope Brown Ives gave the window as a memorial, placing her name on it. Here was an object so totally out of character with the architecture and traditions of the church that its appearance engendered controversy among the members.[92] The decision to accept and install the window was made by the Charitable Baptist Society, which included many non-Baptist, non-churchmember pew owners.

Until the 1860s, baptisms had been performed at varied hours, in various places, often unconnected to the regular worship services.[93] Until at least 1864 some baptisms took place in warm weather, out-of-doors in either the Seekonk River north of the India Point Bridge or in Thurber's Pond, near present-day Branch Avenue.[94] By the 1870s all baptisms were performed in the Meeting House as part of the Sunday worship services, and the new baptistry of 1884 provided a plush, ornate setting for this rite. At the same time the organ was rebuilt and enlarged by Hilborn T. Roosevelt. The sermons and the music took on a more elevated and classical character, and in 1895 the common communion cup was replaced by individual cups for each person.[95] By the turn of the century the deacons began to dress in mourning coats and striped trousers, emphasizing the solemn, formal nature of the services. Old First was a respected, prestigious church, and it might be noted that of those who were dismissed to non-Baptist churches after 1890, more became Episcopalians than members of any other denomination.[96] It may have no significance, but the Meeting House was painted grey for its one and only time in 1900. In the quarter century from 1875 to 1900, while Baptists state-wide experienced a decline, First Baptist continued to grow, ending the century with 647 — the highest number since Gano's revival of 1820.

By the end of the nineteenth century, First Baptist was clearly one of the venerable institutions in the city. By then, the church was 250 years old. Beginning with the 100th anniversary of the dedication of the Meeting House in 1875, a series of celebrations found the speakers emphasizing the unique history and glory of the Providence church. The tone of the celebrations and discourses was congratulatory and self-satisfied. By then it began to present itself as the "Mother Church" of Baptists.

ABOVE William W. Douglas (1841-1929), the eldest son of Rev. William Douglas (1812-1887), entered as a 2d lieutenant in the R.I. Fifth Heavy Artillery Regiment in November 1861 and mustered out as a captain at the expiration of his three-year enlistment in December 1864. He subsequently had an outstanding career as a lawyer, legislator, and judge, sitting on the Rhode Island State Supreme Court as associate justice from 1891 to 1905 and as chief justice from 1905 until he retired in 1908. Baptized at fourteen in 1855, he was a member of First Baptist until his death in 1929. He served as moderator of the Charitable Baptist Society from 1900 to 1914. Engraving from John K. Burlingame, *History of the Fifth Regiment of the Rhode Island Heavy Artillery* (1892).

CHAPTER 6

The Mother Church

In 1896 Dr. Henry Melville King wrote *The Mother Church*, a little book which touted First Baptist Church in America as more than just the first Baptist church. He saw it as the "mother church," the source of the Baptist movement in America. King began the promotion of the church as a Baptist shrine and national church.[1]

His presentation of First Baptist's role as the "mother church" was hyperbole and certainly inaccurate. First Baptist has the distinction of being first, but not the founder of the other early Baptist churches. For example, John Clarke's church in Newport had a completely independent origin, as did the First Baptist in Boston and other early New England churches. Likewise, the appearance of Baptists in the Mid-Atlantic colonies (New York, New Jersey, and Pennsylvania) had beginnings unconnected to the Providence church. On the other hand, King completely ignored the evidence that might allow one to say that First Baptist was a mother church. His account left out this church's role in beginning and promoting the Six Principle Baptists in the seventeenth and eighteenth centuries. And, he did not speak of the daughter churches that First Baptist established in the Providence area. From 1805 to 1919 First Baptist helped to found a dozen churches, beginning with Second Baptist and ending with Federal Hill Italian Baptist Church.

King's history, which focussed entirely on the origins of First Baptist, mostly reflected that odd controversy over who was first: Providence or Newport? The priority of the Providence church had been unquestioned until 1847 when the First Baptist Church of Newport advanced the claim that it was first. Initially this was based on the belief that the Portsmouth Compact signed by the Antinomian followers of Anne Hutchinson in Boston on March 7, 1638, created a church. In fact, the compact created a civil government.[2] The proponents for Newport argued that John Clarke starteded a Baptist church in Portsmouth that May, and that this church went with him when he removed to Newport when that town was founded in April 1639.[3]

The Newport church presented its claim to the Warren Baptist Association meeting in September 1847.[4] A committee of the association looked into it and concluded that the Newport church had been formed "certainly before the first of May, 1639, and probably on the 7th of March, 1638."[5] This provoked such controversy, including a vigorous rejoinder from First Baptist in Providence, that the Warren Association decided to drop the issue, saying "the settlement of contested claims of different churches to priority of constitution does not pertain to the objects of the Association . . . ."[6] The Providence church mounted a counterattack using university professors and colonial history experts who demolished the 1638 founding date for the Newport church.[7] This caused Samuel Adlam, the new pastor of the Newport church, to concede that his church had not been a Baptist church before 1644. However, he advanced another argument: (1) that Roger Williams had not founded a church in Providence, and (2), if he had, it had disintegrated when he withdrew, and (3) the present Providence church was actually started in 1652 when it became a General Six Principle Baptist church. All of which meant that the Newport church, beginning in 1644, was still the first Baptist church.[8] Not content with that, Adlam said, "Among the evils that have resulted from the wrong date of the Providence church has been the prominence given to Roger Williams."[9] Instead, John Clarke was "the true founder of the baptist cause in this country. . . . And when baptist history is better understood [everyone will say of the Newport church] 'THIS IS THE MOTHER OF US ALL.'"[10] While the First [United] Baptist Church of Newport continued (and continues) to maintain its claim to priority, the contest was soon lost among historians.[11] Even the Rhode Island historian, Thomas Bicknell, who regarded John Clarke as greater than Roger Williams, dismissed Newport's claim.[12]

The arguments over priority were a sideshow to First Baptist's real work of planting and promoting churches and Sunday schools in the Providence area, beginning with the Second Baptist Church in 1805. In this respect First Baptist of Providence could truly claim to be a "mother church." As the town grew at the beginning of the nineteenth century, the

OPPOSITE Photo by Warren Jagger (2000).

The arguments over priority were a sideshow to First Baptist's real work of planting and promoting churches and Sunday schools in the Providence area, beginning with the Second Baptist Church in 1805. In this respect First Baptist of Providence could truly claim to be a "mother church."

DAUGHTER CHURCHES

1805	Second Baptist Church of Providence
1805	First Baptist Church of Pawtucket
1806	Pawtuxet Baptist Church
1820	Third Baptist Church
1840	Meeting Street Baptist Church
1847	Eighth Baptist Church
1850	Allendale Baptist Church
1855	Brown Street Baptist Church
1877	Roger Williams Baptist Church
1883	Mount Pleasant Baptist Church
1897	First Italian Baptist Church
1902	Federal Hill Baptist Church

Westminster-Weybosset area rapidly developed on the west side of the Providence River. A group of neighbors gathered themselves as the "Congregational Society in Richmond Street," but in 1804 when they were without a pastor, they called Joseph Cornell, a Baptist minister to preach to them. Cornell sparked a revival and many switched to being Baptists, and these converts joined the First Baptist Church. It was soon decided to establish a Baptist church in the neighborhood where these new Baptists lived. Of the sixteen original members when the church was organized on May 1, 1805, thirteen were from First Baptist. To these were added another eight from First on the following Sunday.[13] A half century later when Second Baptist erected a new building and changed its name to the Central Baptist Church, First Baptist gave $4900 to the building fund.[14]

The second daughter was the First Baptist Church of Pawtucket. Baptists living in Pawtucket village had sought to start a church in the 1790s, even securing a charter for the "Catholic Baptist Society of North Providence" in 1793; but they were unable to organize a church. These few were members of the "ancient Baptist Church in Providence" and continued as such until they finally formed a church

in August 1805. David Benedict, a student at Brown (and soon to wed Stephen Gano's daughter Margaret), began preaching to the Pawtucket group in 1804 and inspired them to launch their church. Neighboring churches convened a council to sanction the new church, and Gano moderated the council while his deacon, Henry Grew, served as clerk. Of the original thirty-nine members on August 27, 1805, thirty-three came from First Baptist, and several more followed in the succeeding weeks.[15]

The third daughter, the Pawtuxet Baptist Church, was born November 18, 1806. While Baptists had gathered in the area since the 1760s, they did not organize a church until 1806. All of the initial thirty-four members were from First Baptist Church of Providence.[16]

Before the end of Gano's tenure, the Third Baptist Church of Providence was begun. It sprang from sixteen members of First Baptist who lived in the Wickenden neighborhood of the East Side. Many of them were new converts in the revival of 1820. In November of that year, they organized a church but continued to worship at First until their own meeting house was raised in 1821. Then they called Allen Brown, a licentiate from First, to be their first minister. Within a year of Brown's installation, Third suffered a split over the issue of free will and was expelled from the Warren Association. Brown adopted the freewill doctrine that everyone had a chance of salvation, with the result that several of the founding members left Third and returned to First Baptist. After Brown resigned in 1828, Third Baptist returned to the Calvinist fold and was readmitted to the Warren Association.[17]

A few individuals from First Baptist Church were involved in the start of the Fourth Baptist Church, but this was a Freewill Baptist congregation in the beginning. Four of the eleven men associated with the Fourth Baptist petition for a charter from the state in 1820 were pew owners or members of First Baptist,[18] but Fourth Baptist was excluded from the ranks of the Regular Baptists in Rhode Island because it originally held freewill principles.[19] While First Baptist welcomed and blessed the creation of Second and Third churches, it wanted little to do with Fourth Baptist. Not until Zalmon Tobey, their first pastor, left in 1833 did Fourth

ABOVE Henry Melville King (1838-1919) was the 22nd pastor of the church and served from 1891 until his retirement in 1906, whereupon he was made pastor emeritus. He began to promote First Baptist Church as the "Mother Church" of Baptists in America. His daughter, Lida Shaw King, was the dean of the Women's College (Pembroke) at Brown from 1905 until 1922. Photo from the archives of the First Baptist Church in America.

The Congdon Street Baptist Church also has roots in the First Baptist Church. Between 1800 and 1830 the number of blacks in Providence nearly doubled with the consequent establishment of an array of African-American community institutions — fraternal, literary, and improvement societies, churches, a choir, and a military group, the African Greys.

Baptist turn to the Calvinist view of limited atonement and was welcomed into a Regular Baptist association. As a matter of fact, Fourth Baptist had experienced the "iron law of creeping respectability" and wanted an educated minister. Unable to find one in the Freewill Baptist denomination, they turned to the Regular Baptists for one. First Baptist had a hand in this conversion when in 1835 Fourth saw sixteen of its Freewill members withdraw over the issue of "closed communion" and then welcomed thirteen transfers from First.[20] Regular Baptists closed the Lord's Supper to anyone who had not been immersed while the Freewill Baptists welcomed believers without regard to their form of baptism.

The Congdon Street Baptist Church also has roots in the First Baptist Church. Between 1800 and 1830 the number of

TOP The second daughter church of First Baptist Church of Providence was the First Baptist Church of Pawtucket, officially organized in August 1905. Pictured here is the second meetinghouse of the church, erected in 1842 to replace an earlier building which the church had outgrown. Although the steeple was later altered, this meetinghouse served until it was destroyed by fire on November 7, 1957. From *First Baptist Church, 91 Cottage Street, Pawtucket, Rhode Island: One Hundred and Seventy-fifth Anniversary, 1805-1980.* Courtesy of The First Baptist Church of Pawtucket.

MIDDLE The first daughter church in the nineteenth century was the Second Baptist Church of Providence. It was gathered from a group of Congregationalists on Richmond Street who became Baptists in a revival in 1804 and were baptized into First Baptist Church. On May 1, 1805, a council of Baptist churches oversaw the official organization of the Second Baptist Church. In 1807 they erected a meetinghouse at the corner of Pine and Eddy on land that was under water at times. They referred to themselves as "The Muddy Dock Church." That meetinghouse was completely destroyed on September 23, 1815 by the Great Gale (a hurricane) which blew into Providence and demolished the waterfront. Pictured here is the Second or Pine Street Baptist Meeting House, built in 1817 and sold in 1857 when Second Baptist moved to Weybosset Street near Empire and then called itself Central Baptist Church. Photo from *The Central Baptist Church, Sesquicentennial Observance, April 24 - May 1, 1955.* Courtesy of the Central Baptist Church.

BOTTOM The present home of the Congdon Street Baptist Church was erected in 1871 after the congregation was forced to move from its Meeting Street location when vandals destroyed their old meetinghouse. This church's founders were among those, such as George Willis, who made the plans in 1819 in the vestry of the First Baptist Church to organize the African Union Meeting and School-House. The African Union Meeting was meant to be non-denominational, but in the 1830s revivalism carried away large portions of the members into several denominations, leaving a faithful remnant, most of whom were still officially members of the First Baptist. These organized the Meeting Street Baptist Church in December 1840, and George Willis was deacon. Photo by J. Stanley Lemons.

blacks in Providence nearly doubled with the consequent establishment of an array of African-American community institutions — fraternal, literary, and improvement societies, churches, a choir, and a military group, the African Greys. The central institution was the African Union Meeting and School Society, begun in 1820.[21] The principal African-American leaders in this development, especially George C. Willis, were members of First Baptist. They received major encouragement from Henry Jackson, a young, white First Baptist licentiate, who was superintending a Sunday school for African-American children. In April 1819 they met in the vestry at First Baptist to make plans for the construction of a meetinghouse on a lot on Meeting Street donated by the abolitionist Quaker, Moses Brown. When the people gathered to work on the building, Stephen Gano offered the prayer, and they began. On the first Sunday in June 1820, the new building opened for church services, and Henry Jackson preached the first sermon. Although the African Union was supposed to be nondenominational, it was not immune to the sectarian ferment of the 1830s with the result that a Freewill Baptist and two Methodist congregations carried away all but seven men and two women of the Union members. The remnant included Deacon Willis and three others who officially transferred their membership from First Baptist on December 3, 1840, to begin the Meeting

Street Baptist Church. During the entire period from 1819 to 1840 the Sunday school at the African Union was supported by contributions and teachers from the First Baptist Church Sunday School.[22] And, in the decades after 1840 regular contributions went from First Baptist to the African-American church to help support its ministers.[23] (The Meeting Street Church moved to Congdon Street in 1870.) Such aid was not confined to the Meeting Street Church inasmuch as First Baptist raised money for "the Colored Freewill Baptist Church [later Pond Street Baptist] in this city" to help pay their minister.[24]

In 1855 First Baptist aided another daughter church on the East Side by transferring a corps of its own members to a new church. As early as 1844 some had sought to establish a colony somewhere between First and Third Baptist churches, but little was done until November 1855. The new church, which was called the Brown Street Baptist Church when its building was completed on the corner of Brown and Benevolent, had a robust beginning with sixty-five members from First and forty-six from Third. Those who transferred from First included Francis Wayland, who had just retired as president of Brown University after twenty-eight years, several Brown professors, both the superintendent and assistant superintendent of the First Baptist Sunday school, along with fourteen teachers and fifty students of the Sunday school, the wife of Governor Charles Jackson, and the sister of Lieutenant Governor Samuel Greene Arnold.[25] As a result, the Brown Street Baptist Church began with a level of respectability that almost matched that of First Baptist. On the other hand, all of the other churches that resulted from First's efforts from the 1840s to the end of the century were aimed at the mill villages and working class, immigrant neighborhoods.

ABOVE The Eagle Mills of the American Screw Works were about four blocks north of the Meeting House, and these mills were one of Providence's "Five Industrial Wonders of the World." In 1849 the company had invented the first practical machine to make pointed screws, and by the late 19th century had nearly monopolized screw production in America. The smoke pouring from the smokestacks was meant to demonstrate prosperity. Courtesy of the Rhode Island Historical Society.

TOP The Allendale Baptist Church. Zachariah Allen, an Episcopal vestryman, was deeply concerned about the state of religion among the workers in his Allendale mill village in North Providence, so he had a chapel constructed for them in 1847. The architect was Thomas Tefft, a member of First Baptist, who designed a Gothic Revival building. Although intended to be a nonde-nominational chapel, teachers from First Baptist Church established a Sunday School, and within three years the congregation organized itself as a Baptist church. Photo by J. Stanley Lemons.

BOTTOM The Roger Williams Baptist Church. In 1867 the Metcalf family built a mill village around their Wanskuck Mill and began a nondenomina-tional chapel for the workers. Quickly the Sunday school was taken over and run by members of First Baptist Church, and during the next decade the chapel's people were baptized in the baptistry of the Meeting House. When the church officially constituted itself in February 1877, it was a Baptist church. The original one-room chapel was built in 1867 and then added to several times, including a memorial tower in 1906-7 by Sophia Metcalf Baker. Photo by J. Stanley Lemons.

When Zachariah Allen expanded his Allendale Mill in North Providence in 1847, he constructed a mill village, complete with a chapel for the workers. Allen, a vestryman at St. John's Episcopal Church, was greatly concerned about the moral character of his workers, and he commissioned the talented young architect Thomas Tefft (a member of First Baptist) to design the meetinghouse.

The intermittent revivals in the city spurred churches to attend to the state of faith of the working class of Providence. In addition, the suffrage controversy and the Dorr War highlighted profound changes that were taking place in Rhode Island in general and in Providence in particular. Industrialization created industrial neighborhoods and mill villages, and many of these filled with immigrants. Already the increase in the number of Roman Catholics aroused anti-Catholic feelings which spilled over into politics. Many Protestants opposed the suffrage movement because they saw it as an effort by Irish Catholics to take over the state. Thus, the home mission and Sunday school ideas converged with a concern which the Protestant churches felt for industrial neighborhoods and the immigrants who filled them. Church members felt a clear imperative to establish Sunday schools for the children of the poor and the mill workers and to send missionaries among the foreign born. These efforts produced six more Baptist churches: Eighth Baptist, Allendale, Mt. Pleasant, Roger Williams, Federal Hill, and the First Italian Baptist Church.

By the mid-1840s, Baptists sought to organize a church in the working class neighborhood on Smith Hill, and the success of that effort depended heavily upon direct and continuing support from First Baptist. The *Proceedings of the Rhode Island Baptist State Convention* (1847) reported: "The Chapel, a neat and convenient edifice, 35 feet by 50, was erected by the liberality chiefly of members of the First Baptist Church."[26] The chapel was dedicated in November 1846 by which time a flourishing Sunday school was being superintended by Albert Harkness, a member of First Baptist.[27] When Eighth Baptist Church formally organized in May 1847, thirteen of the twenty-nine founding members were transfers from First Baptist.[28] For many years afterwards, financial aid and personnel support flowed to the struggling church. For example, in 1849-1850 the Young Ladies' Bible class was directed by John Jolls from First Baptist.[29] The following year three members of First paid off half of the indebtedness of Eighth Baptist.[30] When the church built a new meeting house and changed its name to the Jefferson Street Baptist Church, $2000 was given by First Baptist for the construction.[31] Again when a financial

crisis threatened Jefferson Street Baptist Church in 1873, First Baptist contributed another $1132.[32]

When Zachariah Allen expanded his Allendale Mill in North Providence in 1847, he constructed a mill village, complete with a chapel for the workers. Allen, a vestryman at St. John's Episcopal Church, was greatly concerned about the moral character of his workers, and he commissioned the talented young architect Thomas Tefft (a member of First Baptist) to design the meetinghouse. It started as a nondenominational chapel, but quickly teachers from First Baptist Church established a Sunday school, and within three years the church organized as a Baptist Church.[33]

Likewise, Roger Williams Baptist Church began as a nondenominational chapel established by the Metcalf family in 1867 for workers at their Wanskuck Mill. The mill superintendent was Thomas Sampson, a member of First, and he assumed the superintendency of the chapel Sunday school and brought in a number of young people from First Baptist to help in the work. In the nondenominational chapel's first decade, its most prominent helpers were Baptists, especially First Baptist pastor Edward Taylor, who baptized forty-two of the chapel's people in the baptistry of the Meeting House. Not surprisingly, then, when the church officially constituted itself in February 1877, it was a Baptist church. Its second minister, Frederick L. Denison, was a member of First Baptist in August 1877 when called to the Roger Williams pastorate.[34]

A nondenominational Sunday school and library association for working class people had started in 1868 on Chalkstone Avenue, but it foundered and threatened to sink in 1878. Taylor, a vigorous champion of Sunday schools, came to the rescue and took charge of the religious services. In October 1878 First Baptist bought the mission property for $1, and it became known as the "First Baptist Mission." This connection provided leadership, money, and even members, enabling the Mission to constitute itself as the Mt. Pleasant Baptist Church in February 1883.[35] Of the twenty-five initial members, eighteen were transfers from First Baptist Church.

Edward Taylor had such an interest in Sunday schools that for a time he took over the job of superintendent of the

Although some feared that the tides of immigration were bringing swarms of people from southern and eastern Europe who were thought to be too alien and beyond assimilation, others sought to improve the condition of the poor and immigrants.

First Baptist Sunday School himself. He felt that Christian education was a necessary companion to revivalist preaching. Under his leadership, the promotion of Sunday schools continued to be a major emphasis at First Baptist. But Sunday school could not reach everyone, it seemed. H.P. Lovecraft, who later became famous as a writer of horror and science-fiction stories, was brought by his mother to First Baptist's Sunday school in 1895. Unfortunately, by age five, little Howard had rejected Christianity. Consequently, he was expelled from Sunday school for disputing the word of the teachers and siding with the lions against the Christians. Still, the weird and melancholy Lovecraft loved the old Meeting House, calling it his "maternal ancestral church," and he occasionally prowled about the place. Once in 1923 he brought a friend to climb the steeple and look at the bell; and he tried to play "Yes, We Have no Bananas" on the organ, but could not figure out how to turn it on.[36]

The final efforts of First Baptist to establish new churches in Providence began in the 1890s. One was a failed attempt to settle a new church at Wayland Square. The idea originated in 1892 among some members who lived in that area.[37] The effort lasted until 1906 when it was surrendered to Union Baptist Church.[38] More significant and successful was the work among the Italian immigrant population. The church planted and nurtured missions, and between 1900 and 1920 it commissioned eleven young Italian-Americans to be missionaries to the Catholic immigrant communities in Rhode Island and Massachusetts.[39] This effort to establish churches in the Italian immigrant neighborhoods reflected the deep concern felt by most Protestant churches about the

burgeoning Roman Catholic population. Indeed, Rhode Island would have a Catholic majority by 1905.

The first Italian mission was begun in 1893 on Marietta Street in the north end of the city. A second mission opened in 1902 on Dean Street on Federal Hill. These served as both religious and social service institutions in the poor neighborhoods. Some of their Roman Catholic neighbors referred to those who attended as "potato Baptists," implying that people joined to get the food provided to its members by First Baptist Church.[40] Father Antonio Bove, a priest at St. Ann's Roman Catholic Church, charged that Protestants were luring the immigrants with promises of food, clothing, and jobs.[41] It was a slow process that brought in only twenty-two members in the first eight years. Those who joined the chapels were baptized into the membership of First Baptist Church and remained on its rolls until 1919 when the Marietta mission organized as the First Italian Baptist Church and the Dean Street mission became the Federal Hill Italian Baptist Church. (First Italian changed its name to Emmanuel Baptist Church in 1942; Federal Hill Baptist merged with Church of the Master in 1958.)

As the nineteenth century drew to a close, many at First Baptist Church felt that they were handling the great changes in Providence quite well. They took pride in being

ABOVE This is the 1897 Brown University class photo of John D. Rockefeller, Jr. During his student days, John D., Jr., was a member of First Baptist and taught Sunday School in its mission church at Wayland Square. In 1957 he gave FBCIA $500,000 in Standard Oil stock which was used for a massive restoration of the Meeting House. Courtesy of Brown University Archives.

the "mother church," and they believed that they were making a proper response. Although some feared that the tides of immigration were bringing swarms of people from southern and eastern Europe who were thought to be too alien and beyond assimilation, others sought to improve the condition of the poor and immigrants.[42] While the emphasis in the women's circles remained on foreign missions, they also knitted and sewed for the local poor. In 1889 T. Edwin Brown, the twenty-first pastor, boasted that the church had several missionaries "exploring mills and factories, frequenting tenements," but the purpose was still traditional evangelism, the saving of souls. However in the 1890s, the missions among the Italians added food and clothing for, at least, the needy of the chapel. Then, the twentieth century brought Elijah Hanley who had a much larger vision of First Baptist Church's role in serving the downtown population. He brought the new perspectives of the Social Gospel.

ABOVE Italian immigrants began arriving in substantial numbers in the 1890s, and First Baptist started mission stations in the Italian neighborhoods, first on Marietta Street in the north end in 1893 and then on Dean Street on Federal Hill in 1902. A young man with the un-Italian name of James Pratt, baptized on December 31, 1893, was the first convert in the Marietta mission. At first the work was slow as was evidenced by the fact that the next baptisms did not occur until September of 1896. Even though few of the mission members spoke any English, they were baptized into membership of First Baptist until their churches were able to stand on their own. Pictured here is the Daily Vacation Bible School, July 1934, of the First Italian Baptist Church (formerly the Marietta Mission). They changed their name to Emmanuel Baptist Church in 1942. Photo from the archives of the First Baptist Church in America.

CHAPTER 7

Providence in Decline

As the twentieth century began, Newell Dwight Hillis, pastor of the Plymouth Congregational Church in Brooklyn, expressed the high optimism of the time: "Laws are becoming more just, rulers more humane; music is becoming sweeter and books wiser; homes are happier, and the individual heart [is] becoming at once more just and more gentle."[1] The civic leaders of Providence felt a similar pride and satisfaction as they boasted that the city's population and economy were booming.[2] At First Baptist the church fathers pointed to membership lists that were the longest in its history and to the respect that the church commanded in the community. The city and state continued to mark great civic moments with ceremonies in the Meeting House, such as the state's memorial service for the assassinated William McKinley in 1901.[3] Few saw much to complain about, but the unfolding century brought unexpected and unwelcome decline.

The mission work among the immigrants in industrial neighborhoods was a sign of a rapidly changing Rhode Island. In the nineteenth century Rhode Island went from being a rural, Yankee state to America's first urban, industrial, ethnic state. By the end of the century, it had become the most densely populated, most ethnic, and most Roman Catholic state in the union. In fact, by 1905 Rhode Island was the first state to have a Roman Catholic majority. Providence, which had been a small town on the eve of the American Revolution, was in 1900 the twentieth largest city in the nation and was counted among the industrial powerhouses.[4] All of these factors had a profound impact upon the situation of America's oldest Baptist church.

In the nineteenth century, as the city developed, the population within the immediate area of the church increased greatly. Indeed, First Baptist was not alone in increasing its membership; all churches grew. Moreover, many new congregations and denominations sprang up. While Providence had had only one Baptist church in 1800, by the Civil War there were at least a dozen of them, including six on the East

Side. By 1910 one found twenty-eight Protestant churches within three-quarters of a mile of the central Market Square.

At first the booming economy drew people from depressed rural areas, but as the century passed, increasingly non-Protestant immigrants poured in from Europe. These people crowded into the available housing near the factories and mills, especially in the double- and triple-deckers that sprang up in working class neighborhoods. The result was that by 1910 Providence's population was 70 percent foreign-born or children of immigrants. One effect of this could be seen in the decline and fall of the Third and Brown Street Baptist churches, which were situated in an area of the East Side that changed from a Yankee Protestant neighborhood into a largely Roman Catholic immigrant area. Third and Brown Street merged in 1878 into Union Baptist, and the fading Union merged with the collapsing Sheldon Street Congregational Church in 1967 to create Faith Community Parish. Likewise, as Smith Hill became an immigrant neighborhood, the Jefferson Street Baptist Church sold its building in 1913 to Saints Sahag and Mesrob Armenian Apostolic Church and merged with the Park Street Baptist Church to form the United Baptist Church. In 1968 the dwindling congregation moved to Smith Street, merged with a struggling Presbyterian church, and finally disappeared in 1987.

The changes in the city were not confined to ethnicity or religious preferences, because the continuing development of downtown Providence eventually eliminated the residences in the business district. The Meeting House now stands on the edge of the downtown business section almost in the shadow of tall buildings. Moreover, as the twentieth century advanced, suburbanization drew off increasing numbers of people. The population of Providence reached its maximum in 1925 at 268,000 people and then declined. It plunged 16.5 percent in the 1950s, so much so that Providence's percentage loss was the second highest in the nation.[5] By 1980 the city had 157,000 inhabitants, which was fewer than it had counted eighty years before.[6]

First Baptist, along with most Providence Baptist churches, lost members as a result of the population migration. Their constituencies moved to the suburbs, and several Baptist churches folded completely. For example, in 1950 the

Cranston Street Baptist Church had a membership of nearly 600, but by 1970 it had closed. On the other hand, Meshanticut Park Baptist Church in suburban Cranston, which had just sixty members in 1945, had over 600 members by 1975. The magnitude of the change becomes clear when one realizes that between 1950 and 1986 nine American Baptist churches in Providence closed their doors and membership in the city's Baptist churches fell 3,482 in that period.[7] In addition, the Providence Baptist Church, a Southern Baptist colony, gave up and moved to the suburbs.

The residential neighborhood behind First Baptist changed greatly after World War II. Brown University expe-

rienced substantial growth after the 1940s. In the process of expansion the university razed several city blocks of houses in the 1950s in order to build new dormitories, and it continues to acquire former residences in a widening area. The increased size of the student body did not add to the opportunity of the church because the religious preferences of the students came to reflect those of the nation, not of Baptists. Few Baptists are now found in the enlarged student body. The interests of the students and faculty are those of any contemporary secular university, not those of a denominational college. Once allied institutions, the church and university are quite separate and unrelated, except that the Meeting House is still "for holding Commencement in." Ironically, it was William H. P. Faunce, Brown President (1899-1929), a member, great friend and favorite of First Baptist Church, who persuaded the Rhode Island legislature to change Brown's charter to delete the provision that the president must be a Baptist. As a result, since 1937 no president of Brown has been a Baptist. Then, in 1945 the charter was amended again to eliminate any denominational tie.

Brown University was not the only cause of local change. The Rhode Island School of Design, whose buildings are on three sides of the Meeting House, has grown significantly; and its students, added to those of Brown, fill many of the apartments in the general area. The immediate neighborhood now is mainly populated by a transient population of students for whose attention First Baptist competes with eight or nine other near-by churches and with Brown University's chaplaincy program. First Baptist is no longer a neighborhood church in the usual sense. Most of its members live miles away; however, its decline as a neighborhood institution began a century ago.

First Baptist entered the twentieth century under the leadership of a scholarly pastor in the twilight of his career. Henry Melville King was born in 1838 and served in a number of places before coming to his last pastorate in 1891. He

A B O V E The development of Providence turned the block on North Main Street just beyond the Meeting House into a busy commercial area, but by the 1890s this area was deteriorating as the commercial center of the city had shifted to the Westminster-Weybosset district. Photo from *Art Work of Providence* (1896).

presided at the time when the church listed the most members, but that total was misleading because it included both the members of the Italian missions who actually attended elsewhere and an increasingly large non-resident membership. The membership appeared to rise from 1900 to 1910, but the Italian missions accounted for the entire increase. At First Baptist itself, the active membership declined in the first decade of the century. When King retired, he was succeeded in late 1907 by the dynamic Elijah Abraham Hanley, a product of the Social Gospel movement.

In the last quarter of the nineteenth century, a number of ministers, seminary professors, and laymen attacked the marriage of the main Protestant denominations to American capitalism and rugged individualism. As the nation had industrialized, most clergymen and their congregations condemned the labor movement, regarded poverty as a sign of individual sin, and supported the use of force, if necessary, to put down strikes. The Social Gospel advocates reacted strongly against these attitudes and argued that the problems of the industrial society could be solved by applying Christ's teachings to the political and social institutions of the day. Of special concern were the class divisions in the cities and the role that urban churches ought to play in bridging the gap. Some felt that producing social unity and equality would usher in the Kingdom of God.

One approach of the Social Gospel to the urban crisis was the establishment of "institutional" churches which provided services, such as soup kitchens, food pantries, legal aid, counseling, clothing, and household goods. They had basketball and baseball teams and added gymnasiums, theaters, and bowling alleys. In this era the churches began to sponsor vacation Bible schools, scout troops, clubs of all sorts, and daycare centers. Another thrust of the Social Gospel was a movement toward unity among the denominations, which led to the establishment of the Federal Council of Churches.

ABOVE By the turn of the twentieth century the neighborhood of the First Baptist Church included part of the upper class area of the East Side as well as the industrial and ethnic slums along North Main Street. This scene shows some of the slums along the Moshassuck River near Randall Square, about four blocks north of the Meeting House. Photo from the *Providence Magazine* (1914).

The immediate neighborhood now is mainly populated by a transient population of students for whose attention First Baptist competes with eight or nine other near-by churches and with Brown University's chaplaincy program. First Baptist is no longer a neighborhood church in the usual sense. Most of its members live miles away; however, its decline as a neighborhood institution began a century ago.

In addition, a few proponents of the Social Gospel became Christian Socialists, holding that the only way to overcome predatory capitalism and heartless individualism was for the state to own the utilities, mines, railroads, and major manufacturing concerns. A Baptist leader of "social Christianity," Walter Rauschenbusch, professor of church history at Rochester Theological Seminary, regarded capitalism as incompatible with Christianity.[8]

Elijah Hanley favored the institutional church, hoped for Christian unity and the decline of denominational exclusiveness, but, while progressive, he was not a Christian Socialist.[9] Hanley chafed at the conservative, narrow-minded attitudes of many in the church in general and in First Baptist in particular.[10] One of his initiatives at First Baptist was toward open church membership, but he was stymied. The Standing Committee dissuaded him from delivering a talk in New York on the subject and prevented him from offering his idea of admitting people baptized by other methods than immersion.[11] His wife, Sarah Hanley, wrote a friend, telling her, "there is always that everlasting *drag* when we try to do anything new or different from what they have done for [sic] time immemorial."[12]

Another impulse in Protestant churches in the early twentieth century was an effort to attract men by making Christianity more masculine; this culminated with the Men and Religion Forward Movement in 1911-1912. American

ABOVE Elijah Abraham Hanley, "standing 6 feet 2, broad shouldered, well proportioned, stalwart and athletic," was described as "a man's man." He came to Providence in 1907 after rebuilding a failing church in Cleveland, and he left in 1911 when his financially-troubled alma mater, Franklin College, implored him to accept the presidency. Dynamic and imaginative, Hanley sought to reinvigorate First Baptist by special efforts to involve men. Recognizing that old First was ceasing to be a neighborhood church, he tried to expand its outreach and secure a firmer financial base by building the endowment and getting denominational support for downtown churches. *Providence Sunday Journal*, August 4, 1907. Courtesy of Providence Journal Company.

ABOVE Elijah Hanley with his secretary in October 1910 in the church office, which was located in the southwest corner of the building. One of Hanley's innovations was the opening of a regular office to conduct church business. After the 1957 restoration of the building, this office became the "Manning Room." Photo from archives of First Baptist Church in America.

Hanley recognized that the whole context for First Baptist was being transformed by the changes in Providence, and he sought to find ways to make the church and its message more accessible and attractive. He wanted an open church and was a fountain of new ideas for the old institution.

church membership had been two-thirds female since the seventeenth century, but by the late nineteenth century this condition began to be regarded as a "crisis" by church leaders. They felt that feminized Christianity was irrelevant to the masculine world of business and industry and lacked appeal to men.[13]

Feminized Christianity was emotional and domestic. The virtues of Jesus in this version were the traditional female virtues: self sacrifice, submissiveness, gentleness, loving-kindness, meekness. He was a meek and mild Jesus. Some church leaders began to emphasize the manly Jesus who was courageous, virile, vigorous, practical, and business-like — the kind of man who was decisive, drove the moneychangers out of the temple, faced down a mob about to stone a woman, and went bravely to his death. Women found that Jesus attractive, and he was in demand for Jerusalem dinner parties. Religious leaders wrote books calling for a manly Christianity, such as Carl Case, *The Masculine in Religion* (1906), and Harry Emerson Fosdick, *The Manhood of the Master* (1911). They formed new denominational men's clubs, connected religion to sports, promoted business-like approaches, such as using advertising, and focused on the practical application of Jesus's message to daily life.[14]

The *Providence Journal* article which introduced Elijah Hanley bore this headline: "Rev. E. A. Hanley, a Man's Man." He told an interviewer from the *Journal* that what the church in America needed was virility — more men. But in order to attract men, the church had to become business-like and practical. "It is the business of the church to make [religion] real and practical."[15] Beginning a campaign to attract men, Hanley visited them in their places of work, preached sermons for them, and established "Dr. Hanley's Class for Men."[16] His class soon outgrew the space available in the Meeting House, so it was moved over to Franklin Hall at 54 North Main Street.[17] For several months in 1908-1909 Hanley spoke every Tuesday at noon to about 200 men in shop meetings at the Gorham Manufacturing Company.[18] He urged them to "live by the spirit of Jesus Christ." He told

ABOVE The 1911 Vacation Bible School posed on the steps of the Meeting House. The Bible School was one of the new outreach programs begun by Elijah Hanley at First Baptist. He hired the church's first Director of Christian Education to oversee this and the Sunday school. A young Albert Thomas (standing on the left end of the fourth row, in shirt sleeves and bow tie) served as director from 1911 to 1912 and returned as the twentieth-seventh pastor from 1941 to 1954. Standing on the right end of the fourth row, dressed in suit and tie, was Noah Wesley, church sexton from 1882 to 1928. Photo from the archives of the First Baptist Church in America.

Downtown churches, Hanley argued, deserved support from other churches, just like missions would. He suggested that the national denomination contribute to the maintenance of its old, central churches as city missions.

them to read their New Testaments and advised, "Don't bother about the theology, but take the simple life of Christ. . . . . There is only one thing that can save the industrial system to-day, and that is the spirit of Jesus Christ."[19] Not surprisingly, when the Men and Religion Forward Movement came to Providence in 1911, First Baptist took part and helped to underwrite its costs.[20]

Hanley recognized that the whole context for First Baptist was being transformed by the changes in Providence, and he sought to find ways to make the church and its message more accessible and attractive.[21] He wanted an open church and was a fountain of new ideas for the old institution. To be more business-like, he opened a church office, hired the first secretary, and employed the first director of Christian education. A sign was put on the corner of Main and Waterman Streets to identify the church, and he began advertising heavily in the newspapers. The church bulletin blossomed with information, announcements, and exhortations. He moved the Sunday evening services from the ground floor to the auditorium. Hanley disdained the doctrinal approach and, instead, preached how to apply Christianity to the ills of society.[22] He believed that the churches had been emphasizing "little things like creeds and forms" and neglecting the larger questions of "How do I live a Christian life?"[23]

In his first summer he experimented with evening services on the back lawn. He explained, "Our auditorium is so very warm summer evenings that we really cannot expect people to attend the service in large numbers. But thousands go to [Roger Williams] Park to hear a musical program. Why cannot we have services on our lawn which people could attend with both pleasure and profit?"[24] Everyone was amazed when nearly a thousand people attended the lawn service the first time,[25] so he continued the program every summer during his tenure. Once they were rained out, and Hanley observed that a "great number, however, who came for the service on the lawn went away without entering the church." In fact, he estimated that ten times as many came to the outdoor services as could be induced to come inside.[26]

Those services on the back lawn of the Meeting House seem to have been the thing which stuck most in the minds of some members decades later. In the 1970s Anne Stevens, Mary and Clara Crosby, and Norman Watson still recalled those programs, with the lantern slide shows projected on a screen on the back of the Meeting House, the Sunday school orchestra playing, a brass band, hymn singing, and special choruses. (Hanley's successor, John F. Vichert, continued the backyard evening services through 1915, but they then lapsed.)

Hanley initiated a number of other programs to expand the church's audience. He opened the first Vacation Bible School in the summer of 1909, and over 100 children from Fox Point to Olney Street attended. Then beginning November 15, he took his ministry to the Providence Opera House where he and the church choir held a series of Sunday evening services. Intending them to run five weeks, Hanley extended the services to eleven weeks and had an average attendance of over 1200 people. The following winter he repeated the experiment and attracted between 1000 and 1200 people to each service. Unfortunately, because the offerings were insufficient to meet the expenses at the Opera House, the services were discontinued. Later, he instituted a

"Neighborhood Night" on Friday evenings and talked on various subjects. In an effort to reach out to the foreign-born, the church sponsored services conducted by an Armenian pastor every Sunday afternoon and continued to nurture the Italian missions.[27]

The decline of the Baptist churches in the center of Providence was a great concern to Hanley. In 1910 he noted that First, Central, Jefferson Street, Stewart Street, and Union Baptist churches had together gained a net total of 120 members since 1890 but that they annually raised $8500 less, paid lower salaries, and had seen the total Sunday school attendance decline by 375 students.[28] The signs of decline were evident. Central Baptist agonized about what to do; and their pastor, John R. Brown, resigned when he felt that his congregation was unwilling to face up to the new realities.[29] Would they build a new edifice that would serve the new situation? Would they dispose of their building and relocate in a residential area where their members had moved? When the city widened Empire Street in 1914, Central seized the opportunity to sell their old building at a substantial price and moved to the East Side.

Hanley wanted First Baptist to strike out in a different direction, to attempt what some of the other Providence churches, such as Calvary Baptist, Grace Church (Episcopal), St. John's Episcopal, Beneficent Congregational, and the Mathewson Street Methodist Church had done. They could no longer remain neighborhood churches, but had become "institutional" churches, serving the special needs of the central city. This involved new facilities, especially a parish hall with a gymnasium, new programs, and a new definition of the church itself.[30] Hanley urged First Baptist to build a parish hall, expand its mission in the downtown area, and promote an endowment to support the ministry. Unfortunately, the changing demographics meant that the older, wealthier families drifted from the downtown churches, and those who joined were less able to bear the cost. He felt that the churches should combine efforts and work through central agencies of charity instead of each trying to undertake individual, little programs.

Downtown churches, Hanley argued, deserved support from other churches, just like missions would. He suggested that the national denomination contribute to the maintenance of its old, central churches as city missions.[31] Shortly before he ended his pastorate in 1911, Hanley wrote a brief appeal on the back of the church bulletin entitled, "The Future of This Church." While he began by saying, "Let no one who loves this church be troubled for its future," his comments pointed to steps that needed to be taken for its preservation. Significantly, he wrote, "One thing should be truly laid to heart—bequests for our future work. There are those now living among us into whose hands God has given power to strengthen our work throughout coming generations."[32] The fact is that the endowment became a key to survival by the 1970s. Without it, or some other help, old First would have had to abandon its Meeting House or merge with another church.

Hanley considered a parish hall to be vital if First Baptist were to survive. He began his effort in February 1909, stressing that the beginners class of the Sunday school had to meet in the kitchen, that his men's class met in the auditorium, and that no place existed to start a new women's class, for the Young People's Society to hold entertainments, or to

TOP One of Elijah Hanley's strongest recommendations was for the construction of a parish house so the church could better serve the kind of city that Providence had become by the twentieth century. Even after Hanley departed to become the president of Franklin College, the parish house idea persisted, at least to the extent that the church had an architect, Gorham Henshaw, present a proposal. This rendering, dated April 7, 1913, was superimposed on an actual photograph taken at the time that the East Side tunnel was under construction in the foreground. Photo from the archives of the First Baptist Church.

BOTTOM The Vestry, shown here c. 1911, was where Sunday evening worship services, prayer meetings, business meetings, Sunday school, the sewing school, and the women's societies met. Overlooking the scene was a large oil portrait of James Hervey Reed, who owned a successful wholesale drygoods business on North Main Street just a few doors south of the Meeting House, and who was a deacon from 1843 until his death in 1893. Photo from the archives of the First Baptist Church in America.

Hanley considered a parish hall to be vital if First Baptist were to survive. He began his effort in February 1909. "Such a Parish Hall would afford a splendid material basis for our growing work, and would make the First Baptist Church in fact what it is in name, the center of Baptist enterprise in our City."

ABOVE Noah Wesley (1854-1928) was the sexton and bell-ringer for the church from 1882 to 1928. The Providence City Council contributed $125 annually to his salary to ring the big bell at sunrise, noon, and 9 p.m. curfew. A native of Baltimore, Wesley moved to Providence after his marriage in 1876. He and his wife became members in 1900. Longtime members stated that the attendance at Wesley's funeral at the Meeting House was the largest in memory. Only a handful of African-Americans remained in First Baptist Church after the organization of black churches in the 1820s-1840s. Until then, ten percent or more of the membership of First Baptist had been people of color. At the beginning of the twentieth century, several African-Americans, including Wesley and his wife, were baptized into the congregation. Photo from the archives of the First Baptist Church in America.

have large dinner gatherings. Further, he said a parish hall would provide a home for the Rhode Island Baptist Social Union and the Baptist state convention.[33] "Such a Parish Hall would afford a splendid material basis for our growing work, and would make the First Baptist Church in fact what it is in name, the center of Baptist enterprise in our City."[34] The church bulletins contained many items which agitated for a parish hall, including a note from February 26, 1911: "At a recent meeting of the Boy Scouts there was cheering when the Pastor finished a story of some experiences in the far west; there was more cheering when the vote was passed 'to have chocolate at our next meeting;' there was most cheering when the boys decided to meet at St. John's Parish House, each paying five cents, in order to play basket ball."[35] The church responded in 1910 by appointing a committee to make plans for a parish house.[36] However, Hanley had been gone two years before the Charitable Baptist Society voted unanimously to approve the proposal to build a parish house, but since it was "about to solicit funds for repairs and renovations to the Meeting House, it was deemed wise to defer action." Then again in 1915 the church established one committee to study the financing of a parish house and another to plan it.[37] But nothing came of it.

Hanley departed for the presidency of Franklin College in June 1911, amid great grief from the shocked members of his church.[38] What they did not know was that Franklin College, desperate for decisive and able leadership, had been pursuing Hanley for over a year before he accepted its call.[39] The college promised to raise an endowment of $500,000 so he could carry out his educational reforms and programs. By this time, also, Hanley was feeling discouraged by the nar-

rowness and conservatism of the pastoral ministry and thought he could accomplish more in education.[40]

He was followed by two relatively short pastorates of John F. Vichert and Albert B. Cohoe.[41] Vichert began in January 1912 and resigned in January 1916 to become the Dean of Colgate Theological Seminary. Albert Cohoe came to the church in October 1916 from Halifax, Nova Scotia, but resigned in May 1920 to follow Harry Emerson Fosdick at Montclair, New Jersey.[42] Vichert was cautious where Cohoe was "impatient of any restraint."[43] This discontinuity of pastoral leadership probably aggravated the deflationary spiral of the church. Little more was heard of building a parish hall after the Charitable Baptist Society turned to meetinghouse maintenance and painting. In fact, the auditorium was prepared for Brown University's 150th anniversary in 1914 by installing electric lights and repainting the large colored panels on the ceiling.[44] When Sarah Durfee died in 1915, she left her house at 34 Waterman Street to be used as a parish house; but the Charitable Baptist Society, run by men who thought they could save money, sold it in 1920 over the protests of the Women's League. The summer lawn services ended, and the Men's Class was turned over to a deacon and gradually faded. By 1917 the Sunday school was

in such dire straits that it was described as having suffered a "compound fracture," and the church dispensed with the position of Director of Christian Education. The membership of the church fell from 710 in 1911 to 585 in 1919, and 26 percent of the remnant were non-resident members. (Sixty of the losses were to the two Italian Baptist churches, which officially organized in June 1919.)[45]

The programs of First underwent significant change. The 1919 report of First Baptist to the Warren Association summarized some of the major changes of that year: "The general character of the mid-week meeting has entirely changed. The former prayer and conference feature has given place to a lecture, talk, or discussion by the pastor. The Sunday evening service was omitted and a meeting for conference

ABOVE Looking west from College Hill, this view of downtown Providence was photographed from the top of the Christian Science Church in 1908. The steeple of the Meeting House of First Baptist is barely visible in its coat of grey paint, begrimed and blackened by the haze of coal smoke that always lay over the city. To the right sprawled the new Union Station over the recently filled Cove Basin where over 300 trains came to Providence daily. The intensified commercial and industrial development had virtually eliminated residential housing to the west of the Meeting House, and a deteriorating building was rapidly ceasing to be the home of a neighborhood church. Courtesy of the Rhode Island Historical Society.

and discussion of matters of general public interest was held in the afternoon. These meetings were well attended, and while not of a distinctly religious character, were appreciated by many who do not ordinarily worship with us."[46] Nevertheless, it is not evident that these developments helped because Cohoe soon departed, causing the church to wonder aloud, "Are the problems of an old down-town church too great for the average minister?"[47] Indeed, President Faunce of Brown University told Cohoe that "he could see no future for the Old First Baptist Church. . . ."[48]

There were plenty of observations and prescriptions about the situation. One person maintained that the church was "indissolubly" linked to Brown and would "commit suicide if it does not see its task and destiny *there*." Another felt that the church should be painted every year and that the Brown students be required to attend the church in a body every Sunday. Several pointed to the drab and deplorable physical condition of the Meeting House, but one man observed something even more depressing. He said that "some of the sickness of the First Baptist Church, Providence, R.I., is due to the *spirit of exclusiveness typified by the closed pew door.* . . ." He recalled an incident when a pew owner arrived late one Sunday morning to find a visitor in his pew. He waited

while the woman stepped from the pew; and then he entered and closed her out, leaving her standing in the aisle in the nearly empty auditorium.[49]

An examination of the situation in 1921 found that non-residents constituted nearly one-third of the membership, that many others were elderly and unable to participate, and that deaths among the aging congregation were mounting. Worse, the Pulpit Committee was having difficulty finding a new pastor. Consequently, the church decided to experiment. "Realizing that it is a difficult task to secure a clergyman who can be depended upon for brilliant preaching, expert executive direction and tireless parish service," they divided "the ministerial office, relieving the pastor of all preaching responsibility and filling the pulpit with the best available preachers from other churches and communities, and from various denominations."[50] And so, beginning in March 1921 the experiment was attempted. They had a series of renowned and brilliant preachers, each supplying the pulpit for a month at a time; but no clergyman wanted to become the nonpreaching administrator. At last, Arthur W. Cleaves accepted the administrative pastorate and began in September 1922, but he gradually brought the experiment to an end and had recombined the duties by 1924.[51]

One idea that Cleaves promoted was that of First Baptist as a national church and shrine for Baptists. In 1925 the church used the occasion of the 150th anniversary of the Meeting House to celebrate its place in Providence. In anticipation, in 1923 the larger community, led by a Unitarian, Henry D. Sharpe, president of Brown & Sharpe Manufacturing Company, had raised $2700 for the Old Meeting House Fund with the hope of providing an endowment for the upkeep of the building itself.

Cleaves pastored the church until 1940, and during his tenure the congregation stabilized. He oversaw a major effort to restructure the organization of the church, to move toward more open membership requirements, and to reinvigorate ties to the Northern Baptist Convention.

These efforts produced growth through 1928, raising the membership to a pre-1920 level.[52] It slipped once more during the the Great Depression of the 1930s, only to recover somewhat as the world slid into World War II. When Cleaves began in 1922, the resident membership was 344; when he died on October 12, 1940, it was 376.[53]

A significant effort was made to open membership in the way that Elijah Hanley had advocated. First, in order to encourage college students to attend, the church voted in November 1922 to give "affiliate membership" to students while they studied in Providence. As a result, the first batch of seventeen students affiliated within three months.[54] Next, in 1923, the church created the "Associate" status for persons coming from churches which did not practice immersion. Associate members could not vote on matters of membership, denominational affiliation of the church, or the election of deacons.[55] One woman was admitted from a Congregational church "*to the full membership and fellowship of the church without further baptism,*" but this was a special case of physical disability.[56]

Cleaves tried to hold Sunday evening services again, but gave up on April 20, 1924 because of low attendance. Since then, the church has never had regular Sunday evening services. Also, the growing popularity of radio in the 1920s cut sharply into attendance at the mid-week prayer meeting,[57] but in 1932 the church began biweekly broadcasts of Sunday services on station WEAN.[58] Inasmuch as Cleaves had been the editor of *The Baptist*, a weekly publication of the Northern Baptist Convention before coming to First Baptist, he stressed the programs of the denomination. He reemphasized the missionary tradition of the church by listing the three current foreign missionaries from the congregation on the front of the bulletin each week and sponsored a "school of missions" in the church.[59] Once again the church met its mission and convention apportionments.[60]

The church consulted an efficiency expert from the Northern Baptist Convention to streamline the general structure of its committees and organizations.[61] As a result, the Women's League, an umbrella organization which covered all of the distinct women's groups in the church, was replaced by a single body, the Women's Society.[62] The Standing Committee was abolished, the Executive Committee was created to include the chairs of all the principal committees and the Women's Society, and the administration of the Sunday school was reorganized.[63]

One idea that Cleaves promoted was that of First Baptist as a national church and shrine for Baptists. In 1925 the church used the occasion of the 150th anniversary of the Meeting House to celebrate its place in Providence. In anticipation, in 1923 the larger community, led by a Unitarian, Henry D. Sharpe, president of Brown & Sharpe Manufacturing Company, had raised $2700 for the Old Meeting House Fund with the hope of providing an endowment for the upkeep of the building itself.[64] As part of this increased historical emphasis, beginning in 1927-1928, the church bulletin included an historical statement on the back, and an expanded version was distributed to visitors to the Meeting House. On May 15, 1930, "Olde Meeting House Day" was celebrated for the first time.[65] In 1935 the Executive Committee voted to have the church designated as the "First Baptist Church in America" when its sermons were broadcast over the radio.[66] Subsequently, the church adopted this as its official title during the celebration of its 300th anniversary in 1938, and it tried that year to get the Northern Baptist Convention to officially declare the church as a denominational shrine. It also gained considerable attention in 1936 during Rhode Island's 300th anniversary celebration. Much was made of Roger Williams and his principles in that year, and First Baptist gained significance as one of the results of Williams' struggles.[67] The church again reminded everyone that it believed in freedom of conscience and had never adopted a written creed or statement.[68]

Cleaves' sudden death at a Brown football game caused the church to turn to a former pastor for an interim. Elijah Abraham Hanley, now retired, served briefly until his own

health caused him to step aside.[69] Even in those few months, he encouraged the creation of the Business and Professional Women's Club which was open to women "actively engaged in a business or profession."[70] Then Albert Thomas, son and grandson of missionaries to Burma, became the twenty-seventh pastor in November 1941. For him, coming to First Baptist was actually a return. He had been the Director of Christian Education under Hanley and Vichert back in 1911-1912. He was the first Brown graduate to become the pastor since Jonathan Maxcy in 1791, and he served on the Board of Fellows and Executive Committee of the Brown Corporation after 1946. Like Cleaves, Thomas supported denominational initiatives and brought First Baptist into the special fund-raising drives in the late 1940s, including the World Mission Crusade, Crusade for Christ, and the Northern Baptist Convention's Stewardship Advance program.[71]

While the war years temporarily reversed the population decline of both Providence and the First Baptist Church, the slide resumed in the post-war era, especially with the exodus to the suburbs in the 1950s. Although the membership rolls of First Baptist appeared to remain fairly stable over the

ABOVE As part of its preparation for the 300th anniversary of its founding, the church began peeling off the Victorian decorations and additions. The elaborately painted ceiling panels gave way to a light yellow color for the plaster, and the woodwork was painted white. However, these were not the original colors of the auditorium, and an authentic restoration was not made until 1957. Photo from the archives of the First Baptist Church in America.

course of Thomas' pastorate, in fact the active membership fell. The nonresident membership had risen to nearly 40 percent by the time Thomas retired in September 1954, and the whereabouts of many members was unknown.[72] One of the tasks undertaken by the church under the next pastor, Homer Trickett, was the identification of the actual membership and a purging of the books. The sudden shrinkage of the reported membership by 218 names between 1955 and 1957 was an exercise in reality.[73]

For years Thomas had been extremely active in Baptist convention affairs, both on a state and national level. He had been president of the Massachusetts State Baptist Convention while pastor at Fall River, and was a leader in the New York State Baptist Convention before that. In addition, he was program chairman for the Northern Baptist Convention in 1942-1944 and a member of the national board of the American Baptist Foreign Mission Society for nine years. He continued the effort to impress upon the denomination the significance of the First Baptist Church in America and to get the convention to aid the church in its efforts to survive in the declining context of downtown Providence. The simple cost of maintaining one of America's architectural treasures was a constant drain on the resources of a shrinking constituency. The physical decay of the old Meeting House was evident to the community; in fact, the *Providence Journal* featured the problems in a series of stories and launched a campaign in 1947 to raise funds to aid in the repair of the building.[74] The church's effort to gain denominational recognition culminat-

ABOVE In 1947 the buildings in front of the Meeting House were cleared
away for the construction of the Providence Washington Insurance building,
opening a unique scene. Through all the years, before and since, other structures have obstructed this distant view of the Meeting House. Work was being
done to the severely deteriorated steeple elements in 1947, and the *Providence
Journal* campaigned to raise funds for the repairs. Courtesy of Providence
Journal Company.

First Baptist itself turned to other sources to try to find the money for the urgent repairs to the Meeting House, and they found their benefactor in John D. Rockefeller, Jr., an 1897 graduate of Brown University and former Sunday school teacher at First Baptist.

---

ed in May 1948 when the Northern Baptist Convention, meeting in Milwaukee, declared the First Baptist Church in America to be a national denominational shrine and authorized a nation-wide campaign to raise a $200,000 endowment fund for its preservation. The slogan was "Wanted: 200,000 Baptists" who would give one dollar each to "Our Denominational Homestead."[75]

The campaign was a fiasco, and it had unfortunate and unforeseen consequences. The church borrowed $5000 to conduct the drive but received only $3010 from the whole Northern Baptist Convention (compared to the $8500 raised in Rhode Island by the *Providence Journal's* effort in 1947), and it caused disillusionment in the church with the denomination. At the same time the campaign generated considerable resentment in other Rhode Island churches. The state had quite a number of struggling churches, especially in Providence; and they needed help as much as First Baptist, but they could not claim national significance. As a result, even thirty years later denominational officials were reluctant to entertain appeals from First Baptist in Providence. As one former American Baptist executive put it, "The ABC hardly dared to boost First Baptist too much or get taken to task for it."[76]

First Baptist itself turned to other sources to try to find the money for the urgent repairs to the Meeting House, and they found their benefactor in John D. Rockefeller, Jr., an 1897 graduate of Brown University and former Sunday school teacher at First Baptist. Harold Tanner, the Chancellor of Brown University, approached him with a proposal for a thorough restoration of the building and received a favorable response.[77] Rockefeller dispatched a team of engineers and experts from New York to survey the condition of the Meeting House, and they found serious problems, not the least of which was the sagging floor of the auditorium and the fact that the floor joists of the south gallery had separated from the sill beams by six or seven inches. In short, the gallery was hanging with little support on one side. They discovered that the organ was sitting on little more than lath and plaster because the floor joists under it lacked seven feet of reaching a supporting beam. Rockefeller responded by turning over $500,000 worth of securities to the Charitable

Baptist Society for the restoration,[78] and they set about fixing the building to last another 200 years.[79]

The congregation moved to Sayles Hall on the campus of Brown University in March 1957 and returned for a grand rededication in April of the following year. The whole ground floor was redesigned, the walls strengthened, the steeple reinforced, the organ rebuilt by the Wicks Organ Company, and the auditorium restored in a major way to its original appearance. The 1832 pews were retained, but the high pulpit and the sounding board were recreated, the 1884 addition closed off, and the colors of woodwork and walls returned to their original "meeting house sage" and white. Even the great chandelier was stripped of its Victorian accretions and returned to its 1792 appearance.[80]

Such an undertaking had at least two consequences. It brought the church back into high profile in the community, and attendance increased. It raised the morale of the congregation to see the Meeting House in such magnificent condition. The number of tourists increased to several thousand each year, so that a systematic guiding program was created. On the other hand, the restoration experience heightened the concern of some members so that preservation of the Meeting House took precedence over anything else. Over the years these would become what their critics called the "museum keepers," but they were numerous and influential enough to thwart most things that they opposed. One victim of this conservatism was the pastor, Homer Trickett, who became discouraged in the end and left for another pastorate.

Trickett began his tenure in October 1955 and set about to promote life within the walls and recognition outside. He was involved in the restoration project in addition to having the task of keeping the congregation together while they were in exile at Sayles Hall. In 1957 he saw the church finally adopt the open membership idea that Elijah Hanley had sought in 1909. They eliminated the "Associate" status and accepted as a full member a person "who has experienced the baptismal ceremony of the particular denomination in which he was brought up in."[81] The church used the rededication of the Meeting House to draw attention to the church, and a series of services involved national, state, and

local religious and political leaders. Virgil Fox, the organist at Riverside Church in New York, presented an inaugural concert on the rebuilt organ; and Brown University awarded honorary degrees to Trickett and Edward Tuller, general secretary of the American Baptist Convention.[82]

When Trickett began his ministry in Providence, he held the view that the most urgent task of the church was to serve in the community and to attack the great issues of racism, war, declining moral standards and practices, rampant humanism in education, and materialism.[83] He believed that the congregation could be revitalized if it could lose itself in those social issues. The church made an effort to engage the local college students and hired an assistant minister who served as Baptist chaplain to the colleges. The chaplain organized student groups which met on Brown's campus; however, the student unrest of the early 1960s saw these groups dwindle away. In the 1960s a grave concern was the alienation of young people, and Trickett supported the idea of sponsoring a coffee house as a means of reaching them.

The Mouthpiece Coffee House opened its doors in March 1967 at One Benefit Street.[84] From being in the talking stages in 1965-1966, it moved to reality after a new assistant minister, Stanford Bratton, was given the responsibility of organizing and finding a site. It was to be a neutral meeting

ground between the youth who loitered on Westminster Mall and the college students. The coffee house had room for forty-two, but within a few months it attracted as many as 150 each night that it was open. Among those drawn to it were some motorcycle gang members, with the result that at least two instances of gang fighting took place outside. With those coming to the coffee house spilling into the streets, the police came to regard it as a nuisance. As a result, the landlord would not renew the lease in 1968, so the coffee house moved to 244 North Main Street, in one of the buildings slated for demolition in the urban renewal program. Despite the problems, several other churches became interested in the project and began to help.

The coffee house was a controversial issue at First Baptist. As Trickett said, "Most of the older members of the church raised serious questions, and some opposed it outright. We have people in this church who wouldn't want to be reconciled with these long-haired young people." On the other side he noted that the youths in the coffee house "aren't about to go to an architecturally nice and culturally refined church."[85] Still, he admitted that Bratton had altered the mission of the coffee house from what the church had intended. Bratton shared a bias against the institutional church that afflicted so many young seminarians of the 1960s, and he regarded any attempt to use the coffee house to draw the youth into the church as "seeking the aggrandizement of the institution."[86] Therefore, between the hostility of many in the congregation and the direction which Bratton gave to the coffee house, the project was in deep trouble. The deaths of some major contributors to the

ABOVE The auditorium was filled with a forest of scaffolding as the painting was done during the great restoration. This picture, dated July 29, 1957, shows the chandelier encased in a protective box. It was taken before the east jut of the building was walled off and the reconstructed high pulpit installed. Photo by Norman Watson from the archives of the First Baptist Church in America.

ABOVE The pillars in the auditorium are solid oak trees, but over time they
dried out and became cracked and twisted. This photo, taken May 18, 1957,
shows how they were repaired to make them look as good as new. Each
column was notched and strapped, pulling the cracks together as much as
possible, and then wood putty filled the rest. Photo by Norman Watson
from the archives of the First Baptist Church in America.

church produced a financial problem for the church, and this was used as the excuse to cut loose from the coffee house and eliminate the position of assistant minister in early 1969.[87]

The demise of the coffee house was just one sign of the state of the spirit of the church. Trickett believed that getting additional space was a high priority, but when the church had an opportunity to buy the building across the street at 188 Benefit Street for a parish house, it refused. Budgetary concerns provoked strong feelings and a few members cut or discontinued their pledges, causing Trickett to write that at least "our people are not indifferent." He pleaded for restraint and asked, "Should we try to decide issues in the church by the power of money. . . ?"[88] When Albert Thomas, the minister emeritus, died in January 1969, some members wanted to purchase a communion set in his memory. The state of mind of the congregation was revealed when they voted one evening to abolish the office of assistant minister, and then voted an additional $800 to complete the purchase of the Thomas Memorial communion service. They cut a major program and invested in memorializing the past. When concerns were raised about the faltering condition of the Sunday school, the moderator of the Charitable Baptist Society, Norman Watson, expressed the opinion that we should have an "adult church" and just concentrate on bringing the very best speakers possible to the pulpit. "It should be open to anybody who has anything to say," he declared.[89]

The minister's report in January 1970, after observing that during the 1960s First Baptist had suffered a decline in attendance in church and Sunday school and in giving to local expenses and world outreach, tried to find hope and optimism. Trickett declared that "the mood of the congregation has become more hopeful, optimistic, more joyful; and our budget situation has become stabilized."[90] In fact, he himself had become discouraged and would be gone to Plainfield, New Jersey, by the fall.

The bottom was reached in the 1970s, and the very existence of First Baptist was brought into question. At the time that Trickett resigned, the pastorates of Central, Congdon Street, and Olney Street Baptist churches also fell vacant. Furthermore, Fourth Baptist Church was moribund. Upon their resignations, both Trickett and R. Leroy Moser of Central recommended that the churches explore the idea of merging, and this was urged by convention leaders. The prevailing wisdom among national leaders of the American Baptist Convention in this period was that struggling downtown churches should merge to form "urban parishes." Instead of maintaining several mostly-empty buildings, they

ABOVE The floor of the auditorium was sagging badly before the restoration, and part of the solution was to add new beams, metal straps and braces, and steel truss rods. On the old rafters, previous painters, such as "Edward Clarke, July 2, 1824," left their marks. The view, dated April 20, 1957, is of the present fellowship room, looking northeast. Photo by Norman Watson from the archives of the First Baptist Church in America.

OPPOSITE John D. Rockefeller, Jr., sent his own engineers to inspect the condition of the Meeting House before deciding to lend a hand. They found the building to be seriously deteriorated, as can be seen in this view of the base sill on the south side of the building. This photo, dated March 6, 1957, reveals that large chunks of the sill had rotted away. Photo by Norman Watson from the archives of the First Baptist Church in America.

should consolidate into a larger, stronger body. The process was being carried out elsewhere, and successful examples, such as the Church of the Master, were paraded before the pastorless, faltering churches. The result was a proposal for one new Baptist congregation on the East Side of Providence, to be called the Roger Williams Memorial Baptist Church. "The First Baptist Meeting House shall be maintained as a National Historic Site. . . [and one] of the other buildings shall be used as the center of worship, fellowship and Christian nurture of the new congregation."[91]

The two African-American churches, Congdon and Olney, rejected the merger idea and immediately sought new pastors. Coming as it did right in the floodtide of black pride and consciousness, the idea of merging with white congregations held little appeal. First and Central, the mother church and its first daughter, appointed committees and began serious conversations.[92] These came to naught, broken off by First Baptist essentially because its members feared the loss of identity and the loss of their Meeting House.[93] The Central Baptist church had the newer, larger

facility, and some people suggested that the First Baptist Meeting House could be turned over to the state convention for its headquarters and for the Rhode Island State Council of Churches. (When Fourth Baptist Church closed in 1981, that is what happened to their building.) Both churches then sought new pastors. Central called Thomas Moye, who was, ironically, a member of First Baptist; and he brought new life there. First Baptist called Robert Withers, but he could not arrest the decline.

First Baptist was in trouble by nearly any measure. When Withers became the twenty-ninth pastor in November 1971, the active membership of the church was 142 people whose average age was 55 to 60 years old. As the Pulpit Committee's "Profile of the First Baptist Church in America" put it: "A considerable number of its members are widows and older ladies. The Church, while nearby to college campuses, has few single persons or young married couples."[94] The average attendance at worship services was about 100, and Sunday school had about two dozen adults and children.[95] The church budget was several thousand

ABOVE The present appearance of the auditorium of the First Baptist Church in America. In 1957 the building underwent a restoration, and the auditorium was returned to its original appearance in most respects. While the 1832 pews were retained, the original colors of woodwork and walls were restored. The high pulpit, the Palladian window, and sounding board were returned to their original places when the opening in the wall was closed. The baptistry was raised and placed behind the Palladian window behind the pulpit. The grand chandelier shed its Victorian accretions and appears (though electrified) as it did in 1792. Photo by Warren Jagger (2001).

dollars lower in 1970 than it had been in 1965, and pledge receipts were nearly $10,000 lower than five years before. The endowment became ever more important, and its income exceeded pledges for the first time in 1970. Back in 1910, Hanley had concluded that an endowment would be needed to save and maintain the ministry of old downtown churches; by now it was certainly true.

When Withers resigned, effective June 1, 1975, conditions were worse. The active membership was down to ninety whose average age was nearly sixty. The 1975 "Profile" prepared by the Pulpit Committee noted, "The church has only 8-10 young single people despite being on the edge of two college campuses. Our church, along with all those in the area, saw the college-age population melt away in the 1960s."[96] It pointed out that the number of members over 80 years old was equal to the number that was 20 to 29. Worse, the smallest portions of the membership were the vital age groups of 30 to 50 years old.[97] Because of the thin-

The mid-1970s marked the lowest point in the history of First Baptist since the secession of Samuel Winsor and the Six Principle adherents in June 1771. Still, a number of hopeful developments showed that the Spirit had not fled the premises.

ning ranks, most church committees were reduced in size; for example, the Board of Deacons was cut from fourteen to seven. The average church attendance was only seventy people, and the Sunday school collapsed after Christmas of 1974.[98] While pledge income had risen 14 percent during Withers' tenure, pledges now accounted for only 37 percent of the church's income.

Withers had come to First Baptist during a national religious depression for the so-called "mainline churches." It was a matter of grave concern among many of the major denominations that, far from keeping up with the growth in population, their membership figures were declining. In addition the campus ministries across the nation still resonated to the anti-institutional attitudes of the student population in the Vietnam War era. The worst effects of the turning away from the institutional church or organized religion became manifest in the mid-1970s. One example was an unsuccessful effort by the Brown chaplaincy program to create a nondenominational campus church in Manning Chapel. The chaplains told the neighboring pastors to leave the students alone and stay out of the dormitories. While few students were attending anyway, this attitude cut off the campus even more. This sort of atmosphere made it difficult to recruit students or anyone else. Whether it was the frame of mind of people of the 1970s or something else, the odd fact was that not one person who joined the church during Withers' tenure remained a decade later.

The mid-1970s marked the lowest point in the history of First Baptist since the secession of Samuel Winsor and the Six Principle adherents in June 1771. Still, a number of hopeful developments showed that the Spirit had not fled the premises. Withers drew the church into the Providence Intown Churches Association (PICA) so that it could better serve the downtown area. A major undertaking of PICA was the creation of a foodbank at Mathewson Street Methodist Church to which food was donated by the cooperating churches. A soup kitchen was opened at Mathewson, which was especially needed in the economically depressed period in the early 1980s. Back in 1908, Elijah Hanley had urged the downtown churches to undertake such joint initiatives in order to be more effective. Withers also functioned as a de facto chaplain to the Rhode Island School of Design as part of an outreach program, and in the subsequent decade a small, but steady stream of RISD students attended the church. Part of the attraction, no doubt, was the development of a gallery in the fellowship room where artists displayed their work. The most enduring contribution of Withers was his encouragement and support of the music program. Himself an organist, he wanted the church to revive its moribund music program. This was accomplished by David Mitchell, who became the minister of music in 1972. Finding only a paid quartet, Mitchell issued a call for singers and gradually built a choir which earned the admiration of everyone who heard it. Younger church members also took some initiative during this period; for example, seeing that the 1975 budget anticipated an $8,000 deficit, they staged a May Fair and raised $2,556.[99] Many of them dressed in colonial costumes in the spirit of the bicentennial celebrations of both the Meeting House and the American Revolution. These same people held an ice cream social on the lawn for the college students the following autumn.

It was not an auspicious time for anyone trying to achieve great things. The city and the entire state reeled from population loss and economic depression in the 1970s. Because of the departure of most of the U.S. Navy fleet operations from Rhode Island, the state was one of only two in the entire nation that suffered a decline in population in the 1970s. For its part, Providence lost another 13.7 percent of its people in that decade. What no one could have known was that the nadir had been reached. The following quarter of a century witnessed considerable revitalization in the state, city, and old First Baptist.

CHAPTER 8

Exciting Times

An old blessing says, "May you live in exciting times." One surveying the history of the First Baptist Church in America in the last quarter of the twentieth century will conclude that those were exciting times. From the slough of the mid-1970s, the church experienced some roller-coaster events, including problems with ministerial leadership, to arrive at the twenty-first century in a much stronger position and condition than anyone had imagined possible. No doubt, the church benefited from the revival and growth of the general condition of Rhode Island and Providence, but First Baptist undertook major efforts to restore and maintain its national historic landmark building, to rebuild the organ, and serve the community.

Richard Bausman began a dynamic but troubled ministry on May 1, 1976. Energetic and magnetic, he attracted a growing corps of young adults who subsequently became leaders and helped to revitalize the church. For example, of the nine persons who served as moderator from 1981 to 2001, five joined during Bausman's tenure. These included Diane Vanden Dorpel, Scott Telford, David Coon, Carol Hagglund, and Linda Bausserman. Despite the mobility of the young professionals who came to the church, the congregation revived in both spirit and activity. In the first two years of Bausman's pastorate the church welcomed nearly fifty members, the most in any two-year period in a decade. Small "growth groups" which Bausman began with twelve soon had fifty people. Attendance at worship, which had fallen to 45-60 during the interim between ministers, rose to 85-105 per Sunday. A prayer circle began and became a "Life in the Spirit" seminar within a year. The Sunday school, which had dwindled away for two seasons, was rebuilt, and the church engaged a paid coordinator to superintend the program. The music program under Mitchell's direction continued to develop with a new Masterworks series in 1977 and special choir concerts on Palm Sunday, starting in 1981. The choir grew to such a size

and quality that it was twice asked to join with the Rhode Island College Chorus and Orchestra for the college's annual spring concert.[1]

A costly and long-delayed renovation of the steeple was authorized in January 1977; and $470,000 later it was finally rededicated on May 16, 1982. The money was raised by a special fundraising campaign. Next, the congregation embarked on equally costly projects to restore and repaint the interior and exterior of the Meeting House. These were completed in 1986, which meant that a major effort to maintain the building consumed most of a decade and the energies of many individuals.

Rather than cut programs out of fear of running a deficit, the congregation chose to accept a series of substantial deficit-budgets in the expectation that new life and growth would result from expanded programs. They were not about to repeat the experience of the Cranston Street Baptist Church which had died clutching a large endowment in 1968. They were not disappointed, and most deficits never materialized. Moreover, the budget was increased 85 percent during Bausman's pastorate, and the achievement of the financial goals was made possible by both a 200 percent increase from endowment earnings and an 80 percent increase in pledge giving.

Despite all the apparent gains, by 1981 growing dissatisfaction caused by multiplying personal conflicts with Bausman expressed itself the next year in closing pocketbooks and disappearing members. The 1982 "Profile" written by the Pulpit Committee reflected the state of affairs in the congregation when Bausman's ministry ended. The active membership and the attendance at worship and in Sunday school began falling, reflecting the strains in the relationship. By January 1982, about 100 members took active part and attendance averaged sixty-five.[2] Only the music program continued to flourish as the choir was the one remaining group in the church that maintained an esprit de corps. On occasion the choir in the gallery outnumbered the congregation seated below. Finally, in April 1982 the deacons requested Bausman's resignation, and his tenure ended on May 30.

Despite the tempestuous nature of his administration, the church was stronger than when he started. It had the

TIMELINE

1981-82	Major steeple renovation
1981	Personal computer introduced
1986	First women ordained at FBCIA
1987	First woman called as minister
1988	350th anniversary of the founding of FBCIA
1991	"Desert Storm"
1992	RIght Now! coalition to reform state government
1998	Handicapped access provided
2000	225th anniversary of the Meeting House
2000	Organ rebuilt and enlarged

strength to endure the first dismissal of a minister since 1789 and to rebound quickly under new leadership. It was financially stronger, and the demographics of the congregation had substantially improved. In 1975 when Bausman had arrived, only about 13 percent of the congregation were between the ages of 30 and 50 years old, but by 1982 a third of the members were this age. The average age of the membership was nearly ten years younger.[3]

In a leap of faith First Baptist decided to engage co-pastors for its ministry. Orlando Tibbetts, a retired denominational executive and former missionary, and Dwight Lundgren, a young parish minister, were called simultaneously. Tibbetts assumed his duties in August 1983 with Lundgren following on September 1. The anxiety of many years lifted like a cloud and programs prospered. The monthly church meetings were replaced with quarterly meetings, a reorganized executive committee became the central coordinating body, and the church rolls were pruned of deadwood.[4] In three years the annual budget increased by nearly 75 percent, exceeding $205,000; giving to missions rose 131 percent.[5] All of this went on while the congregation completed the restoration projects that consumed much time and effort. Newly painted inside and out, the Meeting House was all dressed up and ready for the congregation to move ahead.

The membership grew along with this willingness to pledge and participate. One member of twenty years standing, observing the increased size of the congregation, said, "More are present on our worst Sundays now than used to attend on the best days."[6] Some began to worry about parking and Sunday school space again and to consider how the church could expand or build new facilities. The choir cut a record, "Music from the Meeting House," and serious consideration was given to rebuilding the faltering, cantankerous organ.[7] In line with the church's historic commitment to freedom of conscience, members began writing letters for the

ABOVE The audience rose to give a sustained ovation to the Nobel Peace Prize-winning South African Anglican Bishop Desmond Tutu when he spoke at the Meeting House on February 21, 1999, as part of the Brown University-Providence Journal Public Affairs Conference on "Spiritual Life in America: One Nation Under God." Photo by James Wynn.

All of the old histories speak of Roger Williams beginning the church by baptizing Ezekiel Holliman and "some ten more," but those ten or eleven were all men. In fact, several of those men, including Williams and Holliman, had wives who were baptized at the same time.

"urgent action" cases of Amnesty International.[8] In anticipation of its 350th anniversary, the church voted to have a new history written.[9] In short, the atmosphere and spirit were transformed from wondering who would be left to turn out the lights when the doors were shut on the museum to thinking about service and new facilities. For any member who had lived though the decline of the 1960s and 1970s, the new spirit and momentum brought by Tibbetts and Lundgren in the 1980s seemed miraculous.

One major event was the 350th anniversary of Baptist beginnings in America, celebrated in 1988. First Baptist hosted a national "Faith and Freedom Conference," sponsored by the American Baptists and a number of other Baptist denominations. The governor of Rhode Island and the mayor of Providence both proclaimed the conference period of June 5-11 to be "Baptist Heritage Week." Later in November, the services celebrating First Baptist's birthday were featured on CBS on "Sunday Morning with Charles Kuralt."[10]

Increasingly First Baptist followed that path suggested by Elijah Hanley to work through other agencies of charity. Clothes, household goods, and thousands of dollars were donated to the South Providence Neighborhood Ministries, operating from the Calvary Baptist Church. Beginning in 1990, the church packed and supplied hundreds of lunches for Traveler's Aid Society.[11] Several members worked on house construction in South Providence with Habitat for Humanity, and as many as ten volunteers helped in the soup kitchen each week at Mathewson Street Methodist Church.[12] Dwight Lundgren endorsed church members' roles in Interfaith Volunteer Caregivers Network, HELP (Homeless Ecumenical Leadership Project), and various PICA programs, including Community Cafe and Leisure and Learning.[13]

After Tibbetts retired, Kate Penfield joined the ministerial team in 1987, bringing her interest and connections in civic and political affairs in Rhode Island. For example, she was a member in 1981 of the first class to go through Leadership Rhode Island, a training and networking project of the Greater Providence Chamber of Commerce, and she served on the board of directors of Leadership Rhode Island for a number of years after 1986. Her particular concerns were the AIDS epidemic and the low level of ethics in the state

government. The church responded to the AIDS crisis by giving support to the Family AIDS Center for Treatment and Support, sponsoring AIDS worship services, and putting on a "festival of caring" at the Meeting House which raised $5,510 for FACTS House, a facility for treatment of infants with AIDS.[14]

By the early 1990s, the lack of ethics in government had made Rhode Island a scandal in the nation. The chief justice of the state supreme court had been forced to resign because of corruption; the past governor was indicted (and eventually imprisoned) for extortion; the credit union system had collapsed, leaving one-third of the state's people without their deposits; state pension scandals and indictments or imprisonment of the mayors of four of the largest cities in the state all combined to produce a reform uprising. Ironically, the decline in the twentieth century had helped to disentangle First Baptist Church from the state. First Baptist was no longer one of the pillars of the community, and no one spoke of the Christian duty to support the government as some had at the time of the Dorr Rebellion in the 1840s. Consequently, First Baptist was "the first church in Rhode Island to speak out and take a stand about the state of the state."[15] The adult forum had a series of notable speakers on "Fixing the System," and the church worked with a statewide coalition, RIght Now!, to force the state government to reform itself.[16] The Meeting House hosted a service and was the staging area for Baptist marchers on January 5, 1992, who joined thousands of others from the faith community to march to the State House. This coalition was spearheaded by the Rhode Island State Council of Churches whose executive minister was Rev. James Miller, an active member of First Baptist, and whose past president was Kate Penfield.

Although Kate Penfield was a leading spokesperson for First Baptist Church in the ethics and governmental mess in Rhode Island, First Baptist had not been a leader in extending opportunities to women in the ministry. Her election was the capstone to the long history of female participation in America's oldest Baptist church, even if women's role had not been adequately recognized.

All of the old histories speak of Roger Williams beginning the church by baptizing Ezekiel Holliman and "some ten

more," but those ten or eleven were all men. In fact, several of those men, including Williams and Holliman, had wives who were baptized at the same time. If the men did, indeed, outnumber the women that autumn day of 1638, it was probably the last time in the history of the Baptist church in Providence that more men than women were members. Without exception, every extant membership list finds women outnumbering the men, sometimes as much as three to one. For example, in 1780, the membership was 70 percent female; in 1832, it was 77 percent female; in 1884 it was again 70 percent female. In 1910 women constituted 64 percent of the membership, even after Hanley's attempts between 1907 and 1910 to narrow the gap by emphasizing the masculine side of Christianity and to have special programs for men. The constituency list of January 2001 showed that 61 percent of the members were women.[17] None of these figures or proportions is unusual in American religious history.

The role and place of women in First Baptist through the generations generally reflected women's status in the larger society. Although the constituency has always been mostly female, the power and authority was mostly male until well into the twentieth century. While Catherine Scott was credited with convincing Williams that believer's baptism was the Scriptural concept, the rite was administered by men. Women tended to be treated in a more anonymous fashion. For example, an entry from April 29, 1762, told of a church meeting concerned with buying more land so that the meeting house could be enlarged. Listed are eight men's names "and Sundry women."[18]

As we have seen, the place of women in First Baptist was affected by that "iron law of creeping respectability" in the eighteenth and nineteenth centuries.[19] As Baptist leaders sought acceptance from other denominations, they "put their house in order," including silencing women and taking away their vote in church meetings. Initially women could vote, but that was eliminated at some point after 1786.[20] The last clear example of women's voting occurred on August 4, 1791 on that old issue of requiring the laying-on-of-hands before someone could take part in the Lord's Supper. All members were polled, male and female, black and white; and the ritual lost 62-4. The clerk recorded each voter, including two African-American women, Membo Navy and Sophia Davis.[21] However, this vote was exceptional because the "sisters" were not allowed to speak in meetings without permission of the "brethren." This caused one woman to reject membership when it was extended to her. She applied in November 1792 "provided she might be allowed to speak in publick when it was strongly impressed upon her mind." After much debate, the church voted in January 1793 to admit her "in the same manner that other members are admitted, that is to be subject to the rules and order now established amongst us." She refused those

ABOVE The First Baptist Meeting House was dedicated May 27, 1775, "for the publick Worship of Almighty GOD and also for holding Commencement in." Each year the graduating class of Brown University marches down the hill in a colorful procession and into the Meeting House for their commencement exercises. Pictured here is graduation day 1914 as the students filed into the building, accompanied by the music of the American Band. Courtesy of Brown University Archives.

In contrast to the staid and traditional ceremonies of 1914, the graduation festivities now are exceedingly colorful and reflect the racial and cultural diversity of the university.

terms.[22] As described earlier, in 1803 Joanna Gano was not permitted to read her long discourse and indictment against her husband, the pastor of the church, and she was expelled for being disorderly.

When, in 1844, First Baptist issued its first manual of rules and regulations, it clearly limited voting and speaking to men.[23] As noted elsewhere, the women in 1865 had to speak by written petition on the issue of a church choir. It was effective in that instance because the signatories were the most notable women in the church. Still, from time to time, the opinion of women was sought, and special, separate votes were asked. For example, in 1808 the brethren rejected an offer of resignation by Stephen Gano, and "the sisters of the church also manifested their approbation of the vote

ABOVE In contrast to the staid and traditional ceremonies of 1914, the graduation festivities now are exceedingly colorful and reflect the racial and cultural diversity of the university. Pictured here is baccalaureate day 1999 as the students filed into the building to the beat of African drums. Photo by Peter Goldberg. Courtesy of Brown University News Service.

which had past [sic], by rising when the question was proposed to them."[24] The women were asked only to affirm a decision already made by the men. When the church debated the call to Edward Taylor to be the minister in 1874, "The sisters in the church be requested to express their opinions upon the nomination by word and by vote."[25] By the 1880s, the men reconsidered the ban on women's participation, and amended the rules to read: "Every member, not under age, shall be entitled to vote on all questions. . . ."[26] Then the limitation on women's speaking ended in 1890.[27]

In the early nineteenth century as the middle class woman's world narrowed to the "Woman's Sphere" of domesticity and motherhood, women found a new range of opportunities when the missions and Sunday school movements swept American Protestantism. As disestablishment advanced in every state, making religion fully voluntary, the fact that women constituted the overwhelming proportion of the membership of Protestant churches meant that the male leadership depended heavily upon women's support and cooperation. Furthermore, as the Victorian notion of the "Better Half" gained strength, women were seen as the true fount of religion and morality in society. They were thought to be naturally more spiritual than men, with the result that it was regarded as quite normal and proper that women would be involved in matters of education, benevolence, and religion.[28]

What occurred in First Baptist in the nineteenth century was quite typical: women created a network of societies to collect money for missions, Sunday school, ministerial education, women's colleges, and various benevolences, such as the relief of the poor, orphans, blind, and insane. The array of female-run groups, including the Female Mite Society (1806), Female Charitable Baptist Society (1820), Female Foreign Missionary Society (1827), Female Education Society (1830), Maternal Association (1832), Young Ladies' Association for Foreign Missions (1832), Ladies' Western Association for Home Missions (1835), First Baptist Knitting Society (1835), a sewing school for the poor (1837), Young Ladies' Prayer Meeting (1857), First Baptist Sewing School (1860), Young Ladies' Missionary Association (1866), Woman's Baptist Foreign Mission Society (1872), Mission Band of Earnest Workers (1873), Women's Christian Temperance Union auxiliary (c. 1875), Ladies' Home Mission Sewing Society (1878), Young Ladies' Improvement Society (1885), Farther Lights Society (1895), Woman's City Missionary Society (c. 1900),

Woman's Baptist Home Mission Society (1901), and the Girls' Home Mission Circle (1905). Many of these organizations resulted from the recurrent revivals of interest in missions that swept one generation of young women after another. Others were long-lived and disappeared only when all the women's groups were merged into the Women's Society in 1923.

Looking at the organizations of First Baptist through the nineteenth century, one is struck by the fact that while female societies proliferated not one male group was begun. The explanation is not hard to find. The male arena was not confined to home and church; therefore, the religious, moral, and benevolent thrust of men was expressed in public, non-sectarian organizations. Men joined the likes of the Rhode Island Bible Society, Providence Religious Tract Society, Society for the Encouragement of Faithful Domestic Servants, Providence Franklin Society, Providence Washington Total Abstinence Society, Providence Anti-Slavery Society, and the Rhode Island Educational Union. The men did not have to create new organizations inside the church: they were the officialdom of the church itself and the Charitable Baptist Society. A man was always the superintendent of the Sunday school, even though the school was begun and largely taught and run by women. After 1827 a woman was selected as assistant superintendent, and it was said of Emily Eddy, who held that position from 1827 to 1845, that "in reality Mrs. Eddy was the Superintendent, and indeed that she was the life of the whole school at that time."[29]

Emily Eddy had been a seventeen year-old convert in the 1820 revival and helped to establish the Sunday school. She lived in Boston while her husband Richard was treasurer of the American Baptist Missionary Union from 1845 to 1855 and rejoined the church when they returned to Providence. Besides her deep interest in the Sunday school, she was a leader in the Female Mite Society, the Female Charitable Baptist Society (which was begun to minister to the poor women of the church), and the Woman's Foreign Missionary Society. In addition she started the First Baptist Sewing School in 1860.[30] All of this explains why at her death in 1875 she was described as "a sort of sub-pastor to the women." Many women felt that it was sufficient to tell her about their circumstances, instead of going to the pastor.[31] She was a central figure in the female network of First Baptist Church.

The membership of the Charitable Baptist Society, the corporation of the church, was entirely male in the beginning. However, as widows inherited pews, a few women were admitted to the Society. In 1895 ten women were members along with thirty-four men, but no woman was an officer.[32] The 1895 version of the Charitable Baptist Society's by-laws provided that the Committee on Repairs and Sexton "may also elect two ladies, not members of the Society, to assist the committee in superintending the Sexton in the discharge of

ABOVE The Great Awakening of the nineteenth century generated many women's organizations within First Baptist, among which was a sewing school for the poor children of the industrial neighborhoods near the Meeting House. The first sewing school was begun in 1837 but faded out within a few years; then in 1860 Emily Eddy founded the First Baptist Sewing School. Shown here about 1910, the sixty or so students were evidently of different races and ethnicity, aided and superintended by nearly twenty church women. Photo from the archives of the First Baptist Church in America.

Looking at the organizations of First Baptist through the nineteenth century, one is struck by the fact that while female societies proliferated not one male group was begun. The explanation is not hard to find. The male arena was not confined to home and church; therefore, the religious, moral, and benevolent thrust of men was expressed in public, non-sectarian organizations.

his duties."[33] In short, two auxiliaries were added to oversee the housekeeping, something that was well within the Woman's Sphere. No woman was elected to a Society committee until the 1920s, when two women members occupied the "reserved" positions on the Repairs and Sexton Committee and one went on the Music Committee.

The church had its own set of officers, but they, too, were all male. The first woman to hold any church office was Sarah Durfee, who was elected to the Advisory Committee for the Sunday school in 1890. Then, in 1892, the church established the Committee on Social Affairs with responsibilities to make arrangements for social gatherings; naturally, it was a committee of women. But, women did make a significant breakthrough in January 1917 when three were elected to the Standing Committee, the most powerful committee of the church. Its responsibilities included the "general care of the order and discipline of the church. . . . It shall be their duty to watch over the purity of the church; to admonish, in brotherly kindness, the erring; to reclaim the wandering. . . . No application for pecuniary aid, for the purposes of benevolence, shall come before the church, until it has been examined and sanctioned by the Committee."[34]

ABOVE Anna Canada Swain (1889-1979) was the second woman to be president of the Northern Baptist Convention, serving two years, 1944-1946. Normally a person served only one year, but during the war emergency from 1942-1946, the convention switched to a biennial meeting to cut down on travel and to save fuel. She became nationally known through her leadership in the Baptist foreign mission societies. In 1948 she became a member of the Executive Board of the World Council of Churches, and in 1954 she became the first woman to serve on the Central Committee of the WCC. Photo from archives of the First Baptist Church in America.

Over the years the Standing Committee had been the church's executive committee and moral police force, investigating the sins of the congregation and screening applications for admission. By the time of World War I, the stern discipline of earlier days had long since disappeared, and applicants for admission were being interviewed by the pastor and deacons. As noted earlier, in 1923 the Standing Committee was abolished in favor of an executive committee which operated like a pastor's cabinet.

Historians have observed that wars, disasters, and hard times often bring conditions in which the situation of women has improved. The decline of First Baptist in the twentieth century seems to fit this view. Women's progress in the Charitable Baptist Society came after it was forced to open its membership. By the late 1920s the society had trouble finding enough members to hold meetings or to fill its committees. In 1928, two consecutive quarterly meeting were cancelled for lack of a quorum of seven. Only one person appeared at the first, and at the second, only two.[35] As a result, in 1932 pew ownership was abandoned and membership was opened to anyone who was a contributor of record for two years.[36] Consequently, fifty-six new members entered the society, and forty-five of these were women. The society suddenly had a female majority, but none was elected to be a general officer until 1954-55, when Nellie Nelson became the deputy moderator and Clara Crosby was elected deputy clerk.[37]

Until the 1960s, except for work thought to be "women's work," nearly every office in the church was held by a man. The exceptions were so few as to be easily specified:

Margaret Rose and Katherine Tanner were members of the committee of eight which carried through the Rockefeller restoration effort in 1957;[38] Mary Crosby and Margaret Rose were part of a special sub-committee which oversaw the restoration of the auditorium itself. Then in its 195th year, 1969, the Charitable Baptist Society elected Elizabeth Angell as moderator.[39] By this time, the Properties and Sexton Committee, probably the most powerful committee in the society and one which had formerly been a male principality, was completely dominated by its female members. The church itself was slightly quicker than the Charitable Baptist Society in electing a woman to be a general officer— Mildred Walker became church clerk in 1962.[40] This creeping change seems all the more remarkable when you realize that twenty years earlier, in 1944, Anna Swain of First Baptist was elected president of the Northern Baptist Convention, only the second woman to hold that office![41]

The ancient, dual governing structures of the First Baptist Church in America have long puzzled outsiders and bedeviled members. The church itself was always composed of anyone who was admitted, but the society was an incorporated body created by the colonial charter of 1774. Its members did not have to be members of the church, but did have to be financial supporters under the original scheme of things. This is how it was possible for both Nicholas Browns

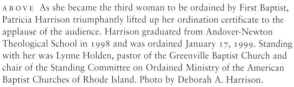

ABOVE As she became the third woman to be ordained by First Baptist, Patricia Harrison triumphantly lifted up her ordination certificate to the applause of the audience. Harrison graduated from Andover-Newton Theological School in 1998 and was ordained January 17, 1999. Standing with her was Lynne Holden, pastor of the Greenville Baptist Church and chair of the Standing Committee on Ordained Ministry of the American Baptist Churches of Rhode Island. Photo by Deborah A. Harrison.

RIGHT Amy Freeman Johnson was the fourth woman to be ordained by First Baptist Church in America. Licensed by FBCIA, Johnson graduated from Yale Divinity School in May 1999, and was ordained October 15, 2000. The centrality of women in First Baptist was further emphasized when Linda Bausserman, the moderator, administered the Vows of Ordination to Johnson. Photo by Dan Blackstone.

to be moderators of the society for so many years despite the fact that neither was ever a member of the church. Each body had its officers and conducted its own business. The society's business was finances, buildings and grounds; the church's business was the ministry, missions, Sunday school, and evangelism. In addition, for many years the Sunday school had its own treasurer and conducted business unaccountable to either church or society. In an effort to create some order and efficiency, the finances were combined in 1919 and one treasurer and a joint committee on budget was adopted. But, the rest of the dual process persisted.

One recommendation made in 1957 by a committee to study the governance of the church and society was that the general officers of both governing bodies be made identical. At last in 1973, J. Stanley Lemons was elected moderator of both, and that became the practice. That same year the first women were elected to the Board of Deacons. Neither innovation provoked much comment; people were just glad to have someone to fill all of the offices. This came at a moment when willing members found themselves filling

multiple positions, and able-bodied males were scarce. Women came to hold virtually any office. The first woman to be moderator of both bodies simultaneously was Alice Forsstrom in 1978. In fact, that year Russell Fox, the treasurer, was the lone male general officer in either the church or society. For the next seven years a woman was moderator, and in 1984 women chaired every major committee in the church and society, including the Deacons, Music, Missions, Budget & Finance, Education, Restoration, and Properties and Sexton Committees.[42]

Women found new opportunities for service in 1958. After the restoration of the Meeting House, the church began a guides program to welcome visitors and inform them about the building and Baptist history. Since then, over 182,000 visitors from all the world have been guided by volunteers, the vast majority of whom were women.

The rise of laywomen to all positions of work and responsibility in the church had a counterpart in the call to the ministry of Nancy Forsstrom, who was licensed in March 1984. She was First Baptist's first female licentiate, and she

ABOVE Nancy Forsstrom Downes received her ordination to the Christian ministry on September 21, 1986. She was the first female licentiate of First Baptist, but was the second to be ordained. The previous Sunday a convert to Christianity from Hong Kong, Florence Li (whose hand rests on Downes' shoulder) completed her ordination in the Meeting House. Also shown are Dwight Lundgren, thirty-second pastor of First Baptist; Janet Aquavella, former pastor of the United Baptist Church; Orlando Tibbetts (hand on her head), thirty-first pastor, and Homer Trickett, twentieth-eighth pastor, who had baptized and officiated at the marriage of Downes. Photo by J. Stanley Lemons.

and Florence Li, a convert of American Baptist missions in Hong Kong, were both ordained in September 1986. All that remained was for the church to call a woman minister, and that was done in 1987.

Penfield served until July 1, 1995, when she left to become the executive director of the Ministers Council of the American Baptist Churches USA. This capped her growing involvement in the work of the denomination, since she had previously held several important positions in the American Baptist Churches of Rhode Island and the State Council of Churches, in addition to being a member of the Executive

Miller noted that, while many Baptist churches faded and died in the long decline of Providence, "First Baptist remained rooted in the city." He said that "the sheer presence of our magnificent building in the heart of Providence . . . helped to keep the congregation downtown," but now "it's a good thing we are right where we are."

Committee of the Ministers Council since 1986 and national vice president of the American Baptist Churches USA from 1993 to 1995. Part of her legacy was to become the inspiration and mentor to other women who felt called to the ministry, and First Baptist Church subsequently ordained Patricia Harrison on January 17, 1999, and Amy Johnson on October 15, 2000.

Within six months of Penfield's departure, Dwight Lundgren left to become the pastor of the First Baptist Church of Philadelphia. Morgan Edwards, the pastor of that old church in 1760s, had been the one to urge the creation of a Baptist college in Rhode Island, and the Philadelphia Baptist Association sent James Manning to start the college which became Brown University. So, Lundgren's going to Philadelphia closed a circle that had been open for over 230 years. During his last months, in October, the Meeting House was the site of a three-day, national conference of Baptists marking the 150th anniversary of the 1845 split of the Baptist denomination. They gathered at First Baptist because the final steps in the division occurred right there.[43] Looking back over the years of Lundgren's pastorate (1983-1996), one found that First Baptist had stabilized and advanced. The involvement of the church and its members in social services in the city had expanded, the annual budget had risen from $117,000 to $320,000, and the effective membership had increased by about thirty.[44]

The church issued the call on June 1, 1997 to Clifford Hockensmith to be its minister, and on June 22 during a violent thunderstorm a bolt of lightning harmlessly struck the steeple of the Meeting House. An intrepid photographer captured the event in a spectacular picture. When a copy was shown to Hockensmith soon after he began his ministry on August 1st, he laughingly remarked, "I wonder if this was a good omen or a bad omen?" Events were to prove that it was a bad omen. Soon enough, it became evident that a mismatch had occurred. The pastor complained that First Baptist did not have a creedal statement, even though the church had long taken pride in the fact that it did not have one. In addition, Hockensmith did not approve of the church's stand favoring a high wall of separation between church and state. He thought, for example, that the Biblical story of Creation ought to be included in his son's public school biology textbooks.[45] These issues and others produced a clash of religious and historical cultures which

resulted in a vote of dismissal on August 1, 1999, exactly two years to the day that he began.[46]

In the colonial era, First Baptist Church found its pastors within the congregation; then in the late eighteenth century, it turned to the wider world of Baptist colleges and seminaries to seek its ministers. In the year 2000, for the first time in 210 years, the church looked within itself and called one of its own to be the new pastor. But, unlike the rough farmers and cobblers of colonial days, the choice to begin the twenty-first century was a man of great experience and national stature. James Miller had been a member of First Baptist since 1992 after he arrived to be the executive minister of the Rhode Island State Council of Churches. He worked hard to have the moral voice of Rhode Island's churches heard in the state's political climate which was rife with corruption, cronyism, and criminal activity. He helped to fashion the "RIght Now!" coalition which produced the January 1992 mass march of thousands to the State House. RIght Now! was a statewide coalition of business corporations, civic agencies, and religious institutions that could not be manipulated in the "Rhode Island way," and it helped to produce significant ethics reform in Rhode Island's government. In addition, because of Miller's leadership in the causes of race relations and social reconciliation, in 1997 the National Council of the Churches of Christ presented the Rhode Island State Council with its "Ecumenical & Interfaith Service Award." Then on May 4, 2000, Miller himself received the "Walter Cronkite Faith and Freedom Award" from the Interfaith Alliance, a national organization. Another honoree at the Yale Club in New York that evening was Tom Brokaw, the anchor of NBC *Nightly News*, and they received their awards from the hands of Walter Cronkite, the distinguished, retired CBS anchorman.[47]

Not only were members of First Baptist aware of the honors bestowed on Miller, they were acquainted with his activities that involved the church in other ways. Over the years he had frequently preached and led services at the Meeting House. He was instrumental in bringing to First Baptist Church the opening service on May 5, 1996, of a city-wide, week-long revival under the sponsorship of the State Council of Churches. In October 1998 he engineered the "University and Interfaith Forum on Religious Liberty," a three-day gathering in conjunction with Roger Williams University's unveiling a new statue of Roger Williams. The concluding

sessions of the conference were held in the Meeting House on Sunday, October 25, and included speakers at the adult forum, the morning worship service, and an afternoon colloquium. In addition Miller gave quiet, welcome help and advice to the church's moderators and leaders during both interims of the 1990s, and he served on the Board of Deacons during difficult times.

Interestingly, Miller had been associated with some of the same institutions as Jonathan Going. They both pastored the First Baptist Church of Worcester, Massachusetts, and both had connections with the First Baptist Church in America. Going was one of the founders of Newton Theological Institution and Denison University, and Miller was on the board of trustees of two American Baptist colleges. Whereas Going launched his ministry at First Baptist, Miller came after a distinguished career as a pastor and executive, bringing almost forty years of religious leadership.

He found the congregation ready for new leadership. After nearly five years of "transition," First Baptist looked positively upon the continuing challenges of being a downtown church. The physical condition of the Meeting House, including a new handicapped entrance, was excellent, and the spirit of the congregation was high. Long-delayed projects had been accomplished, including the production of a professional publicity brochure, a new compact disc featur-

ing the choir, and a website on the Internet. Most significantly, after nearly seventeen years of planning and delay, in 2000 the organ was rebuilt and expanded. Stephen Martorella, minister of music since 1987, had designed the expansion and worked closely with The Foley-Baker Company of Connecticut to assure the best results. The congregation approved the writing of a new history of the church, received acceptance of its invitation to host the annual meeting of the American Baptist Churches of Rhode Island in April 2001, and prepared for the June 2001 biennial meeting of the American Baptist Churches, USA, which was to be held in Providence for the first time.

Miller noted that, while many Baptist churches faded and died in the long decline of Providence, "First Baptist remained rooted in the city." He said that "the sheer presence of our magnificent building in the heart of Providence . . . helped to keep the congregation downtown," but now "it's a good thing we are right where we are." First Baptist is positioned to serve a city undergoing a renaissance. He felt that First Baptist Church would experience a "new vitality of membership and commitment, a renewal of mission and involvement."[48]

First Baptist has a national role to play as well. Miller maintained that being a "legacy church" and an "historic church" were major assets and part of the on-going mission and purpose for the First Baptist Church in America. "It is in the interest of the whole free church movement that we are an historic church, ever having to apply its legacy to the new, contemporary situation." He felt that church-state relations were "paramount in our times" and argued that the First Amendment separation of church and state was seriously threatened. "These issues," he declared, "are beckoning First Baptist to respond. We have a powerful legacy to bring to these issues. We have a new mandate to lead on the issue of religious freedom."

As First Baptist entered the twenty-first century, it sought to be true to its founding principles. The growing threat to the traditional Baptist concept of separation of church and state produced an increased awareness of that heritage. Among the thousands of visitors each year were many Baptists whose spirits were low because of the erosion of Baptist principles in their own churches and denominations. They came, as on a pilgrimage, to the wellspring of Baptist traditions. Perhaps Henry Melville King's boast is true: "The city of Providence is the mecca of the Baptists of all nations, and of all lovers of soul-liberty throughout the world."[49]

ABOVE Shown here officiating at the communion table of First Baptist Church, James Miller became the 35th pastor, beginning December 1, 2000. Miller had been the executive minister of the Rhode Island State Council of Churches from 1992 until he accepted the call to be the minister of FBCIA. Photo by Bryan Cooper.

APPENDIX

Ministers of the Church

1. ROGER WILLIAMS 1638-1639

2. CHAD BROWN 1639 – before 1650

3. THOMAS OLNEY 1639-1652

4. WILLIAM WICKENDEN 1642-1670

5. GREGORY DEXTER 1654-1700

6. PARDON TILLINGHAST 1681-1718

7. EBENEZER JENCKES 1719-1726

8. JAMES BROWN 1726-1732

9. SAMUEL WINSOR 1733-1758

10. THOMAS BURLINGAME 1733-1764

11. SAMUEL WINSOR, JR. 1759-1771

12. JAMES MANNING 1771-1791

13. JOHN STANFORD 1788-1789

14. JONATHAN MAXCY 1791-1792

15. STEPHEN GANO 1792-1828

16. ROBERT E. PATTISON 1830-1836

17. WILLIAM HAGUE 1837-1840

ROBERT E. PATTISON 1840-1842

18. JAMES N. GRANGER 1842-1857

19. SAMUEL L. CALDWELL 1858-1873

20. EDWARD G. TAYLOR 1875-1881

21. THOMAS EDWIN BROWN 1882-1890

22. HENRY MELVILLE KING 1891-1906

23. ELIJAH ABRAHAM HANLEY 1907-1911

24. JOHN F. VICHERT 1912-1916

25. ALBERT B. COHOE 1916-1920

26. ARTHUR W. CLEAVES 1922-1940

27. ALBERT C. THOMAS 1941-1954

28. HOMER L. TRICKETT 1955-1970

29. ROBERT G. WITHERS 1971-1975

30. RICHARD D. BAUSMAN 1976-1982

31. ORLANDO L. TIBBETTS 1983-1986

32. DWIGHT M. LUNDGREN 1983-1996

33. KATE HARVEY PENFIELD 1987-1995

34. CLIFFORD R. HOCKENSMITH 1997-1999

35. JAMES C. MILLER 2000

OPPOSITE The steeple bell, weighing 2,500 pounds, was imported from England in 1775. It was cracked by being rung too vigorously and was recast by the Hope Furnace of Rhode Island in 1787. It cracked again and was recast by the Henry N. Hooper Company of Boston in 1844. Originally it bore the inscription:

> *For Freedom of conscience the town was planted,*
> *Persuasion, not force, was used by the people.*
> *This church is the oldest and has not recanted.*
> *Enjoying the granting bell, temple and steeple.*

Photo by Warren Jagger (2000).

1 ROGER WILLIAMS (c. 1600/1603-1683) was the minister only a few months. He was certainly gone by July 1639 because Governor John Winthrop of Massachusetts noted that fact in his Journal in July. Richard Scott, one of the men that Williams baptized to start the church confirmed this when he said, "I walked with him in the Baptist way, about three or four months, in which time he broke from the society. . . ." Williams was born in London about 1600-1603, earned his B.A. from Pembroke College, Cambridge, in 1627, and was ordained an Anglican clergyman. But he was denied his M.A. in 1628 for refusing to sign the articles of submission to the bishop, and instead he became the chaplain to Sir William Machem in 1629. He and his wife Mary arrived in Boston in February 1631. After Williams fled from Salem in February 1636, he founded Providence in June 1636 as a refuge for persons "distressed of conscience." He baptized his congregation in late 1638, but resigned from the church within a few months and never again attached himself to any church. In 1644 he published *The Bloudy Tenent of Persecution* and again in 1652 *The Bloudy Tenent Yet More Bloudy*, making his the first voice for religious liberty in America, and he continued to contribute to the debate and controversy of the English Reformation in a series of books and pamphlets over the years. He went to England and secured the first charter for Rhode Island in 1644 and was the chief officer of the colony under the charter from September 1644 to May 1647. When in 1651 William Coddington secured a commission to make himself "Governor for Life" over Portsmouth and Newport, Williams and his friend John Clarke of Newport sailed to England and got Coddington's patent revoked in 1653. In 1654 the four towns (Providence, Newport, Portsmouth and Warwick) of Narragansett Bay were reunited, and Williams served as president from September 1654 to May 1657. In other years Williams served in the General Assembly as a representative from Providence. The exact date of his death in 1683 is not known, but he died between January and May. When the International Monument to the Reformation was created in Geneva, Switzerland, Roger Williams was enshrined as the representative of North America because of his contributions to the principles of religious freedom and separation of church and state.

2 CHAD BROWN (? - before 1650), the founder of the Browns of Rhode Island, served as elder until his death. Although the grave marker, erected by this descendents in 1792 when his body was moved to the North Burial Ground, says, "He died about A.D. 1665," later sources flatly state, "It is evident that he died some years earlier than has been supposed, as the name of his widow occurs in a tax list on Sept. 2, 1650." See Abby Isabel Buckley, *The Chad Browne Memorial, consisting of Genealogical Memories of a Portion of the Descendents of Chad and Elizabeth Browne, 1638-1888* (Brooklyn, 1888), 8, RIHS. Rev. William Hague described Brown as being a man of a "cooler temperament" than Williams, a man who was "highly esteemed as a man of sound judgment and of a Christian spirit. . . an arbitrator of individual differences." See: Hague, *An Historical Discourse Delivered at the Celebration of the Second Centennial Anniversary of the First Baptist Church, in Providence, November 9, 1839* (Providence: B. Cranston, 1839), 8. Brown was born in England and came to Boston in July 1638, and then to Providence "for conscience' sake." He was one of the town proprietors who signed the compact which pledged to subject themselves to orders of the whole, but "only in civil things." He was a surveyor and helped lay out the original home lots on Towne Street. He also served on committees trying to settle the disputes over colonial boundary lines of Providence Plantations. By the late eighteenth century it had become a Brown family tradition that Chad Brown, not Roger Williams, was actually the first pastor of the Baptist church in Providence.

3 THOMAS OLNEY (1600-1682) emigrated to America in 1635, followed Williams to Providence from Salem in 1636,

and was one of those excommunicated in July 1639 by the Salem church for being re-baptized in Providence. Isaac Backus regarded Olney as Williams' immediate successor as pastor. When the church opted to become a Six Principle Baptist church, he led a schismatic group out of the Providence church in 1652 and continued as the minister of that group until his death in 1682. His son Thomas, Jr., continued as the elder of the splinter group until he rejoined the main stem by 1718. See: James H. Olney, *A Genealogy of the Descendents of Thomas Olney, an Original Proprietor of Providence, R.I., who Came from England in 1635* (Providence, 1889), 10-12, RIHS; Howard Chapin, "Our Rhode Island Ancestors," #134, RIHS. As the genealogical entry says, Olney was one of the original proprietors of the town and was its first Treasurer; Isaac Backus, *A History of New England with Particular Reference to the Baptists* (New York: Arno Press, 1969, reprint of 1871 edition), I: 92, 405; II: 285, 490.

4 WILLIAM WICKENDEN (? - February 23, 1670) was born in England, came to Providence from Salem in 1639, ordained by Chad Brown in 1642, and his ministry continued officially until his death in 1670. However, he had moved off to "Solitary Hill" (in the Olneyville section of present-day Providence) around 1650 and his presence in the church was intermittent. He was one of the leaders in stressing the need for the laying-on-of-hands, and he helped to establish the Second Baptist Church of Newport in 1656, the second Six Principle Baptist church in Rhode Island. Later that year he was imprisoned by the Dutch authorities in the New Netherlands (New York) for four months for preaching and then was expelled. He was described as "a cobbler from Rhode Island" who "stated that he was commissioned by Christ. He began to preach at Flushing [Vlissingen] and then went with the people into the river and dipped them." Quoted in Albert Henry Newman, *A History of the Baptist Churches in the United States* (Philadelphia: American Baptist Publication Society, 1898), 233. For the report of Wickenden in New Netherlands, see the letters of Rev. Johannes Megapolensis and Rev. Samuel Drisius to the Classis of Amsterdam, August 5 and October 25, 1657, *Narratives of New Netherland, 1609-1664 in Original Narratives of Early American History*, edited by James Franklin Jamison (New York: Charles Scribner's Sons, 1909), 397, 400. Also see: *List of Members* (1832), 8; Chapin, "Our Rhode Island Ancestors," #46, RIHS; William Hague, *An Historical Discourse* (1839), 97-98.

5 GREGORY DEXTER (1610-1700), born in London, was a Baptist preacher in England before he returned with Roger Williams in 1644. He quickly associated himself with the Baptist church and was ordained an elder in 1654 after William Wickenden moved away about 1650. He, too, was a leader in making the Providence church into a Six Principle Baptist church, and he helped establish the Second Baptist Church in Newport as a Six Principle church. At various times Dexter served as commissioner and town clerk of Providence and president of Providence and Warwick from May 1653 to May 1654, during the period when William Coddington of Newport secured a charter to make himself "Governor for Life" over Newport and Portsmouth. See: S.C. Newman, *Gregory Dexter, being a record of the Family Descendents from Rev. Gregory Dexter* (Providence: A. Crawford Green, 1859), 9; "Dexter Family: Genealogical Material on Rev. Gregory Dexter," n.p., RIHS; "Genealogy of Rev. Gregory Dexter, prepared by Hannah Smith Hammond," 3, RIHS; Howard Guild, *Ancestry of Calvin Guild, et al.* (Salem Press, 1891), 32; "Baptists Beneficiaries of 'Statue' Account," *Providence Journal* (n.d., 1970) in FBC Scrapbook (1960s-1973); Hague, *An Historical Discourse*, 97-98.

6 PARDON TILLINGHAST (1622-January 29, 1718), was born in Severn Cliffs, near Beechy Head, in Sussex County, England, and is said to have served in Oliver Cromwell's army. In 1643 he emigrated to Connecticut, came to Providence in

1645 and was admitted as a freeman in 1658. He lived in Newport from 1663 to 1667, returning then to Providence. He was noted for his "plainness and piety." A leader of the Six Principle Baptists, he was ordained an elder in 1681 and served as pastor until 1718. Roger Williams himself in 1672 described Tillinghast as "a leading man among the people called Baptists, at Providence." See: Williams in *George Fox Digg'd out of his Burrow* in *Publications of the Narragansett Club*, V: 320. Tillinghast was one of only five Rhode Islanders who authored a printed work before 1700, writing *Water Baptism Plainly Proved by Scripture to be a Gospel Precept* (printed 1689). In 1700 he purchased a piece of land 30 feet square and constructed the first meeting house for the Baptist church on it. He deeded it to the members in 1711. A cooper by trade, he became a shopkeeper, shipowner, and prosperous trader in coastal commerce after King Philip's War and built the first wharf and warehouse in Providence around 1680. He served as Overseer of the Poor in 1687, six terms in the Rhode Island General Assembly between 1672 and 1700, seventeen terms on the Providence Town Council between 1688 and 1707, and town treasurer 1707-1711. See Howard M. Chapin, "Our Rhode Island Ancestors," #137, RIHS; and Rose Tillinghast, *The Tillinghast Family, 1560-1971* (privately printed, 1972), 9-11; William R. Tillinghast, "Genealogy of the Tillinghast Family: Male Lines" (typescript, presented to RIHS by James A. Tillinghast, April 15, 1942); John Avery Tillinghast and Frederick Wheaton Tillinghast, *A Little Journey to the Home of Elder Pardon Tillinghast* (Providence: Standard Printing Co., 1908).

7 EBENEZER JENCKES (1669-August 4, 1726) was born in Pawtucket (first native-born pastor), and he was described thus: "He was a man of parts and real piety. He refused every public office except the surveyorship of the property of Providence, which required no great attention or time." Morgan Edwards, "Materials for a History of the Baptists in Rhode Island," *Collections of the Rhode Island Historical Society*, (1867), IV: 322. His brother Joseph was the first governor of the colony from Providence (1727-1732) since May 1657. See: William B. Browne, *Genealogy of the Jenks Family of America* (Concord, NH: Rumford Press, 1952), 24; "A Short Sketch of the Family of Jenckses," (privately printed, Frank Wilder, 1926), RIHS. The Jenckes brothers favored relaxing the requirement of laying on of hands.

8 JAMES BROWN (1661-October 28, 1732), born in Providence, was the grandson of Chad Brown. His father, John Brown, was described by Moses Brown as a "preacher but not an elder." See: Moses Brown's letter to Francis Wayland, May 25, 1833, in Reuben Guild, *History of Brown University, with Illustrative Documents* (Providence: Providence Press, 1867), 208. See: Bulkley, *Chad Browne Memorial*. Brown wanted to relax the requirement of laying-on-of-hands, and the church almost suffered another split over the issue. Deacon Samuel Winsor and others even met separately for a while, but an agreement was signed on May 25, 1732, in which it was stated that the ritual of laying-on-of-hands would be strictly observed in the church; see: Guild, *Early History of Brown University*, 210.

9 SAMUEL WINSOR (November 18, 1677-November 17, 1758), born in Providence, was the son of another Samuel Winsor and grandson of Joshua Winsor who married Mercy Williams, daughter of Roger Williams, making him the great-grandson of Roger Williams. He believed in strict adherence to the ritual of laying-on-of-hands before a new member could be admitted to communion. He prevented the church from relaxing its position in the 1730s. See: Kay Kirlin Moore, *Descendents of Roger Williams: The Winsor Line through his daughter, Mercy Williams* (Greenville, RI, 1987), I:1, RIHS.

10 THOMAS BURLINGAME (May 29, 1688 -January 7, 1770), born in Cranston, "was ordained at the same time with Mr. [Samuel] Winsor, but in a measure resigned his care of the

church, a considerable time before his death, in order to preach to a new church in Cranston." See: *A List of Members* (1832), 10. See also: *Burlingame Manuscript*, I: 21, RIHS. Burlingame helped to found a Six Principle Baptist church in Cranston in 1764. Morgan Edwards said that a congregation had developed in the 1740s, but did not constitute itself as a church until 1764; see: Edwards, "Materials for a History of the Baptists in Rhode Island," 347. See also: Samuel Winsor mss, John Hay Library, Brown University for letter from a number of signers stating that they were forming a Six Principle church in Cranston under the care of Elder Burlingame, May 20, 1764; and another letter, dated June 18, 1764, requesting permission to settle a church in Cranston under Burlingame.

11 SAMUEL WINSOR, JR. (November 1, 1722-January 26, 1803), was born in Providence, but his farm was several miles distant in present-day Johnston and it became increasingly difficult for him to minister to those members of the congregation who lived near the meeting house on Towne Street (now North Main). Moore, *Descendents of Roger Williams: The Winsor Line*, 8. He was a prosperous farmer who gave seventy-five acres of land, worth about $150, toward the erection of the College Edifice in Providence, and he was one of the college trustees who supported the location of the college in Providence. See: Reuben Aldrich Guild, *Early History of Brown University, including the Life, Times, and Correspondence of President Manning, 1756-1791* (Providence: Snow & Farnham, 1897), footnote, 213. After Winsor withdrew from the Providence church, he founded a Six Principle Baptist church in Johnston, and the present-day Graniteville Baptist Church traces its roots to that source. Winsor continued as an official trustee of the college until 1791, but never attended a meeting of the Corporation after 1770. He is buried in the family plot in Johnston off Winsor Road.

12 JAMES MANNING (October 22, 1738-July 29, 1791), born in Elizabethtown, NJ, graduated from Princeton in 1762. He was awarded the honorary degree, Doctor of Divinity, by the University of Pennsylvania in 1785. He was founder and first president of Brown University and founder of the Warren Baptist Association. Manning was frequently absent owing to his duties as president of Brown and other activities, such as serving in the Confederation Congress while trying to get Congress to pay for damages that University Hall suffered while being used by the army during the Revolution. In fact, Manning sometimes regarded his appointment as pastor *pro tempore* and urged the church to get another minister. See, Reuben Aldrich Guild, *Early History of Brown University, including the Life, Times, and Correspondence of President Manning, 1756-1791* (Providence: Snow & Farnham, 1897), 217. He expressed this in letters in 1786 and 1788, but he did not preach a farewell sermon until April 1791. He wrote in 1786, "I ever declined the pastoral care of the church as quite incompatible with my engagements to the College, though I have preached, administered ordinances, visited the sick, attended funerals, etc., for the last fifteen years, without assistance." Letter printed in Guild, *Early History of Brown University*, 428. All early church records clearly regarded Manning as the full and permanent pastor, and they voted to pay him £50. He required that they pay him, and he was the first paid minister in the history of the church. All the previous pastors, especially the Six Principle Baptists, regarded the paying of ministers to be simony. According to Isaac Backus, Manning died "in a fit of apoplexy." See: Backus, *A History of New England* II: 493.

13 JOHN STANFORD (October 20, 1754-January 14, 1834), was born in Wandsworth, Surrey, England. A wealthy uncle placed John in a private boarding school from age 10 to 16, but disinherited him when he fell away from the Church of England. Raised an Anglican, he had a conversion experience about 1772 when he was 17 years old and was baptized by immersion. He united with the Baptist church at Maze-Pond in

London and was soon licensed and ordained. His one settled church in England was at Hammersmith, which he served for a few years. He emigrated in January 1786, arriving in Norfolk, Virginia, on April 16, but he moved on to New York in November and opened an academy. He occasionally preached and sometimes assisted John Gano, pastor of the First Baptist Church in New York. He accepted a call to Providence in the spring of 1788, only to be dismissed in September 1789 because of the letter charging him with immoral conduct in England. In that year, Brown had elected him to be a trustee and conferred upon him the Master of Arts. In 1829-1830 Union College in Schenectady honored him with the Doctor of Divinity. The accusation which cost Stanford his position as pastor of FBC, namely that he was guilty of "sodomical practices," was certainly false. In 1802 he forced the retraction of an unnamed libel, adding that a letter from London "calculated to ruin the character of the Reverend John Stanford" was not true. The fact that he continued in the ministry and gained prominence in New York indicates that he overcame the slander. He returned to New York in 1789 and reopened his academy, which remained his principal source of livelihood until he was hired as chaplain for several public institutions. In 1813 he was appointed chaplain of the State Prison and retained this until the prison was moved upstate to Ossining in 1829. Also in 1813 he was appointed chaplain of the Alms House and City Hospital. In addition he ministered to the inmates and residents in the Orphan Asylum, Bridewell Penitentiary, Debtors' Prison, the Lunatic Asylum, and the House of Refuge for Juvenile Delinquents. Declining health and numerous ailments forced him to retire about one year before he died, at age 79, on January 14, 1834. See: Rev. Enoch Hutchinson, "Biographical Sketch of Rev. John Stanford, D.D." *The Baptist Memorial and Monthly Record* [New York], (April 1849), 105-110, courtesy of the American Baptist Historical Society [ABHS]. The libel retraction is found in a deposition by Francis Davis, New York, May 28, 1802, courtesy of the ABHS. Stanford attempted to write a history of the early pastors of the Providence church, and while it has some gross errors, it is still useful. The manuscript is included in the earliest FBC records at the RIHS. The account of his life that appears in Sprague's *Annals of the American Pulpit* was written by Stanford's son and gave no hint of the trouble in Providence: "His sojourn in Providence seems to have been equally agreeable to himself and the people, and his ministry was crowned with a large measure of success." (246). However, this account went on to say that Stanford returned to New York in November 1789, that he reopened his academy, but that "a severe mental affliction, shortly after this overtook him." He came to doubt his faith and the Scriptures, and it took him five months to recover. See: William B. Sprague, editor, *Annals of the American Pulpit*, Vol. VI: *The Baptists* (New York: Robert Carter & Brothers, 1865), 244-249.

14 JONATHAN MAXCY (September 2, 1768-June 4, 1820), born in Attleboro, MA, graduated as valedictorian from Rhode Island College [now Brown University] in 1787, and was appointed tutor in the college, which he held until he was chosen pastor of FBC. He was licensed to the ministry by FBC, April 1, 1790, and assumed the pastorate in 1791, only to resign in one year to become the second president of Brown from 1792 to 1802. Harvard conferred the Doctor of Divinity upon him in 1801. Then he became president of Union College in Schenectady (1802-1804) and South Carolina College until he died in 1820. See: Samuel Caldwell and William Gammell, *History of the First Baptist Church in Providence, 1639-1877* (Providence: J.A. & R.A. Reid, Printers, 1877), 15; Guild, *Early History of Brown University*, footnote, 447.

15 STEPHEN GANO (December 25, 1762-August 18, 1828), was born in New York, son of Rev. John Gano and nephew of James Manning. After studying medicine with his uncle, Dr. John Stites at Cranberry, NJ, he was appointed at age seventeen a surgeon's mate in the army in 1779. He resigned from the

army and signed on a privateer, was shipwrecked, later captured and marooned on an island with thirty other men without provisions. Several starved before they were rescued. On the return voyage to Philadelphia, the ship was captured and Gano was condemned to a prison ship — he bore the mark of the ankle fetter for the rest of his life. He experienced a conversion in 1783 and was ordained to the ministry in 1786. The ordination sermon was preached in his father's church by James Manning. He served churches at Hillsdale and Hudson, New York. In 1789-1790 he travelled west to visit his father, who had moved to Kentucky. While there he helped to organize the church at Columbia, Ohio, the first Baptist church established in the Northwest Territory. He declined to become their permanent minister and travelled instead with his father among churches of Kentucky and North Carolina. In 1792 he was called to the Providence church. He was described as "tall, of large form and fine appearance, save for a wig, which might bring a smile to the observer until he learned that the loss of hair. . . [was] the direct result of the privation and sickness undergone in the prison ship. . . ." Augustine S. Carman, "The Story of Stephen Gano," *Watchman Examiner* (August 8, 1918), 1021. The wig mentioned here was not a formal wig of the sort that Manning wore in the pulpit, but an everyday wig to cover his baldness.

16 ROBERT E. PATTISON (August 19, 1800-November 21, 1874), born in Benson, VT, second son of a Baptist minister, the Rev. William Pattison, graduated from Amherst College in 1826. He received the Doctor of Divinity from Brown University in 1838. In addition to pastorates at Second Baptist Church in Salem, MA (1829-30) and First Baptist in Providence (1830-36, 1840-42), Second Baptist Church in St. Louis (1839-40), he served as corresponding secretary for the Home Department of the Baptist Board of Foreign Missions (1842-45). He had a notable career as an educator as well, serving as a tutor at Columbian College [now George Washington University], 1827-28; professor of mathematics and natural philosophy at Waterville College [now Colby College], 1828-1829; twice president of Waterville College, 1836-39, 1854-57; president of the new Western Baptist Theological Institution at Covington, KY, 1845-1848, until the slavery controversy closed the institution; chairman of Christian Theology at Newton Theological Institution, 1848-54; director of the Oread Institute for Young Ladies (Worcester, MA), 1857-64; professor of systematic theology at Shurtleff College (Alton, IL), 1864-1870; and finally vice president and acting president of the Theological Seminary of the West (Chicago), 1870-1872. He died in St. Louis in 1874. It is of particular interest to First Baptist in Providence to note that when Pattison was called to Shurtleff College, the school had "no funds and no buildings, nothing but students and work. But Dr. Pattison loved work for the Master, and he gave a willing ear to the proposal. His old friends in Providence promised to sustain him until endowments could be secured." That was almost twenty-five years after he left Providence. See: E.C. Mitchell, "Biographical Sketch of Dr. Pattison," *The Standard* [Chicago], December 10, 1874, Colby College Special Collections. For a history of his two terms at Colby College, see: Ernest Cummings Marriner, *The History of Colby College* (Waterville: Colby College Press, 1963), 91-93, 140-142; Edwin Carey Whittemore, *Colby College, 1820-1925: An Account of Its Beginnings, Progress and Service* (Waterville: The Trustees of Colby College, 1927), 62-78.

17 WILLIAM HAGUE (January 4, 1808-August 1, 1887), born in Pelham, Westchester County, New York, the son of a ship's captain in the East Indies trade. His grandfather was a Baptist minister in England, and his father was a sometime lay preacher and superintendent of a Sunday school. Hague was baptized in 1825, graduated from Hamilton College in 1826, studied at Princeton Theological Seminary (1826-1827), and graduated from Newton Theological Institution in 1829. He was honored with the Doctor of Divinity from Brown in 1849

and by Harvard in 1863. He became a trustee of Brown in 1837 and a Vassar trustee in 1861. Having graduated from Newton, he was called by the First Baptist Church of Providence, but he declined it for a church in Utica which he had come to know while a student at Hamilton. He was ordained October 20, 1829, and served as pastor of the Second Baptist Church of Utica in 1829-1830. He resigned because of a throat condition and accepted a professorship of Latin and Greek at Georgetown College, Kentucky. His throat problem healed, and he accepted the pastorship of he First Baptist Church of Boston, where Francis Wayland preached the installation sermon in January 1831. In 1837 he came to Providence "at the urgent solicitation of Dr. Wayland and the First Baptist Church." He was absent in Europe for nine months in 1838-39. He left in August 1840 for the Federal Street Baptist Church in Boston which he served until 1848 when he took the pastorate of the Jamaica Plain Baptist Church in the suburbs of Boston from 1848 to 1850. "Dr. Hague's experimental religion did much to stem the rising tide of error and infidelity which was threatening the religious life of Boston at that time." From 1846 to 1850 Hague also edited *The Watchman and Reflector* in Boston. In April 1850, he went to the South Baptist Church in Newark, NJ, and served until 1853 when he moved on to the Pearl Street Baptist Church [later named Emmanuel Baptist Church] in Albany, NY. In April 1858 he moved again to the Lexington Avenue and Madison Avenue Church in New York City where he served until 1862. He returned to Boston to the Charles Street Baptist Church (1862-1864) and the Shawmut Avenue Baptist Church (1865-1869). He was called to the Baptist theological seminary in Chicago in 1869 to be professor of homiletics, and he pastored the University Place Baptist Church in Chicago (1869-1870). From there he went to the Baptist Church of Orange, New Jersey (1870-1874). He traveled in Europe for the next two years and returned to be the pastor of the Wollaston [MA] Baptist Church (1877-1887). So many pastorates caused Henry Melville King to say, "Dr. Hague conscientiously believed that he could do his best work in short pastorates. The frequent changes were never made to secure personal relief or the relief of the people. . . . His people never wanted him to go." He dropped dead from a stroke near the entrance to the Tremont Temple in Boston on August 1, 1887. Henry Melville King, *Seventy-Five Years of History: Emmanuel Baptist Church* (Albany, New York, 1909), 18-20. He was much in demand because of his powerful preaching style and cheerful, buoyant spirit. "His preaching is more intellectual than practical, and more doctrinal than experimental." *A Souvenir of our Pastor, the Rev. William Hague, D.D.* (Boston: Shawmut Avenue Baptist Church, 1869), 22. A death notice and obituary from the *Providence Journal* were pasted in the front of the Rider Collection copy of Hague's *An Historical Discourse*, John Hay Library, Brown University. Also see: *Appleton's Cyclopedia of American Biography*, (1888), III: 26.

18 JAMES NATHANIEL GRANGER (August 8, 1814-January 5, 1857) was born in Canandaigua, NY. He intended to become an army officer and had an appointment to West Point before a religious conversion in 1831 turned him toward the Christian ministry. He graduated from Hamilton Literary and Theological Institution in 1838. He received the D.D. from Brown University in 1854. He was ordained in 1839 and pastored the Baptist church in Avon, NY, until 1841 when he then became the pastor of the Washington Street Baptist Church in Buffalo until called to Providence in October 1842. He was absent on an official visit of the American Baptist Missionary Union to India from October 16, 1852 to May 4, 1854. He became ill after his return and was able to carry on his pastoral duties only intermittently, and an assistant minister, William Carey Richards, was appointed. He died on January 5, 1857, from "bilious diarrhoea" which the newspapers reported "was thought to have been contracted in the East during an official visit made by him some four years since to the Baptist Missions in the Kingdom of Burmah." He was only forty-two years old. Granger had been president of the Rhode Island Baptist State Convention, president of the Rhode Island Sunday School Union, a member of the board of Newton Theological Institution, and a trustee (1851), fellow (1853), and member of the Executive Board of Brown University. See: *Providence Journal*, January 6, 1857, 2 ; *The Daily Transcript* [Providence], January 6, 1857; Caldwell and Gammell, *History* (1877), 17-18; Francis Wayland, "A Discourse in Commemoration of the Character and Services of Rev. James Nathaniel Granger, D.D., Pastor of the First Baptist Church of Providence, delivered on Sunday January 18, 1857," printed by George H. Whitney, Providence, 1857, bound in *Historical Pamphlets: Rhode Island* in FBCIA Archives, RIHS; also, Rev. Alexis Caswell, "An Address, Delivered at the Funeral of Dr. Granger, On Thursday, Jan. 8, 1857," in *Historical Pamphlets: Rhode Island.*

19 SAMUEL LUNT CALDWELL (November 13, 1820-September 26, 1889) was born in Newburyport, MA, the eldest son of Stephen and Mary (Lunt) Caldwell. He graduated from Waterville College in 1839 and Newton Theological Institution in 1845. He received the D.D. from Waterville College in 1858 and the LL. D. from Brown University in 1884. After graduating from Waterville, he was appointed principal of the Academy at Hampton Falls, NH, and then in May 1840 headmaster of the West Grammar School at Newburyport. After three years of teaching, in November 1842 he entered Newton Theological Institution. The winter after graduation he supplied the pulpit for the Baptist Church of Alexandria, VA. In May 1846 he was called to the First Baptist Church of Bangor, ME, and was ordained to the ministry in August. He remained there twelve years before being called to Providence in 1858. He resigned on August 28, 1873, to become professor of church history at Newton. Five years later he became the president of Vassar College, where he served from 1878 to 1885. His tenure at Vassar came during hard times for the college, and he was forced to resign in the end. Vassar experienced more than a decade of decline which continued right through Caldwell's administration, and he was unable to do anything to arrest the erosion of enrollment. He was basically the wrong man for the time because what the college needed was a vigorous, out-going president who could aggressively spread its message. The official history of Vassar stated, "Dr. Caldwell was constitutionally unfitted for this kind of work. He was a man of modest, diffident spirit, of scholarly habits, accustomed to the pen, to deliberative bodies, to the careful weighing of questions, rather than to the executive realization of ends decided upon. . . . In another period and place his qualities might have shone in the chair of a college executive, but they were not adapted to meet the exigencies of a college that demanded aggressive courage to stay its decline. . . ." He returned to Providence to live his last five years. He served as a trustee of Waterville College from 1850 to 1863 and was a trustee of the Corporation of Brown from 1859 and a member of the Board of Fellows from 1862. He was secretary of the Corporation from 1874 to 1889. He died from septicemia from an internal infection. See: obituary, *Providence Evening Bulletin*, September 27, 1889, 3. The quotation is from James Monroe Taylor and Elizabeth Hazelton Haight, *Vassar* (New York: Oxford University Press, 1915), 144. Also see: *Appleton's Cyclopedia of American Biography*, V:235; *Harper's Weekly*, October 5, 1878; King, *Historical Catalogue*, 6-7.

20 EDWARD GLENN TAYLOR (November 25, 1829 - April 10, 1887), born in Philadelphia, PA, graduated from University of Lewisburg in 1854 and Rochester Theological Seminary in 1856 and was ordained in Terre Haute, IN, in 1857. He held pastorates in Cincinnati and Chicago before going to New Orleans. He was pastor of the Coliseum Place Baptist Church in New Orleans, LA, when called to Providence in 1875. He left Providence in 1881 for the Mount Morris Baptist Church in New York and then had pastorates in Newark, NJ, and Buffalo, NY, where he died. Taylor was a great advocate of Sunday schools and his leadership and support of the Sunday schools at Mt. Pleasant and Wanskuck helped produce the Mt. Pleasant

and Roger Williams Baptist churches He was on the editorial staff of the American Baptist Publication Society for a number of years and prepared notes for the Sunday School Lessons. King, *Historical Catalogue*, 7; *Manual of the First Baptist Church in Providence, August, 1884* (Providence: E.L. Freeman & Co, 1884), 6; "Ministers Deceased," *New York Baptist Annual* (1887), 70.

21 THOMAS EDWIN BROWN (September 26, 1841-January 27, 1924), born in Washington, DC, graduated as valedictorian from Columbian University in 1861, was pastor of the Tabernacle Baptist Church in Brooklyn (1862-1869), and the Second Baptist Church in Rochester (November 1869-1882). After Providence (1882-1890) he went to the Memorial Baptist Church of Philadelphia (1890-1896), First Baptist Church, Franklin, PA (1896-1904), and then to First Baptist in New Britain, CT (1904-1915). While pastor in Philadelphia, he served for a year and a half as chaplain of the University of Pennsylvania. He received a D.D. from the University of Rochester in 1876 and in 1921 the Doctor of Humane Letters from George Washington University [formerly Columbian College]. He died from a heart attack at the home of his daughter in Independence, KS, in 1924. See: obituary, *Independence* [Kansas] *Reporter*, January 27, 1924; King, *Historical Catalogue*, 7; death notice from the *Annual of the New York Baptist State Convention* (1924), 65-66.

22 HENRY MELVILLE KING (September 3, 1838- June 16, 1919) was born in Oxford, ME, baptized in the Free Street Baptist Church in Portland on January 6, 1856, at age 17, and graduated from Bowdoin College with the A.B. in 1859 and A.M. in 1862. That same year he completed his studies at Newton Theological Institution. Colby College awarded him a D.D. in 1877 and Bowdoin gave him a S.T.D. in 1899. Ordained in August 1862 at the Free Street Church, he briefly taught Hebrew at Newton before becoming the pastor of the Dudley Street Baptist Church in Roxbury on April 1, 1863. From there he went in 1882 to the Emmanuel Baptist Church in Albany, NY [formerly the Pearl Street Baptist Church] , and then to Providence in 1891. His pastorate at Providence ended on Easter, April 15, 1906, and he remained as pastor emeritus until his death in 1919. He was chairman of the board of managers of the American Baptist Missionary Union (1884-1887) and member of the executive committee (1874-1882, 1894-1901, 1906-1909); president of the Rhode Island Baptist State Convention (1891-1895), and a trustee of Newton Theological Institution, Vassar College, Hamilton Theological Seminary, Rochester Theological Seminary, Worcester Academy, Hartshorn Memorial College, and Brown University. *Who Was Who*, I: 678; obituary, *Providence Journal*, June 17, 1919, 10; King, *Historical Catalogue*, 7-8; King, *Seventy-Five Years of History: Emmanuel Baptist Church* (Albany, New York,1909), 27; *Dictionary of American Biography*, V: 391.

23 ELIJAH ABRAHAM HANLEY (May 26, 1871- June 22, 1943), born at Prairie Creek, near Terre Haute, IN, graduated from Franklin College in 1895, and was an assistant in rhetoric at Brown University for 1895-96 and received his M.A. in 1896. He was a graduate student at the University of Chicago, 1896-1901. Franklin College awarded him the D.D. in 1903. He pastored the East End Baptist Church in Cleveland from 1901 to 1907 and then served the First Baptist Church in Providence (1907-1911). He was president of Franklin College from 1911 to 1917. From there he became the pastor of the First Baptist Church of Rochester, NY (1917-1921), the First Baptist of Berkeley, CA (1921-1929), and the Park Baptist Church in St. Paul, MN (1929-1936). He was a research student at Union Theological Seminary in New York in 1936-1938 and then at the University of Chicago in 1938. He kept himself occupied by temporarily filling vacant pulpits in Minneapolis and St. Louis. After the death of Arthur Cleaves, Hanley briefly returned as interim minister at First Baptist Church in America from April 1 to July 3, 1941, but failing health forced him to give up the position. He moved to Berkeley, CA, and rejoined his former church. He died of a coronary thrombosis on June 22, 1943, in Soda Bay, CA. See: John F. Cady, *Centennial History of Franklin College* (1934), 170-181, from Franklin College Library; also see: *Providence Sunday Journal*, August 4, 1907; *The Watchman-Examiner*, July 18, 1907; *Providence Sunday Journal*, April 24, 1938; Church Calendars, February 16, 1941, July 6, 1941; *Who Was Who*, Vol. 5. (*Who's Who* has his name wrong, calling him Elijah *Andrews* Hanley.) *The Watchman-Examiner*, July 29, 1943, 715, announced his death, but had the wrong date. The date of death was June 22, 1943: see Certificate of Death from State of California.

24 JOHN FREDERICK VICHERT (August 10, 1874-January 17, 1948) was born in Gobles, Ontario, Canada, graduated from Woodstock College, Ontario, and received his M.A. (1898) and B.D. (1904) from McMaster University in Toronto. Franklin College honored him with a D.D. in 1912, and McMaster awarded him the D.D. in 1919. Ordained in 1899, he was the pastor of the Calvary Baptist Church in Victoria, British Columbia, from 1899 to 1904. Then he pastored the First Baptist Church of Fort Wayne, IN, from 1906 to 1912. After serving in Providence (1912-16), he became dean of Colgate Theological Seminary (1916-23) and then a professor at Rochester Theological Seminary in 1923. He continued when the two seminaries merged in 1928 and retired in 1940. He served as president of the New York State Baptist Convention from 1921 to 1924. A strong supporter of prohibition, he was the New York gubernatorial candidate of the Law Preservation Party in 1932. He moved to Florida in 1943 after retirement and lived there five years before he died of a heart attack. See: undated 1948 obituary in FBC Scrapbook, RIHS; *Who Was Who*, Vol. 2; *Colgate-Rochester Divinity School Bulletin*, April 1948.

25 ALBERT BEDELL COHOE (August 19, 1877-October 17, 1966) was born in North Norwich, Ontario, Canada, and earned his B.A.(1896) and M.A.(1899) from McMaster University. He was awarded the honorary D.D. from McMaster in Toronto and from Acadia University in Wolfville, Nova Scotia. He was also awarded an honorary D.D. by Brown University in 1929. He was ordained in 1901 and pastored the Baptist church in Grimsby, Ontario. He soon resigned and went to the University of Chicago where he remained for six months. He then was called to the Brussel Street Baptist Church in St. John, New Brunswick, and remained there for six years. Next he accepted a call to the First Baptist Church of Halifax, Nova Scotia, before coming to Providence in 1916. The First Baptist Church of Montclair, New Jersey, offered a call to him in 1919, but he declined and remained in Providence for another year. Montclair refused to withdraw the call, and he went to serve them in 1920. Cohoe said that when he received the call the second time, he discussed it with President William Faunce of Brown who advised him that FBC had no future. He remained the pastor of the First Baptist Church of Montclair, NJ, from 1920 until he retired in September 1947. He once sought to retire in 1934, but the church refused to accept his resignation, and he stayed on for another thirteen years. Upon retirement he returned to Canada, where he died in Barrie, Ontario in 1966. See: Obituary, *The Montclair* [New Jersey] *Times*, October 20, 1966; obituary: *Providence Journal*, October 23, 1966; Death Note: *Barrie Banner*, October 27,1966, 6; *The First Baptist Church, Montclair, New Jersey: A Brief Story of Its Beginnings and its Growth, 1886-1936* [50th anniversary history], courtesy of the Montclair Public Library; *75th Anniversary Program of First Baptist Church, Montclair, 1961*, courtesy of FBC, Montclair, NJ. The conversation with Faunce is recalled in an undated, typed biographical sketch written by Cohoe in retirement; FBC mss, Box 2, "Writings of the Pastors," RIHS.

26 ARTHUR W. CLEAVES (March 20, 1876-October 12, 1940) was born in Boston but grew up in Maine. He graduated from Coburn Classical Institute in Waterville, ME, and received his A.B. from Colby College in 1894. Colby awarded him a D.D. in 1920. He received his B.D. from Newton Theological Institution in 1901 and served as pastor of the First Baptist Church of North Scituate, MA, from 1901 to 1906. He then became the pastor of the First Baptist Church of Newburyport from 1906 to 1920. In addition, from 1910 to 1920 he was on the editorial staff of the *Newburyport News* and the *Gloucester Times*. From 1920 to 1922 he was the editor of *The Baptist* [Chicago], a weekly denominational newspaper for the Northern Baptist Convention. He accepted the call to FBC in 1922 and was president of the American Baptist Foreign Mission Society in 1935 and 1936. In 1928 "he engaged in a protracted debate with M.R. Ellis," who had written an essay arguing that Roger Williams was never a Baptist. Cleaves also was a trustee of Andover-Newton Theological School. Governor Norman Case (a member of his church) appointed Cleaves to be Rhode Island's representative to two international conferences in 1929. Cleaves died at the Brown-Cornell football game on October 12, 1940. See: front page obituary in *Providence Sunday Journal*, October 13, 1940; *Who Was Who*, I: 229.

27 ALBERT C. THOMAS (May 2, 1886-January 15, 1969) was born in Henzada, Burma, a son and grandson of Baptist missionaries, and he returned to the United States when he was ten years old. He graduated from Wakefield (MA) High School, received his B.A. from Brown University in 1908, and his B.D. from Newton Theological Institution in 1911. In 1931 Brown University awarded him a D.D. From 1908 to 1910, while in seminary, he was the director of religious education and assistant pastor at the Farm and Trades School on Thompson's Island in Boston Harbor. In 1910 he became the educational director at the First Baptist Church in Brookline, MA, and then to FBCIA in 1911 as educational director under E.A. Hanley. In 1912 he went to Second Baptist in St. Louis as educational director and then in 1916 to the Emmanuel Baptist Church in Brooklyn as educational director. During World War I, as a captain, he served as chaplain to the 306th Field Artillery and spent a year overseas with the unit. Ordained in 1920, he was the pastor of the Charleston Avenue Baptist Church in New York City from 1920 to 1927. At the same time he was a Protestant chaplain at New York University. From 1927 to 1941 he was pastor of the First Baptist Church of Fall River, MA, before coming to Providence. After a ministry of thirteen years at FBCIA, he left in 1954 for the pulpit of the First Baptist Church of Rockport, MA. After retiring in 1960, he moved back to Rhode Island and was named minister emeritus of FBCIA in December 1960.

Active in denominational affairs, Thomas was president of the Southern New York Association (1924-25); president of the New York State Baptist Ministers' Conference (1924-26); president of the New York City Baptist Ministers' Conference, (1926-27); member of the Board of Directors of the New York State Baptist Convention (1923-26); president of the Massachusetts Baptist State Convention in 1935; member of the Board of Directors of the New England Baptist Conference (1928-38) and of the Massachusetts Baptist State Convention (1938-40). He served on the National Board of the American Baptist Foreign Mission Society (1928-37), and was chairman of the Program Committee of the Northern Baptist Convention from 1942 to 1944. He served as a member of the Executive Committee of the Federal Council of Churches from 1940 to 1950. He was a trustee of Newton Theological Institution from 1928 on and became a trustee of Brown (1942-46) and then a member of the Board of Fellows and Executive Committee of the Corporation of Brown University from 1946. Compiled from various biographical items and undated clipping from *Providence Journal* in the FBC papers at RIHS and from *Who's Who in America*, Vol 29, (1956-57). The obituary in the *Providence Bulletin*, January 16,1969, contained a number of errors.

28 HOMER LEROY TRICKETT (October 5, 1913-) was born in rural West Virginia near Independence. His father was a farmer, and Homer was one of eleven children. He attended grammar school at Engleside School and graduated from Newburgh High School. He entered college intending to be an engineer and was graduated *magna cum laude* from Salem College (WV) with an A.B. in 1936. He entered Crozier Seminary in Chester, PA, and was graduated with the B.D. in 1939 and the Th.M. in 1940. In four years he completed all course requirements for the Ph.D. at the University of Pennsylvania, but decided not to write the thesis because the churches in West Virginia, where he expected to minister, were generally opposed to too much education in their ministers. Brown University awarded him the D.D. in 1958. He was pastor of the Prospect Hill Baptist Church in Prospect Park, PA (1940-49), and the First Baptist Church of Reading, PA (1949-55) before coming to Providence in 1955. In 1970 he left to become the pastor of the the First-Park Baptist Church of Plainfield, NJ, where he served until his retirement in 1979. He returned to Providence, resumed his membership in FBCIA, served as interim pastor in four churches and was part-time associate minister at Phillips Memorial Baptist Church in Cranston from 1985 to 1997.

While pastor of FBCIA, Trickett served as president of the Rhode Island Baptist State Convention (1965), president of the State Council of Churches (1968), one of the three non-Catholic members of the Commission on Ecumenism of the Roman Catholic Diocese of Providence in 1967, and a member of the board of the Historical Society of the American Baptist Convention. Interview with Homer Trickett, March 14, 1988. See also: Rhode Island State Council of Churches, *Council Highlights*, September 8, 1970, 3; undated clipping from *Providence Journal*, 1970, and *Watchman Examiner*, April 4, 1957, in Scrapbooks of FBC, RIHS.

29 ROBERT GORDON WITHERS (September 9, 1927 - March 24, 1995) was born in Cameron, West Virginia, and graduated from Alderson-Broaddus College with a B.A. in 1949 and Colgate-Rochester Divinity School with the B.D. in 1954. His grandfather, A. B. Withers, and father, Gordon L. Withers, were both American Baptist ministers in West Virginia, and his younger brother, William, was a pastor there. His twin brother Richard was a professor at Alderson-Broaddus. At first, Robert did not intend to enter the ministry, and studied electrical engineering as an undergraduate. His first pastorates were six mountain churches in Petersburg, WV, which he served from 1953 to 1956, followed by Emmanuel Baptist Church in Albany, NY (1956-1963). He was the pastor of Tabernacle Baptist Church in Utica, NY (1963-1971) before coming to Providence. He left in 1975 to become the minister of the First Baptist Church in Morgantown, WV, which he served until 1981. From 1981 to 1986 he pastored the University Baptist and Brethren Church at State College, PA, and resigned to enter the D. Min. program at Colgate-Rochester Divinity School, in order to become a pipe organ consultant to churches. He completed graduate study for the D. Min. at Colgate-Rochester in 1990. Though retired from the active service as an American Baptist minister, he was minister of St. John's United Church of Christ in McEwensville, PA, from 1987 to 1994, when he became ill with cancer. In his last year he served the First Baptist Church of Lewisburg as technical consultant for their organ restoration project.

He served on the Board of Managers of the New York Baptist Convention, chaired their committee on social concerns (5 years), and was a member of the convention's committees on higher education and urban ministries. He chaired the resolutions committee for the American Baptist Convention (1967) and was a member of the legislative committee of the New York State Council of Churches for fourteen years. He was a member of the Board of Directors of the Rhode Island State Council of Churches and chaired their Long-Range Planning Committee.

He served as the moderator of the Centre Association, ABC, in Pennsylvania, and was vice-chairman of the Board of United Ministries at Pennsylvania State University. He was president of the Roger Williams Fellowship of American Baptists, 1979-1985. His interest in social concerns led him to membership on the board of directors of Planned Parenthood in Albany, Utica, and Providence, the Women's Center for West Virginia University, Chaplaincy Services for the West Virginia University Medical Center, United Way in Utica and Morgantown, and Family Health Services, Centre County (PA). See: Letter from Robert G. Withers to J. Stanley Lemons, July 26, 1988, and resumé, dated 1985, in folder marked "Research Notes for 350-FBC: Notes on Pastors," FBC mss, RIHS. See also: *Providence Evening Bulletin*, October 23, 1971; obituary, *Providence Sunday Journal*, March 26, 1995, B: 10.

30 RICHARD D. BAUSMAN (June 16, 1936-), was born in Dayton, Ohio, and received his B.A. (1958) and M.A. (1959) from Miami University, Ohio, and the B.D. (later upgraded to M. Div.) from Colgate-Rochester Divinity School in 1962. In 1984 he received his D.Min. from Andover-Newton Theological School. He served as assistant minister at the First Baptist Church in Dayton, OH (1962-1964) before becoming a university chaplain with the United Ministry at Cornell University, Cortland Community College, and Ithaca College from 1964 to 1972. He also taught at Cortland Community College from 1968 to 1973. He was pastor of the United Baptist Church in Lewiston, ME, from 1972 to 1976 before coming to FBCIA. He was dismissed by FBCIA in May 1982 and served as pastor of the North Baptist Church, Port Chester, NY, from June 1983 until he became director of the United Christian Center in Columbus, OH, beginning in September 1984. He also served as executive secretary of the Campus Ministry Association from 1984 to 1998 when he returned as pastor to the place of his first employment, the First Baptist Church of Dayton, OH. See: curriculum vita submitted to the Pulpit Committee, 1976; telephone interview, January 17, 2001.

31 ORLANDO TIBBETTS (April 9, 1919 -) was born in Portland, ME, grew up in Boston, received the A.B. from Gordon College (1940), and the B.D. (1943), S.T.M. (1952), and D.Min. (1973) from Andover-Newton Theological School. In addition, Rio Grande College awarded him a D.D. in 1956. He was pastor of the Trenton Street Baptist Church in Boston (1940-46), the founder, professor, and president of the Baptist Seminary in Mexico City, Mexico (1946-53), and pastor of the First Baptist Church of Barberton, OH (1953-58) and Lakewood Baptist Church in Ohio (1958-63) before becoming the city executive secretary of American Baptist Churches in Boston in 1963. In 1970 he became the executive minister of American Baptist Churches of Connecticut. He retired in 1982 and then served as interim executive minister of the American Baptist Churches of Rhode Island during 1982-1983 before receiving the call to FBCIA in 1983. After three years he retired again and moved to Tavares, Florida, and then to Penney Farms. See: Installation Program of Tibbetts and Lundgren, November 20, 1983; curriculum vita in folder "Research Notes for 350-FBC: Notes on Pastors."

32 DWIGHT LUNDGREN (June 20, 1944-), was born in Methodist General Hospital in Brooklyn, NY, and grew up in Connecticut. He was graduated with the B.A. *cum laude* from Trinity College (Hartford) in 1966 and the B.D. *cum laude* from Yale Divinity School in 1969, followed by another year of study in the Graduate School of Yale University. While his grandfather had been a minister in the Baptist General Conference [Swedish Baptist], the grandfather did not influence Lundgren's decision to enter the ministry. Instead he attributed this decision to the inspiring example of Richard B. Hardy, his pastor in West Hartford. His first pastorate was the First Baptist Church of

Shelton, CT (1970-75), followed by the First Baptist Church of Branford, CT (1975-83), and then to Providence. After a ministry of 13 1/2 years, Lundgren left to become the pastor of the First Baptist Church of Philadelphia, PA, beginning February 1, 1996. He finished his ministry at Philadelphia on February 7, 1999, and began the next day as the director of Reconciliation Ministries with the Board of National Ministries of ABC/USA.

He chaired a number of committees and programs for the American Baptist Churches of Connecticut (ABC/CONN). In 1987-1988 he chaired the Planning Committee of the 350th Celebration of the American Baptist Churches of Rhode Island (ABCORI) and the American Baptist Churches of the United States of America (ABC/USA), which resulted in the "Faith and Freedom Conference" in Providence June 5-7, 1988, to mark the beginnings of Baptists in America. The conference was co-sponsored and planned with the Baptist Joint Committee on Public Affairs, Washington, DC, and a number of other Baptist denominations and historical organizations. After 1987 Lundgren chaired the Providence Intown Churches Association, a consortium of nine churches working on central city social issues with a budget of over $60,000. In 1988-89 he was president of the American Baptist Ministers' Council of ABCORI, and after 1989 he served as chairman of the Standing Committee on the Ordained Ministry for ABCORI, which has oversight of all issues related to discipline, ministerial ethics and standards. Interview with Lundgren, March 15, 1988; and publicity statement in the current files of FBC, March 20, 1988; updated, December 8, 1993; December 27, 1995; March 1999.

33 CAROLE "KATE" HARVEY PENFIELD (March 9, 1943 -) was born in Elmira, NY, and grew up there. She earned her B.A. in 1965 from the State University of New York at Albany. She moved with her husband to Cincinnati where she received the M.Ed. in counselling from the University of Cincinnati in 1967. She was a high school French teacher in 1965-1966 and worked as an employment counsellor for International Business Associates in Cincinnati from 1969 to 1970. She came to Providence when her husband became a vice president at Rhode Island College, and she embarked on a second career by entering the ministry and earning the M. Div. from Andover-Newton Theological School in 1981. She subsequently received a D. D. from Central Baptist Seminary in 1996. She served as associate pastor (1981-85) and co-pastor (1985-87) of Central Baptist Church of Providence and Protestant chaplain and instructor in the sociology of religion at Bryant College (1981-84). She was appointed minister by FBCIA, beginning May 1, 1987 and served until June 30, 1995. She was quite active in denominational affairs and held a number of significant offices, including editor of *The Minister*, the ABC/USA Ministers Council journal (1986-89); member of the Executive Committee of the Ministers Council of ABC/USA (1986-95); member of the National Commission on the Ministry of ABC/USA (1986-87); ABC/USA Advocacy Project (1988-90); Eastern Commission on the Ministry (1986-87), president of the Ministers' Council of ABCORI (1982-84) and senator of the Council (1985-86); vice president (1986-87) and president (1987-89) of the Rhode Island State Council of Churches; member of the Standing Committee on the Ordained Ministry (1982-1993) and the Board of Managers of ABCORI (1982-84). She was the national vice-president of ABC/USA (1993-95) and resigned as pastor of FBCIA to become the executive director of the Ministers Council of ABC/USA. She was a member of the first class in 1981 to go through Leadership Rhode Island, a training project of the Greater Providence Chamber of Commerce, and served on the Board of Directors of Leadership Rhode Island for a number of years after 1986. Divorced in 1994, she resumed her maiden name of Harvey on January 4, 1998. Interview with Penfield, March 15, 1988; and curriculum vita in the current files of FBCIA, March 20, 1988. Updated January 5, 1998.

34 CLIFFORD R. HOCKENSMITH (August 22, 1952-) was born in Greensburg, PA. He grew up in Jeannette, PA, was baptized at age eight, and graduated from Hempfield Area Senior High School in 1970. He received an intense call to the ministry when he was sixteen years old. He earned his B.A. in pre-theology and psychology from Indiana State University of Pennsylvania, Indiana, PA in 1974. He attended Andover-Newton Theological School from 1974-1977, and received his M.Div. degree in 1978. He earned the D.Min. from Eastern Baptist Theological Seminary in 1994. He was the assistant pastor of the First Baptist Church of Jeannette for 1977-1978. He was the pastor of the Immanuel Baptist Church in Erie, PA (1978-82); associate pastor, First Baptist Church, Dover, DE (1982-86); and pastor of the Plymouth Valley Baptist Church, Norristown, PA (1986-97) before accepting the call to FBCIA. He commenced his service on August 1, 1997 and was dismissed by the church on August 1, 1999 by a congregational vote of 66 to 57. He became the pastor of the Wickford Baptist Church, Wickford, RI, in 2000.

35 JAMES C. MILLER (July 25, 1937 -) was born in Richwood, West Virginia, and graduated from Alderson-Broaddus College with a B.A. in 1960 and Colgate-Rochester Divinity School with the M. Div. in 1963. Keuka College awarded him an honorary doctorate, the D.H.L., in June 1985. He was ordained September 8, 1963. His first pastorate was at the First Baptist Church, Cooperstown, NY (1963-65). Next he was senior minister of Emmanuel Baptist Church, Schenectady, NY (1965-73) and served as part-time chaplain at Union College, Schenectady (1972-73). Then he was the senior minister at the First Baptist Church, Worcester, MA (1973-80) and Lake Avenue Baptist Church, Rochester, NY (1980-91) before becoming the executive minister of the Rhode Island State Council of Churches (1991-2000). He got an early start in leadership roles, having been state president of the Baptist Youth Fellowship [BYF] of West Virginia (1956-58) and national president of the BYF of the American Baptist Convention (1958-59). He was vice-president of the Massachusetts Council of Churches and president of the Genesee Ecumenical Ministers, Rochester. He had numerous responsibilities with the ABC/USA, including serving on the Commission on Christian Unity, executive committee of the General Board, Board of National Ministries, Commission on Life and Theology, Task Force on the Ministry of the Laity and the Evangelizing Community, and the National Planning Committee of the Evangelistic Life Style Emphasis. He served on the Faith and Order Commission of the National Council of the Churches of Christ [NCC], Personnel Committee of the NCC, and a delegate to the governing board of the NCC. He has been a delegate to two assemblies of the World Council of Churches, one in New Delhi, India, and the other in Harare, Zimbabwe. His community involvement found him as a member of the board of directors and officer of the Urban League of Rochester, board of directors of Charles Settlement House, Rochester, and president of Northwest Community Services, Inc., Rochester. He was on the board of directors of the Urban League of Rhode Island, United Way of Southeastern New England, and Interfaith Health Care Ministries. He was appointed to the Rhode Island Governor's Commission Against Bias & Prejudice and served on the Rhode Island Coalition Against Racial Bigotry, the advisory committee of the Rhode Island Indian Council, and the advisory council of the Poverty Institute, Rhode Island College. He was a founding member of RIght Now!, served on the executive board of Common Cause of Rhode Island and the steering committee of the Rhode Island Coalition Against Casino Gambling. Both Common Cause of Rhode Island and the John Hope Settlement House have honored him with their Community Achievement Awards. The Ministers Alliance of Providence awarded him their Ecumenical Award at the Martin Luther King breakfast, January 15, 2001. He has been a trustee of Keuka College and Alderson-Broaddus College and a member of the Board of Visitors of Colgate-Rochester Divinity School/Bexley Hall/Crozier Theological Seminary. FBCIA issued a unanimous call to Miller on October 1, 2000, and he began his ministry on December 1, 2000. See: "Professional Resume: James C. Miller."

THE AUTHOR

J. Stanley Lemons was graduated with an A.B. from William Jewell College, M.A. from the University of Rochester, and the Ph.D. from the University of Missouri-Columbia. After teaching at Ohio State University, he came to Rhode Island College in 1967 and rose to the rank of professor by 1976. In addition he was visiting professor at Southwest Texas State University in 1979-1980. An historian of American culture, Dr. Lemons' scholarly interests and publications have ranged over the topics of women's history, African-American history, popular culture, American religion, social reform, and Rhode Island history. His publications include *The Woman Citizen: Social Feminism in the 1920s*; *Aspects of the Black Experience*; with Dr. George Kellner, Rhode Island: *The Independent State*, the 350th anniversary history of Rhode Island commissioned by the Rhode Island Historical Society; *The First Baptist Church in America*, the 350th anniversary history of the church; with Dr. Emily Stier Adler, *The Elect: Rhode Island's Women Legislators, 1922-1990*. In addition to more than a dozen articles in scholarly journals, Dr. Lemons was co-creator of award-winning multi-image shows, "Providence: A Century of Greatness, 1832-1932" and "The White City and Packingtown: Chicago from the Great Fire to the Great War." In 1988 Rhode Island College awarded him their Thorp Professorship in recognition of his career of sustained scholarship. In 1998 he received the college's Paul Maixner Award for Excellence in College Teaching.

ENDNOTES

CHAPTER 1

1 Anthony Carlino, "Roger Williams and His Place in History: The Background and the Last Quarter Century," *Rhode Island History*, 58(May 2000), 37-71.

2 "Top Ten People and Events of the Millennium," *Providence Journal* (December 25, 1999), D: 7.

3 For a discussion of the erosion of the traditional Baptist stance among the Southern Baptists, see: Bill J. Leonard, "Southern Baptists and a New Religious Establishment,"*The Christian Century*, (September 10-17, 1986), 775-777. R. Albert Mohler, Jr., president of the Southern Baptist Seminary, attacked the concept of "soul competency" in his annual Founders Day address, see: "E. Y. Mullins: A Millennial Reflection," March 30, 2000, [tape recording from The Southern Baptist Theological Seminary.] The original draft of the 2000 version of the Southern Baptist Statement of Faith and Mission caused Bill Webb, the editor of the paper of the Missouri Baptist Convention, to observe: "A couple of our dear Baptist friends — soul competency and priesthood of all believers — were present in the 1963 document but have not been included in the present version." See: "Opinion," *Word & Way*, 137(June 1, 2000), 2. However, they were restored at the last minute: *Word & Way*, 137 (June 22, 2000), 3. On one level, the attacks upon "soul competency" represent the triumph of old-fashioned Calvinism, with its emphasis upon the "irresistibility of God's Grace" upon the Elect, which has come to characterize the current leadership of the Southern Baptists in their drive to enthrone "inerrancy." On another level, the attack by Mohler on Mullins seeks to undermine the influence that Mullins has exerted on behalf of separation of church and state. Mullins, once the president of Southern Baptist Theological Seminary and president of SBC, was unequivocal in his opposition to any use of public money for religious schools and Bible reading in public schools. The rejection of traditional Baptist tenets is much clearer in the efforts of ministers, such as Pat Robertson and his Christian Coalition and Jerry Falwell and his Moral Majority, to promote school prayer in the public schools, school vouchers and the idea that the First Amendment really does not mean separation of church and state. See Paul D. Simmons, ed. *Freedom of Conscience: A Baptist/ Humanist Dialogue* (Amherst, NY: Prometheus Books, 2000), 44-47, 58-63.

4 For an encyclopedic coverage of the Baptists, see: H. Leon McBeth: *The Baptist Heritage: Four Centuries of Baptist Witness* (Nashville: Broadman Press, 1987). See also, William Henry Brackney, *The Baptists* (Westport, CT: Greenwood Press, 1998), and B. R. White, *The English Baptists of the Seventeenth Century* (Didcot, England: Baptist Historical Society, 1996).

5 McBeth, 21, 35-38; Brackney, 5.

6 McBeth, 22, 39.

7 The story of Roger Williams is now quite familiar and is found in many books. However, the first biography did not appear until 1834 when James D. Knowles, a profes-

sor of pastoral duties and sacred rhetoric at Newton Theological Institution, published the *Memoir of Roger Williams, the Founder of the State of Rhode-Island* (Boston: Lincoln, Edmands and Co., 1834). Knowles, born in Providence in July 1798, was baptized March 21, 1820, by Stephen Gano and served as superintendent of the newly formed Sunday school in 1820-1821. He was licensed for the ministry by First Baptist Church on November 3, 1820, and soon left to study theology in Philadelphia and Washington, D.C. He graduated from Columbian College in 1824. He was the pastor of the Second Baptist Church in Boston from 1825 to 1832. He then became a professor at Newton, but died of smallpox in 1838.

8 The church in Salem first extended an invitation to Williams to become the assistant to the Rev. Samuel Skelton, but Governor John Winthrop, after consulting with the Assistants, wrote to John Endecott warning about Williams. Significantly, one of their charges against Williams was that he "had declared his opinion that the magistrate might not punish a breach of the Sabbath nor any other offence, as it was a breach of the first table. . . ." [The "first table" was the first four of the Ten Commandments which laid out duties to God.] Salem withdrew the offer from Williams. Winthrop's *Journal*, "History of New England, 1630-1649," Edited by James Kendall Hosmer (New York: Charles Scribners Sons, 1908), 1: 61-62; also see: Knowles, 46.

9 Quoted in Edmund Morgan, *The Puritan Dilemma: The Story of John Winthrop* (Boston: Little, Brown & Co., 1958), 119.

10 Quoted in William G. McLoughlin, *Soul Liberty: The Baptists' Struggle in New England, 1630-1833* (Hanover, NH: University Press of New England, 1991), 305, fnt 1 of Chpt 1. Also quoted in Knowles, *Memoir of Roger Williams*, 53. John Smyth (c. 1570-1612) was well-known to Brewster, having been part of the Separatist group that fled to Holland in 1607. There Smyth concluded that only believer's baptism was correct, but lacking what he believed to be either a true church or a valid administrator of baptism, he baptized himself. Roger Williams faced the same dilemma when he wanted to be baptized in 1638.

11 David Benedict, *A General History of the Baptist Denomination in America and Other Parts of the World* (Boston: Lincoln & Edmands, 1813), 1: 475.

12 First on the list of charges of "divers dangerous opinions" was "that the magistrate ought not to punish the breach of the first table, otherwise than in such cases as did disturb the civil peace." Quoted in Knowles, *Memoir of Roger Williams*, 68.

13 These words appear in Williams' statement in the deed he executed December 20, 1661. See: Knowles, *Memoir of Roger Williams*, 113.

14 John Russell Bartlett, editor, *Records of the Colony of Rhode Island and Providence Plantations, in New England* (Providence: Crawford Green & Brother, 1856), 1: 14; Samuel Greene Arnold, *History of the State of Rhode Island and Providence Plantations*

4th edition [original edition 1859-1860] (Providence: Preston & Rounds, 1894), 1: 102-104.

15 Winthrop reported that Williams held religious services on Sundays and on weekdays alike. Winthrop's *Journal*, 1: 286.

16 Winthrop gave Verin's version of the incident, beginning with the comment, "At Providence, also, the devil was not idle." Winthrop's *Journal*, I: 286-287. The Verin episode is reported in Arnold, *History of the State of Rhode Island and Providence Plantations*, I:104-105. [Lieutenant Governor Arnold (1852-1853) was a member of the Charitable Baptist Society, pew owner, and "hearer" in the First Baptist Church, while his mother Frances Rogers Arnold and wife Cornelia were members of the church itself for 30 years and 48 years respectively.] See also: Howard M. Chapin, *Documentary History of Rhode Island* (Providence: Preston & Rounds Co., 1916), I: 71-74; William G. McLoughlin, *Rhode Island: A Bicentennial History* (New York: W.W. Norton & Co., Inc., 1978), 10-11.

17 Winthrop noted in his *Journal*: "Many of Boston and others, who were of Mrs. Hutchinson's judgment and party, removed to the isle of Aquiday; and others, who were of the rigid separation and savored anabaptism, removed to Providence, so as those parts began to be well peopled." Winthrop's *Journal*, I: 273-274. The church begun by Anne Hutchinson, John Clarke, William Coddington and company at Portsmouth in 1638 was an independent Congregational church, practicing infant baptism just like the Plymouth church.

18 The issue of the date of the founding has been repeatedly examined, especially in the 19th century, and most writers concluded that the church was founded before the end of 1638 of the New Style calendar. Part of the confusion has stemmed from the fact that the British marked time by the old Julian calendar until 1752, by which time it was out of phase with the sun by two weeks. New Year's day in the Old Style calendar was March 25. This means that a date which once read "March 1, 1638" (Old Style) would be rewritten as "March 1, 1639" (New Style). On the basis of the conclusions of scholars and historians, the First Baptist Church officially adopted at its regular quarterly meeting, March 21, 1899, the position that the founding occurred in the autumn of 1638, New Style; see: Henry Melville King, *Historical Catalogue of the Members of the First Baptist Church in Providence, Rhode Island* (Providence: F. H. Townsend, Printer, 1908), Appendix A, 185-186. Samuel Lunt Caldwell (pastor from 1858 to 1873 and then professor at Newton Theological Institution and president of Vassar College) and William Gammell (1812-1889), professor of rhetoric and history at Brown University, carefully stated the conclusion, "The probabilities are in favor of the formation of the church, within the year 1637-1638; but as this entry in Winthrop's Journal is the earliest authentic notice of it, the chronology of the church has usually been reckoned from that date." Caldwell and Gammell, *History of the First Baptist Church in Providence, 1639-1877*

(Providence: J.A. & R.A. Reid, Printers, 1877), footnote, 5. The entry referred to was made by Winthrop in his *Journal* on March 16, 1639 (New Style), Winthrop's *Journal*, I: 297. It can be said with complete certainty that Roger Williams was baptized, but it is uncertain what method was used, whether "dipped" (immersed) or "poured" (water poured over the head from a bucket). English Baptists were not settled on the method until about 1641 when they opted for immersion, and this form was used by Mark Lukar, a Baptist from England between 1641 and 1644 who joined John Clarke's church in Newport. Clarke's church baptized by immersion from 1644.

[19] Ezekiel Holliman was born at Tring, Hertford County, England, and came to Massachusetts about 1634. He lived in Salem in 1637 and was hauled before the court in March 1638 for not attending church and for preaching heretical doctrines. He fled to Providence, and in October 1638 he was made one of the "original proprietors" of Providence by Williams. Being "a man of gifts and piety," he was chosen by Williams to baptize Williams, and he served as an assistant to Williams. After settling in Warwick, he was a member of the General Assembly from Warwick for eight years. His first wife Susannah (Oxston) may have died before Ezekiel left England. He married the widow Mary Sweet in 1638. He died in Warwick, September 17, 1659. See: John Osborne Austin, *Genealogical Dictionary of Rhode Island* (Baltimore: Genealogical Publishing Co., 1969), 102-103; Oliver Payson Fuller, *The History of Warwick, Rhode Island* (Providence: Angell, Burlingame & Co., 1875), 41-42; *Biographical Cyclopedia of Representative Men of Rhode Island* (Providence: National Biographical Publishing Co., 1881), 21; Howard M. Chapin, "Our Rhode Island Ancestors," #82, RIHS. Regarding Holliman on Aquidneck, see: Sheila L. Skemp, "Freedom of Religion in Rhode Island: Aquidneck Island's Reluctant Revolutionaries, 1638-1660," *Rhode Island History*, 44 (February 1985), 13-14.

[20] Richard Scott stated this some thirty-eight years later in a letter appended to George Fox's *New-England Firebrand Quenched* (1677), 247. See: Knowles, *Memoir of Roger Williams*, 171. John Winthrop noted in June or July 1639 that Williams "has come to question his second baptism, not being able to derive the authority of it from the apostles, otherwise than by the ministers of England (whom he judges to be ill authority)." Winthrop's *Journal*, I: 309.

[21] Samuel H. Brockunier, *The Irrepressible Democrat: Roger Williams* (New York: The Ronald Press Co., 1940), 122. See also: W. Clark Gilpin, *The Millenarian Piety of Roger Williams* (Chicago: University of Chicago Press, 1979).

[22] Charter of 1663, granted by King Charles II, July 8, 1663. See [pamphlet]: "Constitution and Royal Charter of 1663," (Providence: State of Rhode Island and Providence Plantations, Secretary of State, n.d.), 29-30.

[23] See: Edwin S. Gaustad, *Liberty of Conscience: Roger Williams in America* (Valley Forge, PA: Judson Press, 1999), 194-195.

[24] Gilpin's *The Millenarian Piety of Roger Williams* shows how Williams was an active participant in the transatlantic theological debates.

[25] Roger Williams, *The Bloudy Tenent of Persecution, for the Cause of Conscience* (London, 1644), 2.

[26] Quoted in McLoughlin, *Soul Liberty*, 306, fnt 5.

[27] Edwin Gaustad, *Baptist Piety: The Last Will and Testimony of Obadiah Holmes* (Grand Rapids: Eerdmans Publishing Co., 1978), 33; Gaustad, *Liberty of Conscience*, 119-120.

[28] Gaustad, *Liberty of Conscience*, xi; also see his chapter entitled "Exile No More" for a survey of the rise of Williams, 193-219.

CHAPTER 2

[1] The General Baptist churches were often called Old Baptist or Ancient Baptist churches, especially when the Great Awakening produced such a flood of Separate Baptist and Particular Baptist churches. The tombstone of Samuel Winsor, Jr., in the Winsor family cemetery in Smithfield, described him as having been the "Pastor of the Ancient Baptist Church of Providence and Johnston for 40 years." When recounting the origin of their congregation, the records of the "Baptist Church of Christ in Pawtucket" used the words "ancient Baptist Church in Providence"; see: Record of the Baptist Church of Christ, Pawtucket, 1805-1830, 1837, RIHS.

[2] "Record Book for Baptist Church In Providence under the Care of the Elder Samuel Winsor & Thomas Burlingame, begun the 27th Day of March 1755 by Nich. Tillinghast, Clerk." This material is written on the reverse of scattered pages of "Church Records, 1793 to 1805." It contains the earliest minutes and lists of members running up to 1770.

[3] Roger Williams, *The Hireling Ministry None of Christs* (London, 1652). Also see: Edwin S. Gaustad, *Liberty of Conscience*, 92-96.

[4] Morgan Edwards, a minister from Pennsylvania, said of Winsor that he was "a man remarkable for preaching against paying ministers, and for refusing invitations to Sunday dinners for fear they should be considerations for Sunday sermons." Edwards, "Materials for a History of the Baptists in Rhode Island," *Collections of the Rhode Island Historical Society*, (1867), VI: 322.

[5] Reuben Aldrich Guild, *Early History of Brown University, including the Life, Times, and Correspondence of President Manning, 1756-1791* (Providence: Snow & Farnham, 1897), 191.

[6] See: Isaac Backus, *A History of New England with Particular Reference to the Baptists* (New York: Arno Press, 1969, reprint of 1871 edition), I: 92, 405; II: 285, 490. *List of members of the First Baptist Church in Providence with Biographical Sketches of the Pastors* (Providence: Hugh Hall Brown, 1832), 8. By the end of the eighteenth century it had become a tradition in the Brown family to regard Chad Brown as the first pastor of the church. John Howland wrote a letter to David Knowles stating that Brown was the first minister; see: Knowles, *Memoir of Roger Williams*, footnote, 174, and letter of Moses Brown to Francis Wayland maintained the same view; see: Guild, *History of Brown University, with Illustrative Documents* (Providence: Providence Press, 1867), 207. Guild, in his *Early History of Brown University*, said, "Among these elders, tradition has given to Brown the priority, though the others were contemporaries with him. He was unquestionably a man of superior abilities, professing practical wisdom and plain common sense; and he served as arbiter in many difficulties occurring in the town." 208.

[7] For the report of Wickenden in New Netherlands, see the letters of Rev. Johannes Megapolensis and Rev. Samuel Drisius to the Classis of Amsterdam, August 5 and October 25, 1657, *Narratives of New Netherland, 1609-1664* in *Original Narratives of Early American History*, edited by James Franklin Jamison (New York: Charles Scribner's Sons, 1909), 397, 400.

[8] A detailed biography of Dexter is Bradford F. Swan, *Gregory Dexter of London and New England, 1610-1670* (Rochester: Printing House of L. Hart, 1949). Inexplicably, he has nothing to say about Dexter's role and participation in the Baptist Church in Providence.

[9] Sydney V. James suggested that Dexter was the person who brought the Six Principle teaching from England. See: James, *John Clarke and His Legacies: Religion and Law in Colonial Rhode Island, 1638-1750*, edited by Theodore Dwight Bozeman (University Park, PA: The Pennsylvania State University Press, 1999), 97.

[10] *List of Members* (1832), 9. This description was taken from John Stanford's history of the pastors, found in the Book of Records of the FBC at the Rhode Island Historical Society. Morgan Edwards, "Materials for a History of the Baptists in Rhode Island," has the same story, 321.

[11] For the story of the dispute, see: Samuel Lunt Caldwell and William Gammell, *History of the First Baptist Church in Providence, 1639-1877* (Providence: J.A. & R.A. Reid, Printers, 1877), 8-9; Edwards, "Materials for a History of the Baptists in Rhode Island," 314-315; Guild, *Early History of Brown University*, 208-209.

[12] James, *John Clarke and His Legacies*, 97-102.

[13] See: Janet Moore Lindman, "'Know How Thy Oughtest to Behave Thyself in the House of God:' The Creation of Ritual Orthodoxy by Eighteenth Century Baptists," *Mid-America*, 78(Fall, 1996), 237-257.

[14] Carla Gardina Pestana, *Quakers and Baptists in Colonial Massachusetts*

(New York: Cambridge University Press, 1991), 169.

15 Brackney, *The Baptists*, 67; James, *John Clarke*, 97; Daniel P. Jones, *The Economic & Social Transformation of Rural Rhode Island, 1780-1850* (Boston: Northeastern University Press, 1992), 21.

16 As the Regular (Calvinist) Baptists in the 18th century became more like the Congregationalists in their desire for an educated clergy and greater decorum, women lost their right to speak or vote in church. See: Ezra Stiles, *The Literary Diary of Ezra Stiles*, edited by Franklin Bowditch Dexter (New York: Charles Scribner's Sons, 1901), I: 146. The Philadelphia Baptist Association, in answer to a query from a member church in 1745 as to whether women should vote in church meetings, said, "No." See: Jon Butler, *Awash in a Sea of Faith: Christianity and the American People* (Cambridge: Harvard University Press, 1990), 122-123.

17 William G. McLoughlin, *New England Dissent: The Baptists and Separation of Church and State* (Cambridge: Harvard University Press, 1971), I: 305-306.

18 Governor from 1727 to 1732, Joseph Jenckes was the first non-Quaker, non-Newporter to be governor of Rhode Island since 1663. Such was the relative importance of Newport that Jenckes was forced to reside in Newport while governor. He was in Newport when the First Baptist Church of Newport hired an educated minister who introduced a number of formal aspects to that church's ritual and practices. See: James, *John Clarke*, 150-155.

19 Quoted by Backus, *A History of New England with Particular Reference to the Baptists*, II: 23. See also: Caldwell and Gammell, *History of the First Baptist Church*, 10.

20 McLoughlin, *New England Dissent*, I: 309-311. See also: Guild, *Early History of Brown University*, 210; Guild, *Life, Times and Correspondence of James Manning and the Early History of Brown University* (Boston: Gould & Lincoln, 1864), 154.

21 Records of the First Baptist Church, August 24, 1791. RIHS. The issue arose again in 1807, and the church defeated with only one vote in favor a motion that "it is the wish or desire of the church that [prospective members] should come under hands. . . ." Records, December 24, 1807. That one member stopped attending and later joined a Six Principle Church. See Records, January 28, 1808, December 13, 1813, and April 28, 1814.

22 For a discussion of this decline, see: Jones, *The Economic and Social Transformation of Rural Rhode Island*, 131-140.

23 Jones, 147-154.

24 The Six Principle Baptists might be excused when one considers the deplorable state of music in New England churches. Congregational singing had become simply terrible by the end of the seventeenth century, described as "uncouth noise," and "hideous howling." See: Laura L. Becker, "Ministers and Laymen: The Singing Controversy in Puritan New England, 1720-1740, *New England Quarterly*, 55(March

1982), 79-96. Most people had forgotten the psalm tunes which the Puritans had brought to America, so that only four to ten tunes remained, depending on the congregation. What was called the Old Way of singing "was an essentially oral tradition consisting of a limited number of tunes sung from memory in a slow tempo with considerable embellishment." (Becker, 80). The Old Way "was to sing without regard to the time and pitch of anyone else." Ola Elizabeth Winslow, *Meetinghouse Hill, 1630-1783* (New York: W.W. Norton, 1972), 151. Both the General Baptists and Quakers had theological grounds for dispensing with music, but the anarchistic, discordant character of church singing might have been enough to justify its elimination. In the early eighteenth century a struggle occurred in Puritan churches over the introduction of the New Way, which was singing by note from printed hymn books. Separate Baptists who broke away from the Puritan church in the eighteenth century sought to develop singing in their churches, but General Baptists continued to oppose it. Perhaps it should be noted that the singing controversy among the Puritans was part of the argument about clerical domination as the clergy sought to bring in the New Way while many laity held to the Old Way.

25 When in 1652 the Rev. William Vaughn of Newport wanted to establish a Six Principle church, he heard that such a church existed in Providence, so he went to Providence to receive the rite of laying-on-of-hands from William Wickenden. Later Wickenden and Gregory Dexter accompanied Vaughn to Newport to aid in starting a Six Principle church, which became the Second Baptist Church in 1656. See: William Hague, *An Historical Discourse, delivered at the Celebration of the Second Centennial Anniversary of the First Baptist Church, in Providence, November 7, 1839* (Boston: Gould, Kendall & Lincoln, 1839), 97-98.

26 Richard Knight, *History of the General Six Principle Baptists in Europe and America* (Providence: Smith & Parmenter, printers, 1827), 298; Records of the Old Six Principle Baptist Church, Swansea, Mass., 1680-1853, RIHS.

27 "Common Place Book of William Winsor," May 17, 1807, 23, Joshua Winsor Family Papers, RIHS.

28 Knight, *History of General Six Principle Baptists*, 263.

29 Samuel Winsor mss, John Hay Library, Brown University.

30 See: McLoughlin, *New England Dissent*, I: 281. Some General Six Principle Baptists held that their association began in 1670 when the elders of the three Six Principle churches (Providence, Second-Newport, and North Kingston) gathered to share concerns. See: Henry Jackson, *An Account of the Churches in Rhode-Island, presented at an adjourned session of the Twenty-Eighth Annual Meeting of the Rhode Island Baptist State Convention, Providence, November 8, 1853* (Providence: George H. Whitney, Printer, 1854), 104. However, Knight, *History of General Six Principle Baptists*, says that the association began by the end of the seventeenth century, 322.

31 Minutes of the Six Principle Baptist Association, RI mss, Box 8, John Hay Library, Brown University; also, Knight, *History of the General Six Principle Baptists*, 322-323.

32 John Hutchins Cady, *The Civic and Architectural Development of Providence, 1636-1950* (Providence: The Book Shop, 1957), 16.

33 Knowles, *Memoir of Roger Williams*, 175.

34 The deed was dated April 11, 1711, but was not recorded until April 22, 1749, see: Samuel L. Caldwell, *Historical Discourse on the First Baptist Meeting-House, Providence, 1775-1865* (Boston: Gould & Lincoln, 1865), 7; Guild, *Early History of Brown University*, 210.

35 Jonathan Sprague (1648-1741) was ordained an elder in FBC in 1685 and preached for many years to a small Baptist congregation in Smithfield. He died in January 1741.

36 The story and Sprague's reply is found in Edwards, "Materials for a History of the Baptists in Rhode Island," 308-312; Benedict, *A General History of the Baptist Denomination*, I: 467-471, reprints the full exchange of letters.

37 Cady, *Civic and Architectural Development of Providence*, 25-26.

38 Cady, 26.

39 Edwin M. Stone, *The Life and Recollections of John Howland* (Providence: G.H. Whitney, 1857), 29; also see: Guild, *Early History of Brown University*, 211-212.

40 Guild, *Early History of Brown University*, 43-59, 108-128; also see: Henry Jackson, *An Account of the Churches of Rhode Island*, 70-72.

41 Stiles, *Literary Diary*, I: 49.

42 Stiles, I: 49.

43 Guild, *Early History of Brown University*, 221-222.

44 Winsor was assisted for about six months by Rev. John Sutton from New Jersey beginning in November 1769, but Sutton was on his way to a church in Nova Scotia. Winsor hoped that Sutton would remain, but he left anyway. Guild, *Early History of Brown University*, 42, 213-214.

45 It was reported that Winsor found "singing in public worship was very disgustful to him." See: *Manual of the First Baptist Church in Providence* (Providence: Knowles, Anthony & Co, Printers, 1861), 4.

46 Ironically, women were to lose their right to speak and vote in church meetings as the church evolved in a more formal direction under Manning and subsequent pastors.

47 Stiles, *Literary Diary,* (August 23, 1771), I: 146; also see: Minutes of the September 1770 meeting of the Six Principle Baptist Association, RI mss, Box 6, John Hay Library, Brown University.

48 Guild, *Early History of Brown University*, 215-216.

49 "A Book of Record of the Church of Christ under the Pastoral Care of Elder Samuel Winsor," June 21, 1771, and

November 1771, FBC mss, RIHS.

50 See listing and compilation in the "Annual Report, 1996, First Baptist Church in America," (Providence, 1997), 21-28.

51 Minutes of the September 20, 1771 meeting of the Six Principle Baptist Association, RI mss, Box 6, John Hay Library, Brown University.

52 Jones, *Economic and Social Transformation of Rural Rhode Island*, 26-27.

CHAPTER 3

1 On the changing uses of ritual, see: Janet Moore Lindman, "'Know How Thy Oughtest to Behave Thyself in the House of God:' The Creation of Ritual Orthodoxy by Eighteenth Century Baptists," *Mid-America*, 78 (Fall, 1996), 237-257.

2 While a few historians have sought to dispute the idea that a "great awakening" happened at all, the challenge has been turned back, and the history of Colonial America continues to have the Great Awakening as an organizing feature. A leading opponent of the idea of a "great awakening" is Jon Butler, "Enthusiasm Described and Decried: The Great Awakening as Interpretive Fiction," *Journal of American History*, 69 (September, 1982), 305-325. Scholarly treatments of the First Great Awakening are many, but especially see: Edwin S. Gaustad, *The Great Awakening in New England* (New York: Harper & Row, 1957); Alan E. Heimert, *Religion and the American Mind, from the Great Awakening to the American Revolution* (Cambridge: Harvard University Press, 1966); Frank Lambert, *Inventing the "Great Awakening"* (Princeton: Princeton University Press, 1999); William G. McLoughlin, *New England Dissent, 1630-1833: The Baptists and the Separation of Church and State* (Cambridge: Harvard University Press, 1971), 2 vols.; McLoughlin, *Revivals, Awakenings, and Reform: An Essay on Religion and Social Change in America* (Chicago: University of Chicago Press, 1978); Clarence C. Goen, *Revivalism and Separatism in New England, 1740-1800* (New Haven: Yale University Press, 1962); Stuart C. Henry, *George Whitefield* (Nashville, TN.: Abingdon Press, 1957); Arnold A. Dallimore, *George Whitefield: The Life and Times of the Great Evangelist of the Eighteenth Century Revival* (London: 1970, 1979), 2 vols; Harry A. Stout, *The Divine Dramatist: George Whitefield and the Rise of Modern Evangelism* (Grand Rapids: W. B. Eerdman, 1991); Frank Lambert, *Pedlar in Divinity: George Whitefield and the Transatlantic Revivals, 1737-1770* (Princeton: Princeton University Press, 1994).

3 McBeth, *The Baptist Heritage*, 204-206.

4 McLoughlin, *New England Dissent*, I: 10.

5 General Six Principle = 6; Particular = 3; Seventh Day = 1.

6 McBeth, *The Baptist Heritage* , 201, 203-206.

7 McLoughlin, *Isaac Backus and the American Pietistic Tradition* (Boston: Little, Brown & Company, 1967), 100.

8 John Asplund, *The Annual Register of the Baptist Denomination in North America to*

the First of November, 1790; found in the Archives of the General Six Principle Baptists, Series XIII, Executive Committee/ Annual Conference, RIHS.

9 Rev. Morgan Edwards, a Welsh immigrant to Pennsylvania in 1761, is credited with suggesting Rhode Island as the location for the Baptist college, and he vigorously worked to secure an endowment and a charter; see: Jackson, *An Account of the Churches in Rhode-Island*, 69-70; McLoughlin, *Isaac Backus*, 102.

10 The manuscript and printed *Minutes of the Warren Baptist Association* from 1767 are in the John Hay Library at Brown University. Also see; Guild, *Early History of Brown University*, 73-79, tells of the founding of the Association.

11 McLoughlin, *Isaac Backus*, 106-107.

12 Minutes of the Six Principle Baptist Association, May 16-17, 1765 and June 5, 1766, R.I. mss, Box 8, John Hay Library, Brown University.

13 *Minutes of the Warren Association*, 1782, John Hay Library, Brown University. Isaac Backus had initially feared domination by the Association, and his church refused to join at first. Separate Baptists remembered that Congregationalist associations had started out as voluntary bodies but came to exercise control over local churches; see: McLoughlin, *Isaac Backus*, 105-107.

14 McLoughlin, *Isaac Backus*, 107.

15 McLoughlin, *Isaac Backus*, 96.

16 McLoughlin, *Isaac Backus*, 123-124; from Backus' *An Appeal to the Public for Religious Liberty Against the Oppression of the Present Day* (1773).

17 Quoted in Gaustad, *Liberty of Conscience*, 203.

18 McLoughlin, *Isaac Backus*, 130-133. Also see: McLoughlin, *New England Dissent*, 544-569.

19 McLoughlin, *Isaac Backus*, 130.

20 McLoughlin, *Isaac Backus*, 133.

21 Robert S. Alley, "Jefferson and the Danbury Baptists: The Interaction between Baptists and the Nation's Founders," *Freedom of Conscience: A Baptist/Humanist Dialogue*, edited by Paul D. Simmons (Amherst, NY: Prometheus Books), 42-44; Paul D. Simmons, "James Madison, The Baptists, and Religious Liberty," *Freedom of Conscience*, 50-61; O.K. Armstrong and Marjorie M. Armstrong, *The Indomitable Baptists: A Narrative of Their Role in Shaping American History*, (Garden City: Doubleday & Co., Inc., 1967.), 1-16; H. Leon McBeth, *The Baptist Heritage* (Nashville: The Broadman Press, 1987), 273-283.

22 See: William R. Estrep, *Revolution Within the Revolution: The First Amendment in Historical Context, 1612-1789* (Grand Rapids: William B. Eerdmans Publishing Co., 1990).

23 Manning was an original supporter, but Backus had to be convinced. He was a delegate to the Massachusetts ratifying convention in 1788 and came there, like nearly all Massachusetts Baptists, as an opponent of the Constitution. However, he was converted by

the debates and especially by being convinced by Manning and various Massachusetts Federalists. See: McLoughlin, *Isaac Backus*, 196-200. On Manning, see: Guild, *Early History of Brown University*, 449.

24 Samuel Caldwell, *Historical Discourse on the First Baptist Meeting House, Providence, 1775-1865* (Boston: Gould & Lincoln, 1865), 19.

25 See: manuscript of pew auction results, "pew folders," Box 2, Charitable Baptist Society papers, RIHS. [Hereafter denoted as CBS]. He was not trying to hog the pews, but wanted the church to gain full revenue from pew rents. He bought up the left-over pews in the 1832 auction.

26 Caldwell, *Historical Discourse* (1865), 16, footnote 3, says: "Tradition says that the chandelier was first lighted on the night of her nuptials, when she was wedded to Mr. Thomas Poynton Ives, at the house on the north side of the meeting house." Baptists did not believe in church weddings in the 17th and 18th centuries as a church wedding smacked of Anglican or Roman Catholic practices. Instead, Thomas and Hope were married in the house parlor, and the *Providence Gazette and Country Journal* (March 10, 1792) reported that the wedding party could see through the window of the meetinghouse across the street that "all sixteen candles [were] lighted in honor of the new couple." See: Robert P. Emlen, "A House for Widow Brown: Architectural Statement and Social Position in Providence, 1791," *Old-Time New England*, (Fall/Winter, 1999), 13-14.

27 See the list of subscribers, Appendix C, and list of members of the building committee, Appendix E, in Norman Isham, *The Meeting House of the First Baptist Church in Providence: A History of the Fabric* (Providence: Charitable Baptist Society, 1925), 27, 30. [Hereafter referred to as *History of the Fabric*.] Check these lists against Henry Melville King, *Historical Catalogue of the Members of the First Baptist Church in Providence, Rhode Island* (Providence: F. H. Townsend, Printer, 1908).

28 The story of the origin of the Charitable Baptist Society and the building of the Meeting House in 1774-75 has been told repeatedly, see: Samuel L. Caldwell, *Historical Discourse on the First Baptist Meeting-House, Providence, 1775-1865, Delivered Sunday Morning, May 28, 1865, Ninety Years After its First Dedication* (Boston: Gould & Lincoln, Printers, 1865); Samuel Greene Arnold, *Address Delivered Before the Charitable Baptist Society on the One Hundredth Anniversary of the Opening of the First Baptist Church, Providence, Rhode Island, for Public Worship, May 28, 1875* (Providence: J.A. & R.A. Reid, Printers, 1875); Henry Melville King, *Historical Discourse in Commemoration of the 125th Anniversary of the Dedication of the First Baptist Meeting-House, Providence, R.I., Sunday, May 27, 1900* (Providence: F.H. Townsend, 1900), Isham, *History of the Fabric* (1925); Arthur E. Watson, *Angell's Apple Orchard, 1774-1929* (Providence: Akerman-Standard, 1929).

29 Judge William R. Staples, *Annals for the Town of Providence from its First Settlement*

to the Organization of the City Government in June 1832 (Providence: Knowles & Vose, 1843), 416, is the source of the story of Angell's unwillingness to sell his land for a Baptist meeting house. Copy of letter from J. M. Addeman to Albert Knight, February 1, 1928, recounts the transaction, Watson papers, Misc. Correspondence, FBC mss, RIHS. Also see: Isham, *History of the Fabric*, 2-3; Guild, *Early History of Brown University*, 219-220.

30 The lottery for the parsonage was reported in the *Newport Mercury*, October 5, 1767. Aso see: William McLoughlin, *Rhode Island: A Bicentennial History* (New York: W.W. Norton & Co., 1978), 70. McLoughlin pointed out public streets, roads, bridges, and other urban improvements were built with money raised through lotteries. Guild listed at least sixteen lotteries for such varied purposes between 1748 and 1777; *Early History of Brown University*, footnote, 221-222.

31 See: Appendix B in Isham, *History of the Fabric*, 24-26.

32 The architectural history of the Meeting House is thoroughly covered in Isham, *History of the Fabric*.

33 George Kellner and J. Stanley Lemons, *Rhode Island: The Independent State* (Woodland Hills, CA: Windsor Press, 1982), 38-39, 53-61.

34 These and the churches subsequently mentioned are discussed in Cady, *Civic and Architectural Development of Providence*, 47-87.

35 John Howland is the source of the information that the Boston Port Bill drove many carpenters and shipwrights to Providence; see: Stone, *Life and Recollections of John Howland*, 37.

36 *Providence Gazette*, June 10, 1775, RIHS.

37 Stiles wrote, "Mr Manning. . . is a Tory, affecting Neutrality. . . . But Mr Manning has particuly been against his Country in heart." *Literary Diary* (July 16, 1776), II: 23.

38 This was Stiles' comment upon hearing the death of Manning: see: *Literary Diary*, (August 3, 1791), III: 425.

39 H.E. Starr, "James Manning," *Dictionary of American Biography*, (1933), VI: 250.

40 The College was closed from December 7, 1776 to May 27, 1782, and the College Edifice was used as a barracks and then as a hospital. Manning wrote to Samuel Stennett, November 8, 1783, saying that during the war the town had been turned into a garrison, "This scattered our church and congregation abroad, which has never been collected since, near fifty of our members not having yet returned." In Guild, *Early History of Brown University*, 364.

41 James Manning to Rev. J. Ryland, November 8, 1783, in Reuben Guild, *Life, Times and Correspondence of James Manning, and the Early History of Brown University* (Boston: Guild and Lincoln, 1864), 313.

42 See: James F. Reilly, "The Providence Abolition Society," *Rhode Island History*, 21 (April 1962), 33-48. Also see: Mack Thompson, *Moses Brown: Reluctant*

Reformer (Chapel Hill: University of North Carolina Press, 1962), 175-202.

43 Thompson, *Moses Brown*, 200-201.

44 Membership list of the CBS, June 28, 1790, "membership folder," CBS mss; and Membership list of the Abolition Society, 1790, Quaker Archive at RIHS.

45 John Brown to Charitable Baptist Society, July 2, 1790, CBS folder: John Brown letter, re: slavery, FBC papers, RIHS.

46 For an account of this latter case, see: James B. Hedges, *The Browns of Providence Plantations: The Colonial Years*, (Cambridge: Harvard University Press, 1952), 83.

47 A report of the school committee, chaired by Manning, calling for tax-supported public education, is reproduced by Guild, *Early History of Brown University*, 462-463.

48 Record book of First Baptist Church, I: 96.

49 The charge was false and slanderous even though the church got "confirming" letters from certain Baptist ministers in England. The reason for concluding that it was false is that an effort to locate a conviction in England turned up nothing. Furthermore, Stanford returned to New York and had a long, successful ministry, capped, in 1829-1830 when Union College in Schenectady honored him with a Doctor of Divinity. In 1802 Stanford forced the retraction of an unnamed libel, adding that a letter from London "calculated to ruin the character of the Reverend John Stanford" was not true. The fact that he continued in the ministry and gained prominence in New York suggests that he was able to overcome the slander. He returned to New York in 1789 and opened an academy, which remained his principal source of livelihood until he was hired as chaplain for several public institutions. In 1813 he was appointed chaplain of the State Prison and retained this until the prison was moved upstate to Sing Sing in 1829. Also in 1813 he was appointed chaplain of the Alms House and City Hospital. In addition he ministered to the inmates and residents in the Orphan Asylum, Bridewell Penitentiary, Debtors' Prison, the Lunatic Asylum, and the House of Refuge for Juvenile Delinquents. Declining health and numerous ailments forced him to retire about one year before he died, at age 79, on January 14, 1834. See: Rev. Enoch Hutchinson, "Biographical Sketch of Rev. John Stanford, D.D." *The Baptist Memorial and Monthly Record* [New York], April 1849, 105-110, courtesy of the American Baptist Historical Society [ABHS]. The libel retraction is found in a deposition by Francis Davis, New York, May 28, 1802, courtesy of the ABHS.

50 A brief sketch of Maxcy's life is found in Guild, *Early History of Brown University*, footnote, 447.

51 Augustine S. Carman, "The Story of Stephen Gano," *Watchman Examiner* (August 8, 1918), 1019-1021. Also see: Henry Melville King, *Life and Labors of Rev. Stephen Gano, M.D.: Pastor of the First Baptist Church, Providence, R.I., From 1792 to 1828* (Providence: Preston & Rounds Co., 1903), found in "Writings of Pastors," Box 2, FBC mss, RIHS. King's pious account omits all mention of the problem that Gano had

with his fourth wife, Joanna, who accused him of being an idol worshipper! King said only, "In 1801, on October 8, Dr. Gano married Mrs. Joanna Latting of Hillsdale, N.Y., who survived him many years." (21). Also see: "Memoir of Rev. Stephen Gano," in *A List of Members* (1832), 13-32; and brief sketch in *Appleton's Cyclopedia of American Biography* (1887).

52 Carman, "The Story of Stephen Gano," *Watchman Examiner*, 1020. He cites Dunlevy, *History of the Miami Baptist Association*, as one source of this claim. Also see: King, *Life and Labors of Rev. Stephen Gano*, 24, Appendix B, quotes a source from the Historical Society of Cincinnati.

53 See: table of membership in King, *Historical Catalogue*, 13-14.

54 See: *Minutes of the Warren Association, 1805-1825*, Rider Collection, John Hay Library, Brown University. See: *Minutes of the Rhode Island Baptist State Convention, 1825-1850*, Vol I. Collected and presented to the Library of Brown University by the Rev. Benedict and Reuben A. Guild, Providence, September 6, 1864, Baptist Collection, John Hay Library, Brown University. See also: *The Watchman* [Boston] August 12, 1825. The first president was Gano; the first secretary was his son-in-law, David Benedict, pastor of the First Baptist Church of Pawtucket, and the treasurer was Hugh Hall Brown of First Baptist in Providence.

55 The entire episode is recorded in the First Baptist Church Records, July 3, August 9, August 15 and August 25, 1803, II: 62-68, RIHS.

56 Most New England Baptists probably regarded the Masons as being anti-Christian. Isaac Backus certainly disapproved of them in the 1790s, and by 1798 some Baptist associations held that membership in the Masons was grounds for excommunication. See: McLoughlin, *Isaac Backus*, 212-213.

57 The clerk recorded that "this church did not exclude Mrs. Gano on account of her opinions against Masonry, but on account of her hard and unchristian language and conduct towards our brethren, who are Masons; toward our Elder, her husband; towards several of our brethren, who are not Masons, towards the Committee of the church; and, indeed, towards the whole Church, as expressly specified in the eleven charges which Elder Pitman brought against her." Minutes of August 25, 1803.

58 Joanna wrote on September 27, 1810, requesting that she be restored to membership, but the church refused on November 4; see: Records, II: 130-131. "What you mention respecting your wish to live with your Husband, and the reason of his passing your door from year to year without calling and the like, fills us with concern. . . ." 130. She petitioned again in 1817, but they refused to readmit her. However, they voted that she could join another church if she wished without opposition from FBC. See: Minutes for December 4, 1817. Subsequently, the West Baptist Church of Hillsdale, New York, (her former home town) wrote asking for some explanation for the letter that Joanna had received from the church in December 1817. See: Minutes for April 2, 1818.

CHAPTER 4

1 Much has been written about the Second Great Awakening, and some of the useful interpretations are found in Martin E. Marty, *Pilgrims in Their Own Land: 500 Years of Religion in America* (New York: Penguin Books, 1985), especially pages 169-250; Nathan O. Hatch, *The Democratization of American Christianity* (New Haven: Yale University Press, 1989); William G. McLoughlin, *Revivals, Awakenings, and Reform: An Essay on Religion and Social Change in America, 1607-1977* (Chicago: University of Chicago Press, 1978), 98-140; Alice Felt Tyler, *Freedom's Ferment: Phases of American Social History from the Colonial Period to the Outbreak of the Civil War* (New York: Harper & Row, 1944); Whitney Cross, *The Burned Over District: The Social and Intellectual History of Enthusiastic Religion in Western New York, 1800-1850* (Ithaca: Cornell University Press, 1950); John B. Boles, *The Great Revival, 1787-1895* (Lexington: University of Kentucky Press, 1972); Paul E. Johnson, *A Shopkeeper's Millennium: Society and Revivals in Rochester, New York, 1815-1837* (New York: Hill & Wang, 1978); Winthrop R. Hudson, *Religion in America: An Historical Account of the Development of American Religious Life* (New York, Charles Scribner's Sons, 1973); John L. Thomas, "Romantic Reform in America, 1815-1860," *American Quarterly*, 17 (Winter 1965), 656-681; H. Leon McBeth, *The Baptist Heritage* (Nashville: The Broadman Press, 1987), esp. 343-392.

2 Hatch, *The Democratization of American Christianity* , 3-4.

3 "Population of Rhode Island," *Rhode Island Manual, 1991-1994* (Providence: Secretary of State, State of Rhode Island and Providence Plantations, 1994), 800-803.

4 Mark Schantz, "Piety in Providence: The Class Dimensions of Religious Experience in Providence, Rhode Island, 1790-1860," (Ph.D. dissertation, Emory University, 1991), 224-225.

5 See: membership tables in Henry Melville King, *Historical Catalogue of the Members of the First Baptist Church in Providence, Rhode Island* (Providence: F. H. Townsend, Printer, 1908), 13-14.

6 Henry Melville King, "Historical Address," *Minutes of the Proceedings of the 75th Anniversary of the First Baptist Sunday School, Providence, R.I. June 3, 1894* (no publisher), 7. The first Sunday school, in Gloucester, England, was begun by Robert Raikes in 1781; also see: Robert Grieve and John P. Fernald, *The Cotton Centennial, 1790-1890: Pawtucket Cotton Centenary Celebration* (Providence: J.A. & R.A. Reid, 1891), 31.

7 Edward Field, *State of Rhode Island and Providence Plantations at the End of the Century* (Boston: Mason Publishing Company, 1902), II: 94. See also: Grieve and Fernald, *The Cotton Centennial,* 31-32.

8 King, "Historical Address," *Minutes . . . 75th Anniversary* (1894), 9, says: "It is certain that these movements [to start Sunday schools] in different parts of the town of Providence were nearly if not quite simulta-

neous, and that the churches as churches had nothing to do with them. It is equally certain that they were begun by Christian women, . . . by Christian girls, who had recently given their hearts to the Savior and were prompted by a fresh love of him and a desire to do good."

9 John L. Lincoln, *Historical Address on the First Baptist Sunday School, Providence, 1819-1869* (Providence; Providence Press, 1869), 8-10.

10 Ibid., 9.

11 I have relied on Lincoln's account, *Historical Address* (1869). John L. Lincoln (1817-October 16, 1891) was the superintendent of the Sunday school from 1855 to 1876 and personally knew many of the founders of the Sunday school. Lincoln was a Latin professor at Brown University, a deacon from 1869 to 1891, and president of the Rhode Island Sunday School convention for nine years. A tribute to Lincoln is found in King's "Historical Address," in the *Minutes. . . 75th Anniversary* (1894), 20-24.

12 Lincoln, 11. When Jonathan Going began a Sunday school in Worcester about the same time, it provoked controversy for the same reasons. Some regarded it as a sacrilege; see: clipping in the Jonathan Going folder, Brown University Archives, John Hay Library.

13 The hearse was used for the first time for the funeral of James Manning in 1791, see: Reuben A. Guild, *Life, Times and Correspondence of James Manning, and the Early History of Brown University* (Boston: Gould and Lincoln, 1864), 451; also see: Arnold, *Address Delivered before the Charitable Baptist Society* (1875), 26-27, who added that by 1795 fees for the use of the hearse were paid to the sexton. "These soon became one of his perquisites, and in 1821, the hearse was abandoned to him." (By then it could no longer be stored in the basement of the Meeting House.)

14 Lincoln, *Historical Address* (1869), 12-13, describes the basement.

15 King, "Historical Address," *Minutes. . . 75th Anniversary* (1894), 12.

16 Lincoln, *Historical Address,* 19.

17 Lincoln, 18. See also, the Reports of the Sunday School Superintendent and the various versions of the *Catalogue of the Library of the First Baptist Sabbath School,* FBC mss, RIHS. One "Supplement to Catalogue. No. 2" listed 525 books. The 1854 catalogue listed 550 books; the 1864 catalogue had 897 volumes.

18 Notes from records of the Beneficent Congregational Church, provided by Mrs. Millie Smith, Historian of Beneficent, to J. S. Lemons, June 13, 1993. Her entries showed 1000 to 1200 attended on May 21, 1828; 1200 to 1400 attended June 5, 1830. Also see: *The Fifth Annual Report of the Rhode-Island Sunday School Union, read at their Annual Meeting, held in Providence on Wednesday evening, April 7, 1830* (Providence: H.H. Brown, Printer, 1830).

19 Lincoln, 22.

20 Lincoln, 15. This method was not peculiar to First Baptist; it was the practice in

other churches; see: Schantz, "Piety in Providence," 112-113.

21 Lincoln, 32.

22 Ibid., 19.

23 Minutes of FBC, March 14, 1837.

24 Brayton's school was the Branch [Avenue] Sabbath School. See: Minutes of FBC, June 4, 1838.

25 Re: Woodville, see: Minutes of FBC, July 27, 1865; and re: Smith Street, see: September 27, and October 25, 1867.

26 "History of the First Baptist Sewing School, established December 8, 1860," in Minutes of FBC, November 21, 1867.

27 Ibid.

28 Samuel L. Caldwell, "Historical Discourse," *Two Hundred and Fiftieth Anniversary of the Formation of the First Baptist Church in Providence, Rhode Island, April 28, 1889* (Providence: Snow & Farnham, Printers, 1889), 51. Gano was quite ill the last years of his ministry and unable even to attend church in the final months; see: "Memoir of the Rev. Stephen Gano," in *List of Members* (1832), 24-32.

29 E. C. Mitchell, "Biographical Sketch of Dr. Pattison," *Christian Standard* [Chicago], December 10, 1874, from Colby College Special Collections.

30 Ibid.

31 Caldwell, "Historical Discourse," 51. Caldwell, who died in 1889, had most recently been president of Vassar College (1878-1885) and before that a professor at Newton Theological Institution (1873-1878). Caldwell was a student at Waterville College from 1835 to 1839, so his initial contact with Pattison was while Pattison was president of Waterville.

32 William G. McLoughlin, *Isaac Backus and the American Pietistic Tradition* (Boston: Little, Brown and Company, 1967), 214.

33 Mrs. T. E. Bartlett, *The Rhode Island Mite Society: A Noble History, A New Outlook,* (n.d.), 1-4. Also see other histories of the Mite Society in Box marked "Female Charitable Baptist Society and Mite Society," FBC mss, RIHS.

34 Quoted from the Records of the Cavendish Baptist Church in the notes in the Jonathan Going file, Brown University Archives, John Hay Library.

35 In 1819 Going circulated a plan for a seminary, and when the Massachusetts Baptist Education Society had the opportunity to purchase an eighty-five acre estate in Newton in 1825, Going was one of just fourteen men who funded the entire cost of it. Included in that short list were also Henry Jackson, James D. Knowles, and Nicholas Brown, all with connections to First Baptist Church in Providence. See: Thomas R. McKibbins, "Aiming at the Sun: On the 175th Anniversary of Newton Theological Institution," *Today's Ministry* [Andover Newton Theological School], 17:2 (Summer, 2000), 5-6.

36 The details of Jonathan Going (March 7, 1786 - November 9, 1844) can be found in the *Dictionary of American Biography;*

William B. Sprague, *Annals of the American Pulpit*, Vol 4: *The Baptists* (New York: Robert Carter & Bros., 1865), 591-593; *Who Was Who in America*; and the Jonathan Going file in the Brown University Archives, John Hay Library.

37 The story is recounted in O. K. Armstrong and Marjorie M. Armstrong, *The Indomitable Baptists: A Narrative of Their Role in Shaping American History* (Garden City: Doubleday & Co., 1967), 107-108. Also see: McBeth, *The Baptist Heritage*, 184-185.

38 William H. Brackney, "Triumph of the National Spirit: The Baptist Triennial Convention, 1814-1844," *American Baptist Quarterly*, 4 (June 1985), 166-167.

39 William Gammell, *A History of American Baptist Missions in Asia, Africa, Europe and North America* (Boston: Gould, Kendall & Lincoln, 1849), 278-279; The American Baptist Historical Society, *The Associate*, 11, no. 2 (November 1995). After graduating from Brown, Sears graduated from Newton Theological Institute and taught at Hamilton Literary and Theological Institution. Sears returned from Germany in 1836 to become a professor at Newton Theological Institution, then secretary of the Massachusetts Board of Education (succeeding Horace Mann) in 1848, and then president of Brown University from 1855 to 1867. *Appleton's Cyclopedia of American Biography*, (New York: D. Appleton & Co., 1887), V: 447. See also: *Biographical Encyclopedia of Representative Men of Rhode Island* (Providence: National Biography Publishing Co., 1881), 61-62.

40 Solomon Peck was baptized on January 3, 1818, licensed in 1822, and ordained December 23, 1823.

41 Love eventually became ill and returned to the United States in 1843. In the summer of 1841 Rufus Buel joined him in Corfu. Buel provoked a riot in December when he sought to distribute tracts to the crowds celebrating St. Spiridion's festival. The mob pursued him to his house and wrecked it, burning the Bibles, tracts, and books that they could find. Buel and his family were rescued by the arrival of British soldiers who escorted them to safety. Buel then withdrew to Malta. Later, in 1847, near Athens, while running a school in his home, he was arrested and fined for "teaching contrary to the law." Buel continued to be harassed by the political and ecclesiastical authorities until he returned to the United States in November 1855. He and his family joined First Baptist in 1856. See: G. Winfred Hervey, *The Story of Baptist Missions in Foreign Lands from the Time of Carey to the Present Date* (St. Louis: Chauncey R. Barns, 1885), 730-735; *Appleton's Cyclopedia of American Biography*, I: 442.

42 Albert N. Arnold was at Corfu and Athens with Rufus Buel. Arnold was born in Cranston, graduated from Brown in 1838 and Newton Theological Institution in 1841, and was ordained to the ministry in Newburyport, Massachusetts, in September 1841. Appointed a missionary to Greece in 1843, he served there from 1844 to 1855. After returning to the United States, he taught at Newton, Hamilton Literary and

Theological Institution, and the Theological Seminary in Chicago. He retired in 1878 to the old family homestead in Cranston, where he died on October 11, 1883. See: Hervey, *The Story of Baptist Missions in Foreign Lands*, 733.

43 See compilations of names of missionaries (drawn from King, *Historical Catalogue*, and various church calendars) in "Missionaries," in folder marked "Research Notes for 350-FBC: Tabulations and Lists," FBC mss, RIHS.

44 Brackney, "Triumph of the National Spirit," 179-180; McBeth, *The Baptist Heritage*, 384-385; Robert G. Torbet, *A History of the Baptists*, (Valley Forge: Judson Press, 1963), 288.

45 Armstrong and Armstrong, *The Indomitable Baptists*, 165.

46 *Herald of Freedom* [Concord, New Hampshire], August 31, 1839, 106.

47 "Minutes of the Acting Board of the American Baptist Foreign Mission Society," February 24, 1845, Archives, American Baptist Historical Society.

48 For a fuller discussion of these events, see: J. Stanley Lemons, "Why Are We Here?" *Into a New Day: Exploring a Baptist Journal of Division, Diversity, and Dialogue*, edited by Kate Penfield (Macon, GA: Smyth & Helwys, 1997), 35-41.

49 Quoted in Mary Burnham Putnam, *The Baptists and Slavery, 1840-1845* (Ann Arbor: George Wahr Publisher, 1913), 51, found in American Baptist Historical Society.

50 "Minutes of the 31st Annual Meeting of the American Baptist Board of Foreign Missions," May 1, 1845, Archives, American Baptist Historical Society; see also: McBeth, 385-389.

51 W. W. Keen, a student at Brown in 1856, recounted a rousing speech by Wayland after the attack on Senator Charles Sumner: see: *The Memoirs of William Williams Keen, M.D.* (Doylestown, Pennsylvania: A Keen Book, 1990), 153-154. When the Civil War broke out, Wayland made impassioned speeches to the students of Brown and the citizens of Providence. He denounced the "wickedness of slavery" and cried, ". . . slavery! slavery! what man was born to be a slave?" See: *Brown University in the Civil War: A Memorial* (Providence: Providence Print Co., Printers, 1868), 18.

52 See list of signers and resolutions of the Anti-Abolition Meeting, *Providence Daily Journal*, November 4, 1835, RIHS.

53 Myron O. Stachiw, "'For the Sake of Commerce: Rhode Island, Slavery, and the Textile Industry," an essay to accompany the exhibit, "The Loom & the Lash: Northern Industry and Southern Slavery," Exhibit at the Museum of Rhode Island History at Aldrich House, Providence, Rhode Island, September 15, 1982 - January 2, 1983. Both Nicholas Brown and Moses Brown Ives were partners in the firm of Brown & Ives, which was extensively involved in cotton manufacture.

54 John S. Gilkeson, Jr., *Middle Class Providence, 1820-1940* (Princeton: Princeton University Press, 1986), 43-44.

55 King, *Historical Catalogue*, 18, 54. Also see: the various lists of members, 1832, 1843, 1850, 1855. Hugh Brown became a book publisher and printed all the church's publications from 1832 to 1855. Brown was also the printer of the Tax Lists for the City of Providence in the period. He signed the call for the Antislavery convention: See: *Pure Testimony* [Pawtucket, R.I.], January 12, 1836. RIHS. H.H. Brown was an early member of the Providence Anti-Slavery Society and "initiated a successful plan to attach an anti-slavery pamphlet to the RI almanac which he printed for 1833 (or 1834)." Deborah Bingham Van Broekhoven to Stanley Lemons, October 18, 1987.

56 Officers of the State Antislavery Society, *Proceedings of the Convention* (1836), 12, RIHS.

57 See pew auction list for 1832 in the CBS papers for the location of Richard Jackson's pew. The record of Phebe's subscription to William Lloyd Garrison's *Liberator* is found in the list of subscribers, Vol. 1, 1839-1845, Care mss. Collection, Boston Public Library. (Information courtesy of Deborah Bingham Van Broekhoven.)

58 *Pawtucket Record and Free Discussion Advocate*, March 12, 1836. Copy in American Antiquarian Society. In particular, Wayland was accused of preaching against Reverends John Blain and Asa Bronson, the two abolitionist ministers in the Warren Association, of the Pine Street Baptist Church [Second Baptist] of Providence and the Fall River Baptist Church.

59 See account in *Pawtucket Record and Free Discussion Advocate*, December 3, 1836.

60 This information came from a journal mistakenly identified as the "Journal of Rev. William Hague (June 25,1837-September 19, 1839)" which belonged to a book dealer, Ric Garren, Nashua, N. H. The manuscript was offered for sale to the RIHS, but they declined to purchase it. I was able to examine it at the RIHS before it was returned to Garren. It was actually written by a Sunday school teacher in Hague's church. Her entry: "Monday evening, April 23, 1838. Heard Miss S. Grimke lecture on the sin of slavery: Tuesday Afternoon, Miss Angelina Grimke on the same subject. Was much gratified; think they reason well."

61 When a faction in the Pine Street [Second Baptist] Church wanted to form a new church on abolitionist principles, a council of churches met to hear their petition. Three men from the Standing Committee represented FBC, and they voted 2-1 to disapprove of the new church, but the majority of the whole council approved the new church, called the West Baptist Church. Minutes of FBC, September 3, 1840.

62 "Report of Treasurer," 1851-1852, in box labeled "Baptist Female Charitable Society," "Mite Society," FBC papers, RIHS.

63 *Providence Journal*, January 6, 1857, 2.

64 See: "Missionaries," in folder marked "Research Notes for 350-FBC, Tabulations and Lists," FBC mss, RIHS.

65 Edith Wilcox (November 3, 1872 - September 2, 1947) was a missionary at

Himeji from 1910 to 1930 and was principal of the girls' school there. See: obituary, *Providence Evening Bulletin*, September 3, 1947.

66 See: Henry Melville King, *Historical Discourse Delivered at the One Hundredth Anniversary of the Rhode Island Bible Society in the First Baptist Meeting House, Providence, September 29, 1913* (Providence: S.L. Freeman Co., 1913). King himself was the president of the Bible Society in 1913.

67 Quoted in C. Allyn Russell, "Rhode Island Baptists, 1825-1931," *Rhode Island History*, 8 (1969), 36.

68 Only First Baptist remained as Second Baptist stayed away from 1821 through 1823, Third Baptist was expelled in 1824 and was restored to the Association in 1829, and Fourth Baptist was begun as a Freewill Baptist church and did not join the fold until 1833. See also: Schantz, "Piety in Providence," 145-146, 160-161.

69 *Minutes of the Warren Association, Held at the Meeting-House of the First Baptist Church Providence, Rhode-Island, September 12 and 13, 1820* (Providence: Brown & Danforth, 1820), 4.

70 Nicholas Brown was a classic example of the upright, religious individual who did not have a conversion experience. He owned sixteen pews in the Meeting House in 1832, two in Second Baptist Church, two in Third Baptist, and one in the Grace Episcopal Church. In addition he gave the church its organ, the clock in the auditorium, land for a parsonage, was moderator of the Charitable Baptist Society for nearly forty years and president of the Rhode Island Bible Society from 1823 until his death in 1841, and gave such an endowment to the Baptist college that it was named for him in 1804.

71 Quoted in Irving H. Bartlett, *The American Mind in the Mid-Nineteenth Century*, 2d edition (Arlington Heights, IL: Harlan Davidson, 1982), 17.

72 From 1776 to 1857 at least 20 members were expelled for espousing Universalism. See: "Erasures from FBC in folder marked "Research Notes for 350-FBC: Tabulations and Lists." The Union services for years included FBCIA, Central Baptist, Central Congregational, Beneficent Congregational, First Unitarian, First Universalist, Westminster Unitarian: see, for example, *Providence Evening Bulletin*, June 19, 1943; June 21, 1947. Also, FBC pastors exchanged pulpits with the First Universalist, see *Bulletin*, November 26, 1943.

73 See Minutes of FBC, February 2, 1837; April 17, 1838; October 4, 1838; November 29, 1838.

74 Russell, "Rhode Island Baptists, 1825-1931," *Rhode Island History*, 46. See also: H. Leon McBeth, *The Baptist Heritage: Four Centuries of Baptist Witness* (Nashville: Broadman Press, 1987), 714, says that the merger caused tensions among Northern Baptists and that by the 1980s many former Freewill churches had withdrawn.

75 Schantz, "Piety in Providence," 408-410.

76 See: Kathryn Teresa Long, *The Revival of 1857-1858: Interpreting an American Religious Awakening* (New York: Oxford University Press, 1998); Timothy L. Smith, *Revivalism and Social Reform: American Protestantism on the Eve of the Civil War* (Baltimore: Johns Hopkins Press, 1980), esp. chapter IV, "Annus Mirablis —1858," 63-79.

77 Schantz, "Piety in Providence," 416.

78 *Providence Daily Journal*, March 23, 1858. Also see: March 30, 1858.

79 *Providence Daily Journal*, May 19, 1858.

80 *Providence Daily Journal*, March 17, 1858; March 20, 1858; March 23, 1858; March 26, 1858; March 27, 1858; March 30, 1858; April 10, 1858; April 13, 1858; April 21, 1858; April 24, 1858; May 8, 1858.

CHAPTER 5

1 Edwin Gaustad, "WHERE ARE THE LIONS . . . when we really need them?" *Christian History*, 4 (1984), 26-29.

2 In addition to the 1789 celebration of the Constitution, other events marked in the Meeting House included the 1783 Treaty of Paris, ending the American Revolution, and a service in 1800 to honor the death of George Washington. See: Samuel L. Caldwell, *Discourse delivered in the First Baptist Meeting House, Sunday, May 28, 1865* (Boston: Gould & Lincoln, 1865), 19; Stephen Gano, *A Sermon on the Death of General George Washington; Delivered Lord's Day, January 5, 1800. Before the Baptist Society in Providence* (Providence: John Carter, Jr., 1800). With respect to the 250th anniversary, see: Providence City Council, *Two Hundred and Fiftieth Anniversary of the Settlement of Providence, June 23 and 24, 1886* (Providence: Providence Press, 1887).

3 For example, see: Jonathan Maxcy [president of Brown University], *An Oration Delivered in the First Baptist Meeting House in Providence, July 4th, A.D. 1794 at the celebration of the nineteenth anniversary of American Independence* (Providence: Carter & Wilkinson, Printers, 1795); Samuel D. Caldwell, *Oration Delivered before the Municipal Authorities and Citizens of Providence on the eighty-fifth anniversary of American Independence, July 4, 1861* (Providence: Knowles, Anthony & Co., Printers, 1861). "July 4th, 1870. Exercises at the First Baptist Church, Providence, R.I., 94th Anniversary of American National Independence," Watson papers, Misc. programs, FBC mss., RIHS.

4 *Providence Courier*, August 5, 1836.

5 "The interior of this large and beautiful edifice, erected in 1775, has recently undergone extensive alterations. In place of the old-fashioned square pews, on the lower floor, the more convenient form of long pews or slips, as they are sometimes called, with reclining backs, has been substituted. A new mahogany pulpit, plain but rich, has taken the place of the old one. The pews and aisles are handsomely carpeted, and the pews all cushioned in a uniform manner, and the windows furnished on the inside with Venetian blinds." *Providence Journal*, October 7, 1832.

6 The assignment of pews was always a major issue in churches since early colonial times, and the ownership of pews was the matter of great concern, especially since where one sat reflected one's standing in the community. It was presumed that the community elite had the best, most prominent pews. One way the "better sort" set standards of social behavior for the "lesser sorts" was to be seen supporting the church. A major committee of the Charitable Baptist Society was the Pew Committee. The way they solved the question of who got which pew in 1832 was to auction the pews to the highest bidders. Accordingly, Nicholas Brown bought a front-row pew, as did his brother-in-law, Poynton Ives. Poor church members could sit in the balcony where the seats were free. Furthermore, the money raised by the auction repaid the whole cost of the new pews.

7 Henry Melville King, "Historical Address," *Minutes of the Proceedings of the 75th Anniversary of the First Baptist Sunday School, Providence, R.I. June 3, 1894* (no publisher), 21.

8 King and Arthur E. Watson, "Historical Statement," (circa 1949); this version of King's 1907 statement was revised by Professor Arthur Watson and used as part of the national campaign to raise an endowment from the Northern Baptists. According to Watson, this remark about the "special place" was originally made by William H.P. Faunce, president of Brown from 1899 to 1929; see: "Lecture given at the First Baptist Meeting House, Thursday, May 15, 1930, being the final part of the Olde Meeting-House Day," 19, in Arthur Watson mss., Misc. Speeches folder, FBC mss., RIHS.

9 William J. Brown, *The Life of William J. Brown, of Providence, R.I., with Personal Recollections of Incidents in Rhode Island* (Providence: Angell, 1883), 46.

10 Samuel L. Caldwell, *Historical Discourse on the First Baptist Meeting-House, Providence, 1775-1865* (Boston: Gould & Lincoln, 1865), 45.

11 Minutes of FBC, August 25, 1803. One might wonder if the struggle to improve the singing drove him to excessive drinking.

12 The emphasis is in the original. See: Samuel Greene Arnold, *Address Delivered before the Charitable Baptist Society* (1875), 30, footnote.

13 For the story of music at FBC, see: William Dinneen, *Music at the Meeting House, 1775-1958* (Providence: Roger Williams Press, 1958), especially 2-11. Also see: King, *Historical Discourse* (1900), 22.

14 Minutes of the Standing Committee, January 26, 1847.

15 Minutes of FBC, July 23, 1857; October 22, 1857.

16 Minutes of FBC, April 21, 1859; May 27, 1859; June 16, 1859; petition March 24, 1865.

17 Minutes of FBC, September 24, 1863; October 22, 1863; December 19, 1863.

18 The petition was presented at the February 24 meeting and is found in the Minutes of FBC, March 24, 1865. The names included the wives of two past presidents and the current president of Brown, the wives of the past and current minister of FBC, as well

as the wives of every significant pew owner. At that point in the church's history women were not allowed to speak in the meetings or vote, but a petition of this nature bore such weight that the men acceded to it.

[19] Minutes of FBC, November 16, 1871. The hymnal was *The Service of Song* (New York: Sheldon & Co., 1871), and it appeared in many editions and printings through the 1880s.

[20] *The Yearly Record, First Baptist Church, Providence, R.I., 1888*; [program] "Two Hundred and Fiftieth Anniversary of the Formation of the First Baptist Church of Christ, (founded before March 16th, 1639,) Providence, Rhode Island, Sunday and Monday, April 28th and 29th, 1889."

[21] Dinneen, *Music at the Meeting House*, 17.

[22] Minutes of FBC, February 19, 1857 (reports the vote to make Wayland the Acting Pastor and his acceptance); January 4, 1858 (Wayland called to be the settled minister); January 29, 1858 (Wayland declined the call).

[23] Minutes of FBC, July 3, 1828.

[24] E. C. Mitchell, "Biographical Sketch of Dr. Pattison," *The Standard* [Chicago], December 10, 1874.

[25] Henry Melville King, *Seventy-Five Years of History: Emmanuel Baptist Church* (Albany, New York: 1909), 18-20; *Appleton's Cyclopedia of American Biography* (New York: D. Appleton & Co., 1887), III: 26.

[26] Minutes of FBC, September 24, 1840.

[27] Minutes of FBC, September 12, 1842. He began at FBC on November 13, 1842.

[28] Caldwell resigned as pastor to become professor of church history at Newton Theological Seminary before becoming president of Vassar College from 1878 to 1885. See: *Appleton's Cyclopedia of American Biography*, V: 235; obituary, *Providence Evening Bulletin*, September 27, 1889, 3.

[29] Minutes of FBC, October 23, 1806.

[30] Minutes of FBC, October 29, 1827; December 17, 1829.

[31] Minutes of FBC, August 25, 1803.

[32] For the story of David Martin, see: Minutes of FBC, November 26, 1807; December 24, 1807; January 28, 1808; December 2, 1808. On December 30, 1813 Martin, who had been "absent for a long time" was threatened with expulsion. His relationship ended when he transferred his membership to the Johnston Six Principle Baptist Church, April 28, 1814.

[33] Minutes of FBC, October 8, 1822.

[34] See: "Erasures from FBC," FBCIA mss, RIHS.

[35] For example, see the case of Mary Billings, in Minutes of FBC, December 26, 1805, December 31, 1805.

[36] Minutes of FBC, May 3, 1787.

[37] Minutes of FBC, August 25-26, 1808 and August 25, 1825; Minutes of the Standing Committee, September 24, 1861; Minutes of FBC, October 24, 1861.

[38] Minutes of FBC, June 29, 1787.

[39] Minutes of FBC, October 24, 1822; January 1, 1824.

[40] For all these examples, see: "Erasures from FBC," FBCIA mss, RIHS. The embezzler, the treasurer of the Sunday School from 1886-1892, was found guilty of taking $2667.50 from the church itself. See: Minutes of FBC, January 23, 1894. Only once in the twentieth century has anyone been expelled for a criminal cause: John L. Jarvis was sent to prison for "carnal knowledge of a girl underage." Minutes of FBC, May 25, 1933; see also: file #16683 Providence Superior Court Records, Judicial Records Center of Rhode Island.

[41] Minutes of FBC, December 24, 1795.

[42] Minutes of FBC, November 29, 1827. They voted "that this church considers it unbecoming and improper for any of our members to visit the theatre or the circus or green cottage (so called) and other places of amusement as sources of dissipation, and those members who do, are the proper subjects of church discipline." The prohibition against theaters and circuses simply faded away in the 1840s and 1850s. No mention of these things occurred as the century advanced, and by the 1920s young adults from the church had their own amateur theatrical group.

[43] Minutes of FBC, July 30, 1826; May 2, 1839. In addition to attending dances, Lucy Lathrop was cohabiting with a married man: Minutes, August 29, 1811; March 31,1814.

[44] W.J. Rorabaugh, *The Alcoholic Republic: An American Tradition* (New York: Oxford University Press, 1979); Ian R. Tyrell, *Sobering Up: From Temperance to Prohibition in Antebellum America, 1800-1860* (Westport: Greenwood Press, 1979).

[45] C. Allyn Russell, "Rhode Island Baptists, 1825-1931," *Rhode Island History*, 28(1969), 43.

[46] "Erasures from FBC," list compiled from Henry Melville King, *Historical Catalogue of the Members of the First Baptist Church in Providence, Rhode Island* (Providence: F. H. Townsend, Printer, 1908), and from the Records of FBC, in folder marked "Research Notes for 350-FBC: Tabulations and Lists," FBC mss, RIHS.

[47] John S. Gilkeson, *Middle Class Providence*, 34, 46. The church heard his confession of repentance, voted to restore him to its membership, and then granted him a letter to join the Third Baptist Church; see: Minutes of FBC, September 1, 1831.

[48] Minutes of FBC, February 2, 1832; see also the annual letter from FBC to the Warren Baptist Association: "This [church] receives no members without a pledge to abstain from the use of ardent spirits," *Minutes of the Warren Baptist Association at Seekonk, Wednesday and Thursday, September 11 and 12, 1833* (Providence: H.H. Brown, Printer, 1833), 9.

[49] "Erasures from FBC," FBCIA mss, RIHS.

[50] These figures and all that follows are based on an analysis of the 1832, 1861, and 1890 membership lists. 1832 was the first to be printed with names and addresses. These lists were checked against the street directories and the tax lists for Providence.

[51] In 1832, when nearly 60 percent of adult males in Rhode Island did not have $134 worth of taxable property, Nicholas Brown owned $535,700, and Poynton Ives had $492,000 in taxable property. Another pewowner, Moses Brown Ives, Poynton's son, was the director of the Providence branch of the Bank of the United States, and had $22,600 worth of taxable property. See: *City of Providence Tax List, 1832*.

[52] For example, Mary Gruetzner was from Switzerland, the Knoblocks, Borks, and Blocks from Germany, the Spencers, Eastwoods, and Nichols from England, Margaret Snow and the Nisbets, McKenzies, and MacMillans from Scotland, the Myers from Sweden, and the MacDonalds from Nova Scotia.

[53] "Report of the Assistant Treasurer," November 22, 1855, and 1863-1864.

[54] Minutes of the Standing Committee, January 21, 1844; February 15, 1844; and June 12, 1844.

[55] "Report of the Assistant Treasurer," October 1857-October 1858.

[56] "Report of the Assistant Treasurer," 1859-1860.

[57] "Report of the Assistant Treasurer," passim. Also see: Minutes of the Standing Committee, January 25, 1845; June 15, 1845. Some pleas for assistance were declined; e.g. the Standing Committee rejected the request from the Baptist Church of Norwalk, Connecticut, (September 28, 1844) and the Baptist Church in Peoria, Illinois (February 3, 1845).

[58] "Report of the Assistant Treasurer," 1871-1872.

[59] "Report of the Assistant Treasurer," September 23, 1851. Twenty-four names were on the list of subscribers from FBC for the $50,175. The $8000 is listed in the November 22, 1855 report.

[60] "Report of the Assistant Treasurer," list of 55 members of FBC in the November 22, 1855 report.

[61] "Report of the Assistant Treasurer," list of 25 names from FBC in 1863-1864 report.

[62] The best history of this development is Patrick T. Conley, *Democracy in Decline: Rhode Island's Constitutional Development, 1776-1841* (Providence: Rhode Island Historical Society, 1977).

[63] A sketch of Knowles's life can be found in *Appleton's Cyclopedia of American Biography*, (New York: D. Appleton & Co., 1887), III: 564. He was born in Providence in July 1798 and died of smallpox in Massachusetts on May 9, 1838. Appointed a tutor at Columbian College in Washington, DC, in 1824, he became the pastor of the Second Baptist Church of Boston on December 28, 1825. Ill health forced him to resign the pastorate in 1832, but he became the professor of sacred rhetoric at Newton Theological Institution. He was the editor of the *Christian Review* and he wrote the first biography of Roger Williams.

[64] July 29, 1824, "Erasures from FBC."

[65] Luther tried to be a bookseller but was jailed as a debtor by 1823. After the failure of

the Dorr Rebellion, Luther was imprisoned again. Released in 1843, he moved to Boston, but was committed to an insane asylum by 1846.

66 Quoted in Mark Schantz, "Piety in Providence: The Class Dimensions of Religious Experience in Providence, Rhode Island, 1790-1860," (Ph.D. dissertation, Emory University, 1991), 326.

67 Schantz, 323- 327. See also: Louis Hartz, "Seth Luther, the Story of a Working-Class Rebel," *New England Quarterly*, 13 (September 1940), 401-418; Carl Gersuny, "Seth Luther — The Road from Chepachet," *Rhode Island History*, 33 (May 1974), 47-55; Marvin E. Gettleman and Noel P. Conlon, "Responses to the Rhode Island Workingmen's Reform Agitation of 1833," *Rhode Island History*, 28(August 1969), 75-94.

68 July 22, 1844, "Erasures from FBC."

69 See: *Providence Tax List*, 1840, 1842, 1844, 1846, 1853, in Providence City Archives.

70 See: *Providence City Directory*, 1850 and 1853.

71 Actually, Barton had been called on the carpet twice before for behavior that the Standing Committee condemned. In 1836 he was charged with "dealing in Lottery tickets." See: Minutes of the Standing Committee, June 28, 1836. Barton first "disclaimed the right of the Committee to call in question his right to purchase Lottery tickets, and that if called upon by the Committee, that he thought he should not appear to answer them in the case." See: Minutes, August 2, 1836. Finally it was reported that "Barton had pledged himself that after the middle of January next he will not purchase, or in any way be concerned in the purchase of Lottery tickets. . . ." Minutes, December 27, 1836. Then he became embroiled in a dispute about ownership of a pew and was forced to surrender his pew: see: Minutes of the Standing Committee, July 2, 1839; August 27, 1839; October 29, 1839; November 26, 1839; March 31, 1840, and finally April 2, 1842.

72 The cases of the Dorrites are recorded in the Minutes of the Standing Committee, May 31, June 14, July 5, July 12, July 19, July 20, August 2, and August 31, 1842; and in the Minutes of FBC, July 7, July 14, July 22, and August 4, 1842.

73 Minutes of the Standing Committee, August 2, 1842. Sisson subsequently stopped attending church and was expelled for non-attendance on April 18, 1844. Robbins died August 9, 1844. As a result, four of the six Dorrites were gone from the church by 1844.

74 Ross was described as "guager and grocer" in the *Providence City Directory* in 1841 and 1847. "Guager" is a variant of "gauger." That word had several meanings, including a dealer in liquor, pawn broker, or one who measures or gauges the worth of items for commerce. He certainly was not a liquor dealer because the church had forbidden any involvement with liquor since 1832. On the other hand, his grocery store on South Main Street put him close to the docks on the Providence River, which meant that he might have been gauging the worth of goods being shipped.

75 Minutes of FBC, July 14, 1842.

76 For examples, see: Henry Jackson, *An Historical Discourse: delivered in the Central Baptist Meeting House, January 8, 1854, also the Articles of Faith, and the Covenant adopted in Church Meeting, January 7, 1847* (Newport, 1854), Article XIV, 40; *A List of Members with the Covenant and Sketch of the History of the Third Baptist Church in Providence, R.I.* (Providence, H.H. Brown, 1855), Article XII, 37-38, in RIHS., *A Brief History of the Waterman Street Baptist Church, Providence, with the Articles of Faith, Church Covenant, Rules and Regulations and List of Members* (Providence: Knowles, Anthony & Co. 1857), Article XIV, 17, in American Baptist Historical Society, Rochester. [The Waterman Street Article on "Civil Government" was identical to the one adopted by the Central Baptist Church in Newport.] Also see: *Mt. Pleasant Church, Declaration of Faith* (Providence: Yankee Notion Publishing Company, 1884), Article XVII, "Of Civil Government," 12, RIHS.

77 King, *Historical Catalogue*, 68, 75. Also see: pew lists in CBS records.

78 See: *Brown University in the Civil War: A Memorial* (Providence: Providence Press Co., Printers, 1868), listed 270 men who fought for the Union after attending Brown, and another twenty-six who came to Brown after their service.

79 Ibid., passim. In 1861 Brown's faculty numbered a dozen, and eight of them, plus the wife of another, were members of FBC.

80 *Providence Daily Journal*, June 10, 1861, 2. That afternoon about 300 of the soldiers attended another worship service at the Central Congregational Church, where the "pulpit was beautifully decked with banners."

81 Samuel L. Caldwell, *A Sermon Preached in the First Baptist Meeting-House, Providence, Sunday Morning, June 9, 1861, before the Second Regiment of Rhode Island Volunteers*, (Providence: Knowles, Anthony & Co., Printers, 1861), 3-5.

82 One ought to remember that May 5 through June 3, 1864 saw some of the bloodiest fighting of the war, from the Battle of the Wilderness, Spottsylvania, North Anna, to Cold Harbor. General Ulysses Grant shifted his forces to attack Petersburg about the time Pvt. Thornton quit. He had been in the 2d R.I. Regt. since December 1861, which means that he had been through the worst of the war. After the slaughter on June 3, Union soldiers developed the "Cold Harbor syndrome," becoming timid to attack and fearful of their chances of surviving. See: James M. McPherson, *Battle Cry of Freedom: The Civil War Era* (New York: Oxford University Press, 1989), 735-742.

83 Appeal of conviction by William H. Smith to Edwin M. Stanton (Secretary of War), April 12, 1865. Document from the Judge Advocate General's Office, National Archives.

84 The captain of Smith's Company A was Thomas W. Fry, the brother of fellow church-member Annie S. Fry. At the court-martial, Fry testified in the defense of the soldier who was wounded in the back of the head.

85 The annual letters to the Warren Baptist Association made only passing references to the war, such as "these times of civil trouble" (September 1, 1861), "the troubles of the present times" (September 7,1862), "the great duties and troubles of a time of war" (August 25, 1864).

86 Minutes of FBC, September 25, 1862.

87 Minutes of FBC, November 28, 1862.

88 Minutes of FBC, April 23, 1863, July 23, 1863, July 21, 1864.

89 Minutes of FBC, September 12, 1865.

90 Fragile newspaper clipping, n.d. (1884), in Watson folders, FBC papers, RIHS.

91 Ibid.

92 Arthur Watson, church historian and long-time member of the Properties and Sexton Committee, said of the window, ". . . no small amount of criticism was evoked at the incongruity of the style of architecture. Beautiful in itself, and prized as a memorial, it is still quite [out] of place in such a colonial house of worship. While convenience has been gained in easy access to platform and baptistry, it has been at the expense of an artistic breach." See: [Lantern-slide] "Lecture given at the First Baptist Meeting House, Thursday, May 15, 1930, being the final part of the Olde Meeting-House Day," 19. Arthur Watson mss, in Misc. speeches folder, in FBC mss, RIHS.

93 For example, baptism of four candidates at 8:30 a.m., in the baptistry, Thursday, June 7, 1857; baptisms took place in the baptistry of the Meeting House, Sunday, October 4, 1857 at 8:30 a.m.; March 7, 1858 — four baptized in the baptistry by Frances Wayland at the close of the forenoon service; Sunday May 2, 1858 —twelve were baptized in the baptistry at the close of the morning worship; Sunday, May 30, 1858, 9 a.m. — fifteen were baptized in the Seekonk River north of the India Point Bridge; Sunday March 27, 1859 — one baptized in the baptistry at the close of the morning service; Sunday Sept 25, 1859 — 2 baptized in the baptistry of the Meeting House at 8 a.m. in the morning; Sunday July 29, 1860 — three baptized in the Meeting House at the close of the forenoon service; December 27, 1863 — four were baptized in the Meeting House at the close of the afternoon service.

94 Addendum to Minutes of FBC, July 21, 1864: reported that two persons were baptized at 9. a.m. in Thurber's Pond. For other outdoor baptisms in the Seekonk River, see: Minutes of FBC, Friday, July 31, 1840: "Mrs. Hope [Brown] Ives and Miss Mary A. Peck were Baptized (in the river) this day," addendum after Minutes of October 2, 1857; Sunday, May 30, 1858, 9 a.m., 15 were baptized in the Seekonk River north of the India Point Bridge, addendum to May 27, 1858 Minutes; Sunday, June 27, 1858, 9 a.m., 12 baptized in the Seekonk, addendum to Minutes of June 24, 1858.

95 Minutes of FBC, February 21, 1895. One factor which propelled the adoption of the individual communion cups all across the nation in the 1890s was the recent discovery of how tuberculosis was communicated. TB was so prevalent that it was called the "White Plague." The first recorded use of individual

cups at communion occurred in 1894 at the Central Presbyterian Church of Rochester, New York. See: William Henry Brackney, *The Baptists* (Westport, CT: Greenwood Press, 1998), 66.

96 "Dismissals to other denominations," in folder "Research Notes for 350-FBC: Tabulations and Lists," FBC mss., RIHS.

CHAPTER 6

1 Henry Melville King, *The Mother Church: A Brief Account of the Origin and Early History of the First Baptist Church in Providence* (Philadelphia: American Baptist Publication Society, 1896).

2 Thomas William Bicknell, *The History of the State of Rhode Island and Providence Plantations* (New York: The American Historical Society, 1920), I: iv, 292.

3 Wilbur Nelson, "History of Baptists in Newport," *Newport Historical Society Bulletin*, 101(January, 1940), 44-45; "Pioneer of Freedom: Dr. John Clarke," a sermon preached at The United Baptist Church, Newport, R.I., by Rev. L. Edgar Stone, Jr., (n.d.); Marie Brownell, "A Brief History of the United Baptist Church," *The United Baptist Church (John Clarke Memorial) 1636-1988: 350 Years* (Newport, 1988).

4 *Minutes of the Warren Baptist Association at Newport, Wednesday and Thursday, September 8 and 9, 1847*, (Providence: H.H. Brown, 1847), 12, John Hay Library, Brown University.

5 *Minutes of the Eighty-second Anniversary of the Warren Baptist Association, held at the First Baptist Church, in Pawtucket on September 12 and 13, 1849*, (Providence: H.H. Brown, 1849), 14, John Hay Library, Brown University.

6 *Minutes of the Eighty-third Anniversary of the Warren Baptist Association, September 11 and 12, 1850*, (Providence: H.H. Brown, 1850), 19, John Hay Library, Brown University.

7 *A Review of a Report, presented to the Warren Baptist Association, meeting in 1848, on the subject of the true date of the First Baptist Church of Newport, R.I., prepared by a committee of the First Baptist Church in Providence, read to the Warren Baptist Association, September 12, 1850* (Providence, 1850), 26 pp. See also: Henry Jackson, pastor of the Central Baptist Church of Newport, *An Account of the Churches in Rhode-Island, presented at the adjourned session of the Twenty-Eighth Annual Meeting of the Rhode-Island Baptist State Convention, Providence, November 8, 1853* (Providence: George H. Whitney, Printer, 1854), 31-32, 79-85.

8 Samuel Adlam, *The First Baptist Church in Providence not the oldest of the Baptists attempted to be Shown* (Newport: Cranston & Norman's Power Press, 1850). See also: Adlam, *The First Baptist Church in America: not founded or pastored by Roger Williams*, edited with introduction by James Robinson Graves (Memphis: Southern Baptist Book House, 1890). Samuel Adlam became the pastor of First Baptist Church of Newport in 1849 and died in 1880. In addition to continuing the argument about priority, he at-

tacked even the civil governance of Providence under Roger Williams, saying its town meeting system was "the least desirable form of government that could be devised . . . ." and that it "disastrously failed." Adlam, *Origin of the Institutions of Rhode Island, a Lecture delivered before the Newport Historical Society, January 10, 1871* (Providence: John F. Green, Steam Book and Job Printer, 1871), 5, 24.

9 Adlam, *The First Baptist Church in Providence not the oldest of the Baptists*, 25.

10 Ibid., 26.

11 The present United Baptist Church (the result of the reunification of First, Second, and Central Baptist Churches of Newport) celebrated its "350th" anniversary in 1988 with a special service on April 17, and the featured speaker was Dr. Edwin S. Gaustad. He shocked them when he told them that regardless of when they might date the founding of the congregation, they were not a "baptizing church" until 1644. In a word, it was not a Baptist church until 1644. Everyone agrees that the Providence church was a "baptizing church" from 1638.

12 Thomas William Bicknell, *The History of the State of Rhode Island and Providence Plantations* (New York: The American Historical Society, 1920), 5 Vols, I: iv, 291-304. See also, Bicknell, *Story of Dr. John Clarke, the founder of the first free commonwealth in the world on the basis of "full liberty in religious concernments,"* (Providence; privately printed, 1915). Presently all the standard accounts of Baptist history and Rhode Island history say that Roger Williams founded the first Baptist church in America.

13 See list in Richard H. Bayles, *History of Providence County* (New York: W.W. Preston, 1891), I: 450. All were dismissed from FBC on April 25, and May 2, 1805; see: Henry Melville King, *Historical Catalogue of the Members of the First Baptist Church in Providence, Rhode Island* (Providence: F. H. Townsend, Printer, 1908). Thirteen of the new members of Second were baptized at First between March 28 and April 25, 1805, and then transferred to the new church the next month. See: *List of Members with the Rules and Regulations and Articles of Faith of the Pine Street Baptist Church, Providence, R.I.* (Providence: M.B. Young, 1851).

14 Report of the Assistant Treasurer, 1855-1865, in box marked "Baptist Female Charitable Society," "Mite Society," etc., FBC papers, RIHS.

15 Records of the Baptist Church of Christ in Pawtucket, 1805-1837, RIHS. All were dismissed from FBC on August 22, 1805; see: King, *Historical Catalogue*.

16 Bayles, *History of Providence County*, I: 450. All were dismissed from FBC on November 16, 1806; see: King, *Historical Catalogue*.

17 *Minutes of the Warren Baptist Association, held at the Baptist Meeting House in Fall-River on Wednesday and Thursday, September 9-10, 1829* (Providence: H.H. Brown, Printer, 1829), 6; *A List of Members with the Covenant and Sketch of the Third Baptist Church in Providence, R.I.* (Providence: H. H. Brown,

1855). Also see: Bayles, *History of Providence County*, I: 452-454. Third Baptist got off to a turbulent beginning because Allen Brown held that he did "not accept personal, unconditional election and perseverance as taught by the Calvinists." The principal founder, Deacon George Dods, and 16 others who believed in strict Calvinism withdrew in 1823, and the Warren Association expelled the church from its membership in 1824. Brown resigned as pastor in 1828 and left the ministry to become a bookkeeper in the Merchants Bank. During his six years, the church had grown from only 30 to 43 members and was in dire financial straits. Third's flirtation with freewill ideas isolated it from most Baptists in Providence and from aid that they might have provided. The next minister was a Calvinist, and the church was readmitted to the Warren Association in 1829. Financial aid came from First Baptist's Nicholas Brown, and the membership tripled by 1836. See: E. H. Johnson, *History of the Third and Brown Street Baptist Churches of Providence, R.I.* (Providence: Union Baptist Society, 1880), 7-14.

18 Bayles, *History of Providence County*, I: 457, lists the names of the petitioners.

19 Some converts in the Providence-wide revival of 1820, living north of Olney street, received baptism from the First General Baptist Church of Cranston. The connection with the Cranston church was fairly nominal even though the organizers of the Fourth Baptist Church were dismissed from their rolls when they officially constituted themselves as a church in the summer of 1823. In fact, the Fourth Baptist Church flirted with Unitarianism. In 1822 the members of the Fourth Baptist Society invited "Rev. Abner Jones, a minister of the Christian Denomination, the Unitarian wing of the Baptist family," to become the pastor, but he declined and the field remained vacant. Finally Zalmon Tobey accepted the call in 1823. Tobey's ideas underwent a series of marked shifts in his lifetime. He was raised a strict Congregationalist of the hyper-Calvinist persuasion of Rev. Samuel Hopkins of Newport, then after graduating from Brown University in 1817 he became a Freewill Baptist, then on to the Christian denomination (Unitarian Baptist), back to the Freewill Baptists, and finally back to the Regular (Calvinist) Baptists. Tobey formally recanted his Unitarian beliefs. See: A.H. Granger, *Historical Discourse, Delivered in the Fourth Baptist Meeting House, Providence, Rhode Island, July 9, 1873, it being the Fiftieth Anniversary of the Organization of the Church* (Providence: Hammond, Angell & Co., 1874), 9-12. Incidentally, none of the four First Baptist people who petitioned the General Assembly for the charter for the Fourth Baptist Society in 1820 was among the members of the church when it organized in 1823.

Baptist Unitarianism was, in fact, like the old Arian heresy of the 3rd-4th century A.D., and at least two notable members of FBC were associated with it. One was the prominent member, Samuel Eddy, who was R.I. Secretary of State (1797-1819), U.S. Congressman (1819-25), and Chief Justice of the R.I. Supreme Court (1827-35). He published an anonymous pamphlet in 1818 advocating Arian ideas, but his identity was revealed and he was excluded from the church on July 3, 1818. The second was Asa Messer (1769-1836), church Clerk (1799-1803), ordained to the ministry by FBC in 1803, third president of Brown University (1802-1826). He denied the heresy, but he offered prayers at the Unitarian church and accepted a D.D. from Unitarian-dominated Harvard in 1820, so his ideas were suspect enough that he was forced to resign as president of the university. While he was never disciplined by FBC, he rarely attended after the controversy and instead frequented a Freewill Baptist church. He owned two farms and a share in a cotton mill, and he ran for governor and lost in 1830. He then served as an alderman in the new city government after 1832. See: *Dictionary of American Biography*, VI: 576. After the Eddy incident, the church voted on July 1, 1819: "That this church has no fellowship with those who openly and avowedly deny the Deity of our Lord Jesus Christ." See: *List of Members* (1842), 46.

20 Tobey left in April 1833 and Fourth was unable to secure a minister, and the congregation dwindled. One problem was the fact that the members of Fourth Baptist wanted an educated minister, but few Freewill Baptist pastors had much education. On the other hand, all the Baptist colleges (Brown, Waterville, Columbian, or Hamilton) were Regular (Calvinist) Baptist. Finally in 1834, Peter Simonson accepted the call, but he was a Calvinist. He demanded "closed communion" [meaning that only persons who had been immersed would be allowed to share the Lord's Supper], and the church accepted his position by a vote of 18 to 13 at their June 1835 meeting. Sixteen "open communion" members withdrew in July 1835 to join other Freewill Baptist churches. "Three days later seven came from the First Church in this city to fill up the vacant places and to strengthen this weak interest. . ." Then others joined so that by the end of the year, Fourth Baptist showed a net loss of only four members. Granger, *Historical Discourse*, 14. In fact, *thirteen* members from First transferred by letter to Fourth on July 2, July 30, and August 2, 1835: Sarah and Harriet Peck, George Peck, Ethan and Sally Whipple, William Hopkins, George Daniels, Ann and Ziba Covell, Sabra Hawes, Anna Aldrich, Jane Thurber, and Rebecca Sessions; see: Minutes of FBC, July 2, July 30, August 2, 1835, RIHS.

21 The story of the Meeting Street Baptist church is told in Jay Coughtry, *Creative Survival: The Providence Black Community in the 19th Century* (Providence: The Rhode Island Black Heritage Society, 1984), 52-58; also see: Robert J. Cottrol, *The Afro-Yankees: Providence's Black Community in the Antebellum Era* (Westport, CT: Greenwood Press, 1982), 57-61,

22 See: John L. Lincoln, *Historical Address on the First Baptist Sunday School, Providence, 1819-1869* (Providence; Providence Press, 1869), 19, mentions the "African School," and on page 110, he wrote, "the colored school in Meeting Street. . . was almost entirely supported by contributions from our school." Regular entries about the African school in the Reports of the Sunday School Superintendent support his claim; FBC mss, RIHS.

23 For example, the March 10, 1842 meeting of the church voted to raise $40 for the aid "of our Colored Brother Rev. Jeremiah Asher," the pastor of the Meeting Street Baptist Church.

24 Minutes of FBC, June 29, 1837.

25 King, *Historical Catalogue*. See also: *A Brief History of the Brown Street Baptist Church, Providence, with the Articles of Faith, Church Covenant, Rules and Regulations, and List of Members* (Providence: Knowles, Anthony, 1866). Dr. Arthur Watson (March 4, 1866 - October 29, 1956), founder of the Electrical Engineering Department at Brown University and FBC church historian for many years, said in 1938 that the creation of the Brown Street church was the result of a "split" which came from "the belief that the First was not doing its duty for the college students. . . . Its life was short, for its motive ceased to yield fruit in attracting college students, and that organization joined hands with the Third church that was located on Tockwotton Street to form the present Union Baptist Church. . . ." See: Arthur Watson, untitled two-page talk, "Read at a meeting of the young people in the vestry of the church some time during 1938." Watson folders, Misc. speeches, FBC papers, RIHS. As no evidence of this "split" was found in any other source, Watson was probably recounting some oral tradition that he heard. (He graduated from Brown in 1888, and after teaching in high school in Massachusetts, he returned to Providence as a physics instructor and joined FBC in 1895. He got his M.A. and Ph.D. from Brown in 1898 and 1905; see: obituary, *Providence Bulletin*, October 29, 1956.) In fact, an 1880 history of the Third and Brown Street Baptist Churches, which gave a fairly unvarnished account of the origins, struggles, controversies, and development of the two churches, provided a wholly different picture of the role of First Baptist in the creation of the Brown Street Church. People at First had been interested and supportive of the idea of a church midway between Third and First a full ten years before it was finally started, and First's pastor, James Granger, was heartily in favor of it. The Brown Street church had substantial financial difficulties that caused it to be weak from its beginning until its merger with Third Baptist in 1878. See: Johnson, *History of the Third and Brown Street Baptist Churches* (1880), 23-28.

26 *Proceedings of the Rhode Island Baptist State Convention* (April 1847), 17. See also: *Minutes of the Providence Baptist Association* (1848), 13; "Reports of the Assistant Treasurer, First Baptist Church," (1847) in box marked "Baptist Female Charitable Society," "Mite Society," etc., FBC papers, RIHS. Also see: Bayles, *History of Providence County*, Vol. I.

27 *Proceedings of the Rhode Island Baptist State Convention* (April 1847), 16. Also see: Harkness' letter, *Minutes of the Proceedings of the 75th Anniversary of the Sunday School, Providence, R.I.* (June 3, 1874), 35.

28 See list of original members in *The Declaration of Faith with the Church Covenant, Rules and Regulations and List of Members of the Eighth Baptist Church, Providence, Rhode Island* (Providence:

Albert Crawford Green, 1850), RIHS.

29 *Proceedings of the R.I. Baptist State Convention* (April 1850), 13.

30 Ibid., (April 1851), 16.

31 "Report of the Assistant Treasurer," November 22, 1855, in box marked "Baptist Female Charitable Society," "Mite Society," etc., in FBC papers, RIHS.

32 Ibid., 1873-1874.

33 The journals of the Allendale Baptist Church begin with the words: "It pleased the Lord to put into the heart of Mr. Zachariah Allen, Esq., owner of the old Allendale Mill, to erect in his village of Allendale in the Spring of 1847, a neat and convenient house of worship. Immediately upon the creation of which a Sabbath school was gathered and organized under the superintendence of Deacon Yeomans of the First Baptist Church of Providence." Quoted in *The Observer* (Greenville, RI), April 8, 1965, 13 [special issue marking the 200th anniversary of the incorporation of North Providence]. Also see: Richard M. Bayles, *History of Providence County, Rhode Island*, II: 188. Their first minister, Christopher Rhodes, was ordained (as a Baptist) and the church was organized officially in April of 1850; see: *Report of the Centennial Celebration on the 24th of June, 1865, at Pawtucket of the Incorporation of the Town of North Providence* (Providence: Knowles, Anthony & Co., 1865). Henry P. Yeomans was a deacon in FBC from February 18, 1836 until he resigned on December 4, 1851. He was baptized into the church on June 5, 1831 and left by letter in October 1864 when he moved to Elmira, New York. King, *Historical Catalogue*, 16, 66. Yeomans started as a baker, but by 1847 he was a prosperous merchant dealing in shoes, leather and hides.

34 *History of the Roger Williams Baptist Sunday School and Church* (Providence, 1915), 3-5, courtesy of Roger Williams Baptist Church, Woodward Road, Providence. Sampson and other key figures are listed in King, *Historical Catalogue*. Also see: *The Observer*, April 8, 1965, 20.

35 While some scattered meetings were held in 1868, the Mt. Pleasant Sunday School and Library Association was actually first organized in 1872. It was non-sectarian, but they voted in a Methodist minister as superintendent. This initial effort folded when the principal benefactor, Henry Armington, was killed in a railroad accident in Pawtucket in the summer of 1873. The school and library did not reopen after the summer vacation of 1873. A Sunday school was started again in 1876 and grew until it needed a larger space. They purchased a building on Chalkstone Avenue in 1878, calling themselves the Chalkstone Mission. However, the purchase plunged them into financial trouble which threatened the continuation of the Mission. They applied without success for help to the Episcopal, Methodist, and Christian denominations. Then Edward Taylor, pastor of First Baptist, came to their rescue. Taylor appointed William K. Andem as superintendent of the Mission Sunday school. Andem was a member of First Baptist (1875-1887) and served as the Sunday school superintendent at FBC from 1884 to 1886. His brother, Eugene Andem, became a member of Mt.

Pleasant Baptist Church. See: Fred. H. Schofield, Jr., editor, *One Hundred Years on Mount Pleasant, serving Christ Yesterday, Today and Tomorrow, 1883-1983* [100th year anniversary booklet] (Providence: Mt. Pleasant Baptist Church, 1983), RIHS; Renaldo E. Leonelli, et al., *Beginnings: Commemorating the History of the Area* (Elmhurst-Mt. Pleasant Neighborhood Jubilee Festival, Providence, June 29, 1986), [part of Providence 350], 12; see also: Bayles, *History of Providence County*, I: 492. On membership of Andem, see: King, *Historical Catalogue*.

36 The best general biography is Sprague De Camp, *Lovecraft: A Biography* (Garden City, NY: Doubleday, 1975). For an account of his expulsion see: H. P. Lovecraft, "Confession of Unfaith," *The Liberal*, 1(February, 1922), reprinted in *Lovecraft Collector's Library*, edited by George Wentzel, Vol. 1 (1952). Lovecraft told of climbing the steeple and trying to play the organ in Lovecraft, *Selected Letters, 1911-1924*, edited by August Derleth and Donald Wandrei (Sauk City, Wisconsin: Arkham House Press, 1965), 277. See, also: Henry L.P. Beckwith, Jr. *Lovecraft's Providence and Adjacent Parts* (West Kingston, RI: Donald M. Grant, 1979), 52.

37 In particular, it was the idea of former Sunday school superintendent, William D. Nisbet (1887-1891). He died in 1894, but individuals, such as John D. Rockefeller, Jr., then a student at Brown University, helped to teach the Sunday school at Wayland chapel. See "Wayland Chapel" folders in FBC papers, RIHS.

38 Minutes of FBC, November 16, 1905.

39 See: "Missionaries," in the folder marked, "Research Notes for 350-FBC, Tabulations and Lists," FBC mss, RIHS.

40 I am indebted to Dr. Carmela Santoro, Professor Emeritus of Rhode Island College, for the story about "potato Baptists." She grew up in the neighborhood of the Marietta Street mission, and her uncle Carmelo became a Baptist. She said that often on Sunday mornings various parts of the Santoro family would encounter each other on Branch Avenue on the way to church. Most were headed for St. Ann's Catholic Church at Hopkins Square, but Uncle Carmelo was going to the First Italian Baptist Church on Charles Street. He would say, "It's too bad you're superstitious or you could hear a good sermon." Lawrence B. Davis, *Immigrants, Baptists, and the Protestant Mind* (Urbana: University of Illinois Press, 1973), pointed out that Catholic hostility to Protestant evangelists was strong. He mentioned that Vincenzo di Domenica was stoned by boys in Providence. When a meeting in Haverhill, Massachusetts, was broken up by a gang of drunken Italian men, the Irish Catholic policeman refused to provide protection, even prohibiting di Domenica from preaching on the streets; see: Davis, 123. Vincenzo di Domenica joined FBC in June 1893, was ordained to the ministry by FBC on December 5, 1900, and moved to Haverhill in May 1902; see: *Historical Catalogue*, 124. In the 1930s the pastor of the First Italian Baptist Church was beaten up and his posters for a revival were ripped apart by a group of Italian Catholics: source of this story was Rev. Paul Aquavella, pastor

of the Emmanuel Baptist Church, October 4, 1987.

41 Robert W. Hayman, *Catholicism in Rhode Island and the Diocese of Providence, 1886- 1921*, Vol. 2 (Providence: Diocese of Providence, 1995), 220. The Methodists and Presbyterians also attempted to evangelize among the Italians, but success was modest. See: Hayman, 217-221.

42 The alarm of Providence Baptists regarding immigration was typical and widespread among Northern Baptists; see: Davis, *Immigrants, Baptists, and the Protestant Mind in America* , 62-128. Baptists generally favored immigration restriction and looked unfavorably upon immigrants from southern and eastern Europe. At the same time, mission work began among these same immigrant communities.

CHAPTER 7

1   Rev. Newell Dwight Hillis, sermon quoted in Walter Lord, *The Good Years: From 1900 to the First World War* (New York: Bantam Books, 1966), 2.

2   George H. Kellner and J. Stanley Lemons, *Rhode Island: The Independent State* (Woodland Hills, CA: Windsor Publications, 1982), 69, 109-115.

3   "Service in Memory of our Deceased President William McKinley, Appointed by the Governor of the State of Rhode Island at the First Baptist Meeting House," (Providence, 1901), RIHS.

4   Providence in the 1890s had become the home of the "Five Industrial Wonders of the World," five factories which were the largest of their kind in the world: Brown & Sharpe (machine tools), Gorham Manufacturing Company (silverware and metal sculpture), Nicholson File Company (metal files), American Screw Company (wood and metal screws), and Corliss Manufacturing Company (steam engines). See: Kellner and Lemons, *Rhode Island*, 63-85.

5   Kellner and Lemons, 148.

6   Population figures, Secretary of State, State of Rhode Island and Providence Plantations, *Rhode Island Manual* (1985-1986), 700-701.

7   See: Yearbooks of the Rhode Island Baptist State Convention, 1950-1987 at American Baptist Churches of Rhode Island headquarters. See also, "Baptist Rolls are Declining: Membership in City Churches Down 18 Per Cent in Decade," *Providence Sunday Journal*, April 28, 1963.

8   Martin E. Marty, *Pilgrims in Their Own Land: 500 Years of Religion in America* (New York: Penguin Books, 1985), 337-355.

9   I am deeply appreciative of Dona Munker for putting me onto the letters of Sarah Hanley to Sara Ehrgott. See: letters from Dona Munker to J. Stanley Lemons, February 5, 2000, and February 14, 2000. Elijah Hanley's wife Sarah wrote a series of expansive and intimate letters to her friend Sara Ehrgott, and in these she explained her husband's stance on such issues as denominationalism and Socialism. Sara Ehrgott's husband was also a Baptist minister, but his adoption of Christian Socialism resulted in

his being fired from his church. While never a Socialist, in 1910 Hanley attended the Sagamore Sociological Conference on Cape Cod, an annual gathering of Socialist thinkers, at the personal invitation of George Coleman, the wealthy sponsor of the conference. Sarah Hanley to Sara Ehrgott, June 21, 1910, tells of the invitation for June 28-30. Also see: Hanley to Ehrgott, August 4, 1909, which reports their reading Walter Rauschenbusch's *Christianity and Social Crisis*. WD Box 145, C.E.S. Wood Collection, Huntington Library.

10 Exasperated, Sarah wrote,"Fie upon the Baptists. They do not honor their Lord." Sarah Hanley to Sara Ehrgott, fragment of letter, n.d. [1910?]. See also: letters, April 1910; June 21, 1910; "Sunday Evening," October 1910.

11 Sarah Hanley to Sara Ehrgott, November 15-16, 1909.

12 Sarah Hanley to Sara Ehrgott, April 1910.

13 Gail Bederman, "'The Women Have Had Charge of the Church Work Long Enough': The Men and Religion Forward Movement of 1911-1912 and the Masculinization of Middle-Class Protestantism," *American Quarterly*, 41(September 1989), 432-465.

14 Ibid., 439-441.

15 *Providence Sunday Journal*, February 2, 1908, IV: 2.

16 See: *Providence Journal*, August 4, 1907. Also see: sermon topics in Church bulletins, October 20, November 3, November 10, November 17, 1907. He created a special Bible class for the men of Brown University, October 27, 1907, and "Dr. Hanley's Class for Men" was first announced on February 2, 1908, beginning February 9.

17 Forty-eight men showed up at the first class (See: bulletin, February 16, 1907), and they had between 69 and 74 within the next three weeks. The class had 114 by November, 1908 (bulletin, November 29, 1908). At the annual banquet of the class, the membership was 134. See: *Providence Journal*, March 30, 1909, 3.

18 Church bulletin, March 14, 1909.

19 *Providence Journal*, May 12, 1909. The hundreds of men who gathered to hear his closing talk at Gorham presented him with a handsome silver pitcher.

20 Minutes of FBC, February 15, 1912.

21 Clara Crosby remembered him as "a breezy Westerner from Indiana who instilled a great deal of enthusiasm among us." She remembered that he began a Vacation Bible School, a Boy's Club and an afternoon sewing class for girls which attracted 75 to 100 girls each Saturday afternoon. The Christian Endeavor Society had 85 members. She recalled the lawn services and the Sunday evening meetings at the Providence Opera House on Dorrance Street. The Neighborhood Nights attracted 100 people for games and refreshments. In fact, half of her entire recollection in 1964 was devoted to Hanley, see: "Reminiscences (A Talk given by Miss Clara Crosby at the Annual Meeting of the First Baptist Church, January 29, 1964)." FBC papers, RIHS.

22 Sarah Hanley to Sarah Ehrgott, August 4, 1909, wrote: "Mr. Hanley rarely mentions [theological dogma] in his preaching. He seeks rather to show men how to live in the world today. . . ." See also: Hanley to Ehrgott, June 21, 1910.

23 *Providence Sunday Journal,* February 2, 1908, section IV:2.

24 Church bulletin, June 12, 1908.

25 "Who that was present did not rejoice over the wonderful service held on our lawn last Sunday evening? The number present must have reached nearly one thousand." Church bulletin, June 28, 1908.

26 Church bulletin, June 20, 1909.

27 "The Down-Town Churches of Providence," *Providence Magazine: The Board of Trade Journal,* 26(August, 1914), 582. In 1918-1919 a ministry to Russians was started by a few Russian Baptists, and they used the vestry of FBC for their meetings. The 1919 report to the Warren Association indicated that eight had been baptized. That work was taken over by the American Baptist Home Mission Society in 1919; see: *Minutes of the Rhode Island Baptist Anniversaries,* (1919), 166.

28 Church bulletin, June 5, 1910.

29 "The Down-Town Churches of Providence," *Providence Magazine,* 581.

30 At the annual banquet in 1909 the athletic committee of "Dr. Hanley's Class for Men" presented plans for a gymnasium to be built at First Baptist , but while these were thought to be good and feasible, no action was taken. See: *Providence Journal,* March 30, 1909, 3.

31 "The Down-Town Churches of Providence," *Providence Magazine,* 582.

32 Church bulletin, May 21, 1911.

33 Church bulletin, February 9, 1909.

34 Church bulletin, March 9, 1909.

35 Church bulletin, February 26, 1911.

36 Minutes of FBC, March 17, 1910.

37 Minutes of FBC, March 18, 1915; March 25, 1915.

38 Sarah Hanley to Sara Ehrgott, July 26, 1911. "Our people were brokenhearted but so kind & sympathetic, trying to be willing to give their beloved Pastor up to a larger work & one for which all felt him so peculiarly fitted. . . . When strong earnest men bid you goodbye with tears streaming down —ah, it was hard!"

39 Sarah Hanley to Sara Ehrgott, June 21, 1910.

40 Sarah Hanley to Sara Ehrgott, April 7, 1911. She wrote, "We are both almost disheartened about the work here. We have taken them just as far as they can go, now, & unless they *do* something they will either cease to exist or jog along on a nice little trot & keep up the worship (?) there in the 'dear old historic building.'" Hanley had proposed a list of reforms for First Baptist in his annual report, "and they haven't even considered one of them - as for instance, the abolition of rented pews, the abolition of the Charitable Baptist Society, the simplification of the financial system and the absolute need for

better equipment for doing down-town work." [By "better equipment" she meant a parish house.]

41 Hanley seems to have relished challenges and had a talent for reforming ailing institutions. His first pastorate was the struggling East End Baptist Church in Cleveland (1901-1907) where he tripled the membership, followed by FBC (1907-1911). See: *Providence Sunday Journal,* August 4, 1907. The financially troubled Franklin College (1911-1917) implored him to take the reins and within four years the College had balanced its budget, and he had introduced new programs and strengthened relations with the churches of Indiana. See: John F. Cady, *The Centennial History of Franklin College* (1934), 170-181. Next he went to the First Baptist Church of Rochester, New York (1917-1921). "Hanley seems to have been a very effective leader here . . . he led the church in considerable growth, was close to denominational work, was something of a strong patriot (he worked at Camp Dix military camp during the first world war as a volunteer from this church), he had some kind of special interest in inter-faith relations in that he had a joint service with a Jewish organization here in the city, and he seems to have done a lot of re-organizing the congregation and administrative structure. He was active in the large community in ecumenical programs, the federation of churches and civic efforts." Letter from Kenneth Dean, pastor, First Baptist Church of Rochester, to J. Stanley Lemons, April 4, 1988. This pastorate was followed by First Baptist Church of Berkeley, California (1921-1929) and the Park Baptist Church of St. Paul, Minnesota (1929-1936). When he retired, he went to Union Theological Seminary in New York as a special student (1936-1938), and then to the University of Chicago. He returned to FBC for a few months in 1941 as interim pastor after Dr. Cleaves died. *Who's Who in America,* (1940-41).

42 Harry Emerson Fosdick had been pastor of FBC of Montclair from 1904 to June 1915, when he resigned to accept the professorship of practical theology at Union Theological Seminary in New York. Arthur Baldwin, D.D., succeeded Fosdick in September, 1916 and resigned in October 1918 to work with the YMCA in France. Montclair was without a pastor until they convinced Cohoe to accept their call. They called him first in 1919, but he remained in Providence for another year. *The First Baptist Church, Montclair, New Jersey: A Brief Story of Its Beginnings and Its Growth, 1886-1936* [50 year anniversary], Courtesy of Montclair Public Library; Obituary of Albert B. Cohoe, *The Montclair Times,* October 20, 1966.

43 In memory of Albert Cohoe, Homer Trickett said: "[He] was a forthright, courageous, liberal-spirited minister of Jesus Christ. During the days of his ministry here he doubtless startled and shocked many with his unorthodox views." *Newsletter,* [FBCIA] October 26, 1966.

44 Report to the Warren Association, 1914; see: *Minutes of the Rhode Island Baptist Anniversaries* (1914).

45 The membership figures are taken from the annual reports to the Rhode Island Baptist State Convention; see: *Minutes of the*

Rhode Island Baptist Anniversaries (1911-1919).

46 *Minutes of the Rhode Island Baptist Anniversaries,* (1919), 165-166.

47 The FBC's letter to the Warren Association noted that the church had lost ground and was without a minister for the third time in recent years, see: "Digest of Letters," *Minutes of the Rhode Island Baptist Anniversaries* (1920), 155-156.

48 Cohoe himself wrote that when he received a second call from the First Baptist Church of Montclair he discussed it with Dr. William H. P. Faunce, President of Brown, who told Cohoe that "he could see no future for the Old First Baptist Church. . ." and advised him to take the offer. See autobiographical statement written after he had retired and returned to Barrie, Ontario, "Albert Cohoe" folder, Box 2, FBC mss, RIHS.

49 The material was reported by Acting Pastor, Frederick B. Greul. See: folder marked "Pastors—Search for 1920-1922: Brother Greul's Letters," Box 3, FBC mss, RIHS.

50 Church bulletin, February 23, 1921. Also see: Minutes of FBC, December 30, 1920 and January 6, 1921; *Minutes of the Rhode Island Baptist Anniversaries,* (1921), 170-171.

51 Minutes of FBC, July 6, 1922.

52 Membership April 1927=529; April 1928=533; April 1929=506. About 20 percent of those totals were non-resident.

53 See: Reports to the Warren Association in Rhode Island Baptist State Convention Yearbooks, 1922-1943. The total membership, including non-resident members, in 1940 was 491; however, the church had no addresses for nearly 14 percent of the total.

54 Minutes of FBC, November 2, 1922. The student had to present a letter from his home church "stating that he is a member in good standing," and the affiliate member had all the "privileges of church fellowship, except the right to vote." Membership automatically ceased when the student left Providence. Minutes of FBC, February 1, 1923, provided the list of seventeen.

55 Minutes of FBC, April 19, 1923. Associate members could not vote to change the status of the church as a Baptist church. See votes on "Associate" members: May 3, 1923; May 10, 1923; September 23, 1923; April 3, 1924; December 18, 1924; January 1, 1925. In all instances these associate members were coming from paedo-baptist churches: Methodist, Congregational, Episcopalian, Lutheran, and Presbyterian.

56 Minutes of FBC, April 5, 1923. A more surprising exception occurred in 1937 when Dr. and Mrs. Haralambia Cicma were admitted by "Christian experience" as full members, "both having been baptized by immersion in infancy in the Greek Orthodox Church." Evidently the form of baptism was held to be more important than the traditional Baptist principle of believer's baptism. Minutes of FBC, April 22, 1937.

57 Interview with Walter Bainton, October, 1987.

58 Church bulletin, November 13, 1932,

announcing the beginning of radio services on November 20, "The Church welcomes also a chance for a larger service."

59 The names of missionaries appear beginning January 14, 1923, and the school of missions was announced February 4, 1923.

60 The church pledged $9,004 to the New World Movement; see bulletin, March 25, 1923.

61 Minutes of FBC, February 18, 1923; April 5, 1923;

62 Church bulletin, April 11, 1923, announcing the April 15 meeting which created the Women's Society.

63 Minutes of FBC, May 17, 1923.

64 See: folder, "Meeting House Foundation, 1923," CBS papers, Box 4; also see: "Saving the Meeting House," *Providence Journal*, June 20, 21, 1923.

65 Minutes of FBC, May 15, 1930.

66 Minutes of the Executive Committee, February 4, 1935, Box 3, Executive Committee folder, FBC mss, RIHS.

67 Many of the publications that appeared about the founding of Rhode Island featured Roger Williams and his ideas of freedom of religion; for example, see: C. S. Lonacre, "A Brief Biographical Sketch of Roger Williams," *Liberty: A Magazine of Religious Freedom*, 31(First Quarter, 1936), 14-15, 25; The Editors, "The Tercentenary of the Founding of Rhode Island by Roger Williams," ibid., 16-17. Also see: The Rhode Island and Providence Plantations Tercentenary Committee, Inc., "Preliminary Statement: Rhode Island Tercentenary Jubilee, 1636-1936," FBC Scrapbooks, RIHS.

68 Repeatedly the past histories had emphasized that no "Church Covenant" or "Statement of Faith" had been adopted by First Baptist even though most other Baptist churches did have such statements. For example, see Caldwell and Gammell's boast, "The church has expressed its judgment on moral and theological points as occasion has required, but it has never adopted any creed or covenant," in *History of the First Baptist Church in Providence* (1877), 19. King proclaims the same in his "Historical Address," *Minutes of the Proceedings of the 75th Anniversary of the First Baptist Sunday School, Providence, R.I. June 3, 1894* (no publisher), 29.

69 One structural effect of the sudden vacancy in the pastoral office was the adoption of a new system of governance in the church. Until Cleaves' death the pastor chaired church meetings. He died on October 12, 1940, and the church elected Arthur Watson to be moderator at the next church meeting on October 31, 1940. Then they made the system part of the by-laws. In March 1941 the church adopted the governance system of the Charitable Baptist Society which had an elected layman serve as the moderator. The first person elected moderator at the annual meeting was Robert E. Brightman. See: Minutes of FBC, February 3, 1941; March 6, 1941; May 8, 1941.

70 See: "Reminiscences" (Talk given by Clara Crosby, January, 1964), mimeograph, FBC mss, RIHS.

71 See: Executive Committee Minutes in the late 1940s; also see, Church bulletins 1946-1949. For example, the Minutes for January 6, 1947, report that FBC had pledged $10,082 to the World Mission Crusade. Minutes for November 1, 1949, voted to participate in the Stewardship Advance Program.

72 Membership figures taken from Reports to the Warren Association in Rhode Island Baptist State Convention Yearbooks, 1940-1955.

73 Ibid., 1955-1958.

74 See packet of clippings August 28, 1947 to December 7, 1947 in FBC Scrapbook, RIHS.

75 [Headline] "The Baptist Meeting House Declared National Shrine," *Providence Journal*, June 18, 1948; "1,300,000 Churchmen Asked for $1," *Evening Bulletin*, April 30, 1949; May 10, 1949; see also: the endowment campaign literature, in CBS papers.

76 L. C. Lemons [former director of periodical circulation of the American Baptist Publication Society] to Stanley Lemons, August 11, 1987. Those at the American Baptist national headquarters in Valley Forge who had Rhode Island connections and who were associates of L.C. Lemons included Herbert Osteye [former business manager of the American Baptist Publication Society], former member of FBCIA and member of the Publicity Committee and Committee on Repairs at the time of the campaign in 1948-1951. (See lists in "A Living Monument and its Preservation.") Another was Dr. Kenneth Cober, former executive secretary of the Rhode Island Baptist State Convention from 1944 to 1952 and then director of education for the American Baptist Convention. A third man was Rev. Hale Thornberry, also executive secretary of the Rhode Island Baptist State Convention.

77 For a sketch and appreciation of Harold Tanner, see: "Harold Tanner: A Great Debt Acknowledged with Esteem and Affection," *Brown Alumni Monthly*, 65(November 1964), 20-23. Tanner (October 30, 1887-December 25, 1968) was born in Pawtucket, graduated from Brown in 1909 and Harvard Law School in 1912. He was a partner in the firm of Tillinghast, Collins, and Tanner from 1916. He was a trustee of Brown from 1929 and chancellor from 1952 to 1964. He was moderator at the church for many years, and in "1957 he was the person most responsible for obtaining a $500,000 grant from John D. Rockefeller Jr. which enabled the renovation of the church." Obituary: *Providence Journal*, December 26, 1968.

78 The sale of the securities brought $525,518.30. And the restoration cost $483,287.56. See: "Report of Special Reserve Fund (Rockefeller) As of October 17, 1958," attached to the "Report of Committee on Preservation and Renovation of the Meeting House," October 14, 1958," FBC mss, RIHS.

79 See: "A Comprehensive Report on the Structural Stability of the First Baptist Church, Providence, R.I.," report of Hegemann-Harris, Inc., New York, FBC mss, RIHS; see also: "To Save the Meeting House," *Brown Alumni Monthly*, 57(April, 1957), 5-7.

80 See: Raymond C. Adams, et al., "Report of Committee on Preservation and Renovation of the Meeting House," October 14, 1958. Some suggestions of the restorers were discarded. For example, the consultant on decoration, Charles R. Strickland, architect, advised, ". . . when the organ is rebuilt, it is recommended that the present mahogany case, if retained, be painted the color of the woodwork, picked out in gold and possibly marbleized." See: "The First Baptist Meeting House, Providence, Rhode Island, 1775: A Report on its' [sic] Decoration, 1955," CBS papers, Restoration Box.

81 Minutes of FBC, April 25, 1957. At the time, about one-third of the American Baptist churches accepted open membership.

82 *Providence Journal*, April 14, 1958; also see: *The Rhode Island Baptist*, 42(May, 1958), 6-7.

83 Pastor's Report, Annual Meeting of the Church and CBS, 1966.

84 Most of the information here is drawn from the "History of the Coffee House," mimeograph, from Coffee House folders, FBC papers. Also see: feature article in the *Providence Journal*, August 12, 1968; and Stanford Bratton, "The Assistant Minister's Report," *First Baptist Church in America: Annual Report, 1968* (January, 1969), 5.

85 *Providence Journal*, August 12, 1968.

86 Ibid.

87 While FBC cut its official support of the Mouthpiece Coffee House, the Mouthpiece itself lived on with the support of other churches and with the continued participation of individual members from FBC. As late as November 1970, a year and a half after FBC pulled away from it, the Mouthpiece tried to launch a temporary job placement service and an arts and crafts cooperative to sell handicrafts. See: Church bulletin, November 29, 1970.

88 FBC, NEWSLETTER, February 8, 1968. The original says: "Should we try to divide issues in the church by the power of money, rather than by the power of love?" Homer Trickett told me that that was a typographical error, that it should have said "decide" rather than "divide." Interview, September, 1987.

89 Norman Watson expressed this sentiment many times over the years that I knew him from 1968 to his death in 1984. He also believed that the preservation of the Charitable Baptist Society was more important than the First Baptist Church, that the CBS should control FBC. I helped to clear out their house at 30 Congdon Street when Selma Watson entered a nursing home after Norman's death. All of the materials that are described as the "Watson papers" and a substantial part of the photographs in the FBC papers were found in that process.

90 Homer Trickett, "The Minister's Report," *First Baptist Church in America, Annual Report, 1969* (January, 1970), 1.

91 "A Proposal for One New Baptist Congregation on the East Side of Providence," mimeograph (1970) in folder

marked, "Research for 350-FBC, Xeroxs," FBC mss, RIHS.

92 For example, see the letter of the First Baptist Melding Committee to the church membership, January 8, 1971, suggesting "a partnership between East Side Baptist Churches. . . ." FBC mss, RIHS.

93 In a stormy Annual Meeting in January 1971, the church voted to discontinue the talks and the merger-melding-partnership idea died.

94 "PROFILE of the FIRST BAPTIST CHURCH IN AMERICA, as prepared by the Pulpit Committee, November 1970," 4, FBC mss, RIHS.

95 The "Scatterization Chart" of the Sunday School prepared by the Melding Committee in January 1971 noted that only 14 families had children, only 30 children were enrolled (though far fewer attended on any given Sunday), only 12 adults attended the Adult Class: see letter to congregation from the First Baptist Melding Committee, January 8, 1971, FBC mss, RIHS.

96 "PROFILE of the FIRST BAPTIST CHURCH IN AMERICA, prepared by the Pulpit Committee, October, 1975," 3, FBC mss, RIHS.

97 Ibid.

98 Ibid., 2.

99 May 3, 1975. The 1975 Annual Report of FBC reported a net income of $2,336.65 from the May Fair after some expenses were charged against the amount raised.

CHAPTER 8

1 May 9, 1983; May 6, 1985.

2 "PROFILE of the FIRST BAPTIST CHURCH IN AMERICA, prepared by the Pulpit Committee, October, 1982," 4.

3 Ibid.

4 First Baptist Church in America, Annual Report (1984) and (1985). Fifty-four names were dropped in 1984.

5 See: Annual Report for 1983, 1984, 1985, 1986.

6 Statement to Sunday morning service during the Every Member Canvass on November 2, 1986.

7 Annual Report (1983), 8-12.

8 Ibid., 6, 15.

9 The book, J. Stanley Lemons, The First Baptist Church in America (East Greenwich, RI: Charitable Baptist Society, 1988), came out in May 1988.

10 Annual Report, 1988.

11 Annual Report, 1990 through 1999.

12 Annual Report, 1988, 1989. See continuing Habitat involvement: 1990, 1991, 1992.

13 Annual Report, 1991.

14 Annual Report, 1988, 1991, 1993.

15 Annual Report (1991), 3.

16 Annual Report (1992), 2.

17 See membership lists of 1832, 1884, 1910, 2001, FBC mss, RIHS.

18 Minutes of FBC, April 29, 1762.

19 On the decline of women in the churches in the 1770s-1790s, including FBC, see: Susan Juster, Disorderly Women: Sexual Politics and Evangelicalism in Revolutionary New England (Ithaca: Cornell University Press, 1994), 122-135.

20 Juster, Disorderly Women, 126.

21 Minutes of FBC, August 4, 1791.

22 The whole episode is found in the minutes for November 29, 1792 through January 31, 1793.

23 List of Members with the General Rules and Regulations of the First Baptist Church in Providence, R.I. (Providence: Knowles & Vose Printers, 1844), 3-4. See Minutes of FBC, March 16, 1844, on the adoption and decision to print the rules.

24 Minutes of FBC, December 2, 1808. The vote of the men was 37-1 with one abstention, but the women's vote was not recorded.

25 Minutes of FBC, December 10, 1874.

26 Minutes of FBC, April 26, 1883; see also: Manual of First Baptist Church in Providence, August, 1884 (Providence, E.L. Freeman & Co., Printers, 1884), 13.

27 Minutes of FBC, April 24, 1890; see also: Manual of the First Baptist Church in Providence, May 1890 (Boston: G. J. Stiles, Printer, 1890), 15.

28 The "Woman's Sphere" has been examined in excellent studies and the classics include Barbara Welter, "The Cult of True Womanhood, 1820-1860," American Quarterly, 18(Summer, 1966), 131-175, and Nancy Cott, The Bonds of Womanhood: "Woman's Sphere" in New England, 1780-1835 (New Haven: Yale University Press, 1977). Women's religious involvement is discussed in Barbara Welter, "The Feminization of American Religion, 1800-1860," in Dimity Convictions: The American Woman in the Nineteenth Century (Athens: Ohio University Press, 1976), 83-102; Nancy Cott, "Young Women in the Second Great Awakening," Feminist Studies, 2(Fall, 1975), 15-29; Mary P. Ryan, "A Woman's Awak-ening: Evangelical Religion and the Families of Utica, New York, 1800-1840," American Quarterly, 30(Winter, 1978), 602-623; Ann Douglas, The Feminization of American Culture (New York: Alfred P. Knopf, 1977); Carl Degler, At Odds: Women and the Family in America from the Revolution to the Present (New York: Oxford University Press, 1980), especially, 298-303.

29 John L. Lincoln, Historical Address on the First Baptist Sunday School, Providence, 1819-1869 (Providence; Providence Press, 1869), 17.

30 "History of the First Baptist Sewing School, established December 8, 1860," Minutes of FBC, November 21, 1867.

31 "Female Charitable Baptist Society," (handwritten, undated account of the society, circa 1905-1906), 9, in box marked "Mite Society, Female Charitable Society," FBC mss, RIHS.

32 In 1895 the church had 554 members, of whom over 69 percent were females.

33 Charter and By-Laws of the Charitable Baptist Society in Providence, With a List of Members (Providence: Snow & Farnham, Printers, 1895), 18.

34 The words of the charge to the Standing Committee were unchanged from its first printing in List of Members with the General Rules and Regulations of the First Baptist Church in Providence, R.I. (Providence: Knowles & Vose, 1844), 7, through the last Manual of the First Baptist Church in Providence, Rhode Island, August 1910 (Providence: F. H. Townsend, 1910), 15.

35 See: Minutes of CBS, August 13, 1928 and November 12, 1928.

36 Minutes of the CBS. November 10, 1930, the CBS voted to abandon the current plan of selling pews. On March 9, 1931, the minutes indicated that a majority favored free pews and wanted to consider a plan whereby the present pew holders would voluntarily deed them to the CBS. The church calendar for May 7, 1933 noted that application cards for membership in the CBS were in the hands of the ushers: "We are anxious to make the membership of the Society coterminous with the actual contributing membership of the Church so far as this is possible."

37 See lists of officers of CBS in CBS papers, RIHS.

38 "Report of Committee on Preservation and Renovation of the Meeting House," October 14, 1958, FBC mss, RIHS.

39 "Officers and Committees of the First Baptist Church and the Charitable Baptist Society for the Year, 1969."

40 Ibid., 1962.

41 Anna Canada Swain (March 18, 1889-April 5, 1979) was born in Versailles, Ohio, the daughter of the Rev. Prentice A. and Adelaide (Spencer) Canada. After graduating from New Bedford (MA) High she attended Oberlin College from 1907 to 1909. She transferred to Pembroke in 1909 and graduated in 1911 with B.A., Phi Beta Kappa. She taught at English High School in Providence in 1917. She married Leslie E. Swain, professor of physical education at Brown University, on June 27, 1911, and they lived in Providence until he retired in 1943, whereupon they moved to their summer home at Craigville, MA, near Hyannis. She was a member of FBC from December 2, 1926 to November 8, 1951. She was awarded an honorary M.A. by Brown in 1945, and received an honorary Doctor of Humane Letters from both Keuka College (1944) and Franklin College (1958). She was president of the Rhode Island Baptist Women's Mission Society from 1925 to 1929. She was vice president of the Women's American Baptist Foreign Missionary Society from 1935 to 1944, except for 1935 and 1942 when she was the president. She was president of the Northern Baptist Convention from 1944 to 1946. She also served as president of the R.I. Federation of Women's Church Societies. She was the first woman trustee of Brown University, serving from 1949 to 1956. She was a member of the committee to set up the Commission on Women's Work of the World Council of Churches. She was a member of the Executive Board of the World Council of Churches from 1948 to 1954, becoming the

first woman to serve on its Central Committee in 1954. *Providence Evening Bulletin*, May 27, 1944, (with photograph) reported her election as president of the convention, as did the church calendar for June 18, 1944. See also: *Evening Bulletin*, June 18, 1945, reported her honorary degree at Brown; *Bulletin*, May 22, 1946; *Bulletin*, September 25, 1948; telephone interview with her nephew, Dr. Richard Brown, executive minister of the Rhode Island State Council of Churches, March 29, 1988. Also, see: *Who's Who*, 1982-1985; biographical file at Brown Archives, and death notice in the *Brown Alumni Magazine*, (June 1979), 2.

42 See: list of officers of FBC and CBS in *Annual Reports*, 1978-1984.

43 See: chapter IV. *Annual Report*, 1995: 7, 22. The papers of the conference were published; see: *Into a New Day: Exploring a Baptist Journey of Division, Diversity, and Dialogue*, edited by Kate Penfield (Macon: GA: Smyth & Helwys Publishing Co., 1997).

44 "Effective membership" refers to the members who attend and contribute. It is impossible to compare membership rolls from before 1983 with current ones because the church purged 54 names in 1984 and 196 more in 1990. Furthermore, a careful search of the membership lists revealed that an accumulation of counting errors over the decades had overstated the membership by forty-one; that is to say that there were numbers but no names! Moreover, since 1990, additional names are removed at each annual meeting so that the membership rolls remain current and accurate. See: *Annual Reports*, 1990-1999. From 1984 to 1999, the pruning of the rolls eliminated 278 names and 41 nameless numbers.

45 The pastor expressed these concerns in a meeting with the church moderator, October 28, 1997.

46 George H. Shriver, professor of church history at Georgia Southern University and former professor at Southeastern Baptist Seminary, has described a "neofundamentalist" strain among current Baptists who are characterized by being "ahistorical, anti-intellectual, and antipluralist." They are hostile "to any and all kinds of pluralism —theological, political, and moral. . . ." See: "The Dangers of Being Tolerant of the Intolerant," *Freedom of Conscience: A Baptist/Humanist Dialogue*, edited by Paul D. Simmons (Amherst, NY: Prometheus Books, 2000), 74-79.

47 *Providence Journal-Bulletin*, May 4, 2000, A-16; see also "Biographical narrative of James C. Miller," The Rhode Island State Council of Churches (n.d.)

48 Interview of James Miller, October 22, 2000.

49 Minutes of FBC, June 15, 1911, includes a copy of King's letter to the delegates to the World Baptist Alliance, meeting in Philadelphia, June 19-25, 1911.

INDEX *Picture captions are in* **boldface type.**